WAR & PEACE
IN THE SPACE AGE
according to Arthur C. Clarke

"The only defence against the weapons of the future is to prevent them ever being used. In other words, the problem is political and not military at all. A country's armed forces can no longer defend it; the most they can promise is the destruction of the attacker...

"Upon us, the heirs to all the past and the trustees of the future which our folly can slay before its birth, lies a responsibility no other age has ever known. If we fail in our generation, those who come after us may be too few to rebuild the world, when the dust of the cities has descended, and the radiation of the rocks has died away."

BOOKS BY ARTHUR C. CLARKE

Non-Fiction

Interplanetary Flight
The Exploration of Space
The Exploration of The Moon
Going into Space
The Coast of Coral
The Making of a Moon
The Reefs of Taprobane
Voice Across the Sea
The Challenge of the Spaceship
The Challenge of the Sea
Profiles of the Future
Voices from the Sky
The Promise of Space
Report on Planet Three
The First Five Fathoms
Boy Beneath the Sea
Indian Ocean Adventure
Indian Ocean Treasure
The Treasure of the Great Reef
The View from Serendip
Spring:1984—A Choice of
    Futures

With the Editors of "Life"
Man and Space

With the Astronauts
First on the Moon

With Robert Silverberg
Into Space

With Chesley Bonestell
Beyond Jupiter

With Simon Welfare & John
    Fairley
Arthur C. Clarke's Mysterious
    World

Fiction

Islands in the Sky
Prelude to Space
Against the Fall of Night
The Sands of Mars
Childhood's End
Expedition to Earth
Earthlight
Reach for Tomorrow
The City and the Stars
Tales from the "White Hart"
The Deep Range
The Other Side of the Sky
* Across the Sea of Stars
A Fall of Moondust
* From the Ocean, From the
    Stars
Tales of Ten Worlds
Dolphin Island
Glide Path
The Lion of Comarre
* The Nine Billion Names of
    God
Prelude to Mars
The Lost Worlds of 2001
The Wind from the Sun
Rendezvous with Rama
Imperial Earth
The Foundations of Paradise
2010: Odyssey Two

With Stanley Kubrick
2001: A Space Odyssey

* Anthologies

ARTHUR C. CLARKE

1984: SPRING
A Choice of Futures

A Del Rey Book

BALLANTINE BOOKS ● **NEW YORK**

A Del Rey Book
Published by Ballantine Books

Library of Congress Catalog Card Number: 83-15643

ISBN 0-345-31358-5

Manufactured in the United States of America

First Ballantine Books Edition: November 1984

Cover Photo: William Coupon, Photographer, *Geo Magazine*,
July, 1983

ACKNOWLEDGMENTS

"Beyond the Global Village," copyright © 1983 by Arthur C. Clarke. First published in *Analog Science Fiction/Science Fact*, December 1983.

"New Communications and the Developing World," copyright © 1982 by Arthur C. Clarke. First published in *Analog Science Fiction/Science Fact*, March 1982.

"War and Peace in the Space Age," copyright © 1983 by Arthur C. Clarke. First published in *Analog Science Fiction/Science Fact*, July 1983.

"Electronics and Education," copyright © 1980 by Arthur C. Clarke. First published in *Omni*, June 1980.

"The Eve of Apollo," copyright © 1969 by *The New York Times* Co., as "Will Advent of Man Awaken the Sleeping Moon?" in *The New York Times*, July 17, 1969. Reprinted by permission.

"Apollo Plus Ten," copyright © 1979 by Arthur C. Clarke. First published as "The Best is Yet to Come," in *Time Magazine*, July 16, 1979.

"Predictions," copyright © 1981 by David Wallechinsky, Amy Wallace, and Irving Wallace. By permission of William Morrow & Co., Inc.

"Of Sand and Stars," copyright © 1983 by Arthur C. Clarke. First published in *The New York Times Book Review*, March 6, 1983.

"Last and First Books," copyright © 1983 by Arthur C. Clarke. By permission of Dodd, Mead & Co., Inc.

"Shaw and the Sound Barrier," copyright © 1959 by Arthur C. Clarke. First printed in the *Virginia Quarterly Review*, Vol. 36, No. 1, Winter 1960.

"Richard Jefferies," copyright © 1948 by *The Field*, May 1948.

"With Brendan Behan," copyright © 1981 by Peter Arthurs. By permission of St. Martin's Press, Inc.

"The Science Fiction Hall of Fame," copyright © 1982 by The Science Fiction Writers of America, for *The Science Fiction Hall of Fame, Vol. III*, edited by Arthur C. Clarke and George W. Proctor (Avon, New York, 1982).

Foreword

It is not only good manners, but good sense, to acknowledge sources of inspiration; a writer who freely admits his borrowings is seldom accused of plagiarism. The title of this book was actually suggested by the excellent movie *Summer of '42*, but I readily admit that it contains resonances of a far more famous work.

As I have (with a little help from Stanley Kubrick) already annexed two dates in the future, it may seem inexcusably greedy to trespass on the territory which George Orwell staked out thirty-five years ago. However, when this book appears, 1984 will belong to all mankind, as it recedes into our common past. I am using the date as a marker, to pin down a moment of time. Or you may compare it with a railway-station name-board, glimpsed for a moment through the window of an express, which arouses disquieting memories before it flashes by into the darkness, hopefully never to be seen again...

So much has been written about Orwell's *1984*, and will doubtless be appearing in the year itself, that I have no intention of adding unnecessarily to the verbiage. I never liked the book (but it was not meant to be liked) and thought it unsatisfactory as a piece of scientific prediction (again, something that was not its main objective). My discomfort, I suspect, was that of the typical liberal optimist when forced to confront the harsher realities of political life. On the other hand, I did not react as violently as some of my left-wing friends — being prepared to confess, even at this late date, that I have *never* been a member of the Communist party. (In retrospect, I feel rather hurt that no one ever invited me to join.)

Perhaps my strongest objection to Orwell's thesis lay in a feeling that its basic premise was impossible; one could not have a state of continuous war, at least between great powers, in a nuclear age. But it must be remembered that Orwell wrote (and died) before the invention of thermonuclear weapons multiplied kilotons into megatons. It did not seem unreasonable, in 1948, to imagine that civilization might absorb an occasional Hiroshima or Nagasaki. Unfortunately, too many people are still living in 1948: I hope that some of the following essays — particularly "A Flash of Golden Fire" — may help to disabuse them.

Today, we can recognize that Orwell's book is a unique work of genius, beyond both praise and criticism. It fulfills perfectly — better even than *Brave New World* — Ray Bradbury's claim: "I don't try to describe the future — I try to *prevent* it."

For, thanks at least partly to Orwell's warning, his worst fears have not come true. Yet we have other fears, more terrible than his wildest nightmares. Some of these I consider in the essays and speeches that follow, but against his ominous date I have deliberately set the hopeful word "Spring," which uplifts the heart with its message of renewal and rebirth.

Though it may be an illusion brought on by wishful thinking, it does seem that despite the horrors and miseries of the present time, there are faint signs that the worst of the world's long winter may be over. The pessimism, violence—even despair—so characteristic of the past two decades are no longer quite as fashionable as they used to be.

Apocalypse may yet be canceled; let us dare to be hopeful.

Colombo:
Spring 1983

Author's Note

The essays and speeches that follow have been grouped into four sections, but there is considerable overlapping of subjects and they can be read in any order. For this reason—and to keep each item self-contained—there has been no attempt to remove the occasional duplication of ideas or phrases.

The address given at the Marconi International Fellowship Award ceremony ("In the Hall of the Knights") also appears as the first item in *Ascent to Orbit: A Mathematical Autobiography*, the collection of my technical papers. It serves as a link between the two books.

A. C. C.

Contents

I. The Weapons of Peace

II. Apollo and After

III. The Literary Scene

IV. From the Coast of Coral

I

The Weapons of Peace

Beyond the Global Village

There is always something new to be learned from the past, and I would like to open with two anecdotes from the early days of the telephone. They illustrate perfectly how difficult—if not impossible—it is to anticipate the social impact of a truly revolutionary invention.

Though the first story is now rather famous—and I must apologize to those who've heard it before—I hope it's unfamiliar to most of you.

When news of Alexander Graham Bell's invention

Address on World Telecommunications Day, United Nations, New York, 17 May 1983, as delivered in the General Assembly.

reached the United Kingdom, the Chief Engineer of the
British Post Office failed to be impressed. "The Americans," he said loftily, "have need of the telephone—but
we do not. We have plenty of messenger boys...."

The second story I heard only quite recently, and in
some ways it's even more instructive. In contrast to the
British engineer, the mayor of a certain American city
was wildly enthusiastic. He thought that the telephone
was a marvelous device and ventured this stunning prediction: "I can see the time," he said solemnly, "*when
every city will have one.*"

If, during the course of this talk, you think that I am
getting a little too fanciful, please remember that mayor....

We have now reached the stage when virtually anything we want to do in the field of communications is
possible: the constraints are no longer technical, but economic, legal or political. Thus if you want to transmit the
Encyclopaedia Britannica around the world in one second, you can do so. But it may be a lot cheaper if you're
prepared to wait a whole minute—and you must check
with the *Britannica*'s lawyers first.

Yet while recognizing and applauding all these marvels, I am only too well aware of present realities. In Sri
Lanka, for example, a major problem is that the village
postmaster may not even have the stamps he needs—to
put on the telegrams that must be *mailed*, because copper
thieves have stolen the overhead wires. And Sri Lanka,
compared to some countries, is rich. It has already im-
ported over a hundred thousand TV sets and thousands
of videotape recorders. That would have been unthink-
able only a few years ago—but human beings need information and entertainment almost as much as they need
food, and when an invention arrives which can provide
both in unprecedented quantities, sooner or later everyone manages to find the money for it.

This is particularly true when the cost of the hardware
drops tenfold every decade—look at the example of pocket
calculators! So please don't dismiss my future because
no one can afford it. The human race can afford anything
it really needs—and improvements in communications
often pay for themselves more swiftly than improvements
in transportation. A developing country may sometimes

be better advised to build telephone links than roads to its outlying provinces, if it has to make the choice.

Let me now focus on the only aspect of the communications revolution which I am at all competent to discuss, and which has profoundly affected my own life-style—not to mention that of millions of other people

Until 1976, making an international telephone call from my home in Sri Lanka was an exercise in frustration that might last several days. Now, thanks to the Indian Ocean satellite, I can get through to London or New York in slightly less time than it takes to dial the thirteen-digit number. As a result, I can now live exactly where I please, and have cut my traveling to a fraction of its former value.

Comsats have created a world without distance and have already had a profound effect on international business, news-gathering and tourism—one of the most important industries of many developing countries. Yet their real impact has scarcely begun: before the end of this century—only seventeen years ahead!—they will have transformed the planet, sweeping away much that is evil, and unfortunately, not a few things that are good.

The slogan "A telephone in every village" should remind you of that American mayor, so don't laugh. I believe it is a realistic and (equally important!) desirable goal by the year 2000. It can be achieved now that millions of kilometers of increasingly scarce copper wire can be replaced by a handful of satellites in stationary orbit. And on the ground we need a simple, rugged handset and solar-powered transceiver plus antenna, which could be mass-produced for tens rather than hundreds of dollars.

At this point I would like to borrow an expression from the military—"force multipliers." A force multiplier is a device which increases, often by a very large factor, the effectiveness of an existing system. For example, it may take fifty old-fashioned bombs to knock out a bridge. But if you give them TV guidance, you will need only one or two, though the explosive power per bomb remains exactly the same.

I suggest that the "Telephone in the Village" would be one of the most effective force multipliers in history, because of its implications for health, animal husbandry, weather forecasts, market advice, social integration and human welfare. Each installation would probably pay for itself, in hard cash, within a few months. I would like to see a cost-effectiveness study of rural satellite telephone systems for Africa, Asia and South America. But the financial benefits, important though they undoubtedly would be, might yet be insignificant compared with the social ones. Unlike its military equivalent, *this* force multiplier would increase the health, wealth and happiness of mankind.

However, long before the global network of *fixed* telephones is established, there will be a parallel development which will eventually bypass it completely—though perhaps not until well into the next century. It is starting now, with cellular networks, portable radiophones, and paging devices, and will lead ultimately to our old science-fiction friend, the wristwatch telephone.

Before we reach that, there will be an intermediate stage. During the coming decade, more and more businessmen, well-heeled tourists and virtually *all* newspersons will be carrying attaché-case-sized units that will permit direct two-way communication with their homes or offices, via the most convenient satellite. These will provide voice, telex and video facilities (still photos and, for those who need it, live TV coverage). As these units become cheaper, smaller and more universal, they will make travelers totally independent of national communications systems.

The implications of this are profound—and not only to media news-gatherers who will no longer be at the mercy of censors or inefficient (sometimes nonexistent) postal and telegraph services. It means the end of closed societies and will lead ultimately—to repeat a phrase I heard Arnold Toynbee use forty years ago—to the unification of the world.

You may think this is a naive prediction, because many countries wouldn't let such subversive machines across their borders. But they would have no choice; the alternative would be economic suicide, because very soon they would get no tourists and no businessmen offering foreign currency. They'd get only spies, who would have no trouble at all concealing the powerful new tools of their ancient trade.

What I am saying, in fact, is that the debate about the free flow of information which has been going on for so many years will soon be settled—by engineers, not politicians. (Just as physicists, not generals, have now determined the nature of war.)

Consider what this means. No government will be able to conceal, at least for very long, evidence of crimes or atrocities—even from its own people. The very existence of the myriads of new information channels, operating in real time and across all frontiers, will be a powerful influence for civilized behavior. If you are arranging a massacre, it will be useless to shoot the cameraman who has so inconveniently appeared on the scene. His pictures will already be safe in the studio five thousand kilometers away; and his final image may hang you.

Many governments will not be at all happy about this, but in the long run everyone will benefit. Exposures of scandals or political abuses—especially by visiting TV teams who go home and make rude documentaries—can be painful but also very valuable. Many a ruler might still be in power today, or even alive, had he known what was really happening in his own country. A wise statesman once said: "A free press can give you hell; but it can save your skin." That is even more true of TV reporting—which, thanks to satellites, will soon be instantaneous and ubiquitous. Let us hope that it will also be responsible. Considering what has often happened in the past, optimism here may well be tempered with concern.

A quarter of a century ago, the transistor radio began to sweep across the world, starting a communications revolution in all countries, developed and undeveloped. It is a continuing revolution—a steady explosion, if I may be permitted the paradox—and it is nowhere completed. Indeed, it will accelerate when the cheap solar-powered radio eliminates dependence on batteries, so expensive and difficult to obtain in remote places.

The transistor radio has already brought news, information and entertainment to millions who would otherwise have been almost totally deprived of so much that we take for granted. But TV is a far more powerful medium, and thanks to the new generation of satellites, its time has now arrived.

I hesitate to add to the megawords—if not giga-words—written about educational TV and direct-broadcast satellites. But despite all this verbiage, there still seem to be a number of points that are not generally understood, perhaps because of the human dislike for facing awkward truths.

Attempts have been made, in some quarters, to regulate or even prohibit direct broadcasting from space. But radio waves do not recognize frontiers, and it is totally impossible to prevent spill-over. Even if country A did its best to keep its programs from reaching its neighbor B, it could not always succeed. During the 1976 Satellite Instructional Television Experiment (SITE) the beam from the ATS 6 satellite was deliberately slanted toward India to give maximum signal strength there. Yet good images were still received in England, a quarter of the way around the globe!

Those who would promulgate what might be called "permission to receive" laws remind me of the fabled American state legislature, which, back in the last century, ruled that the value of pi is exactly 3, as given in the Old Testament. (Alas, this delightful story isn't true: but it can be matched by similar absurdities at this very moment.)

In any event, technology has once again superseded politics. All over the United States, the Caribbean and South America, small "receive only" dishes are sprouting like mushrooms, tuning in to the hundreds of satellite channels now available—and there's little that anyone can do about it, without spending a lot of money on scramblers and encrypting devices which may sometimes defeat their own purpose.

In Sri Lanka, radio amateurs with quite simple equipment have been receiving excellent pictures from the Soviet Union's powerful EKRAN satellites; thanks to these, we were able to enjoy the Moscow Olympics. I would like to express my gratitude to the Russian engineers for their continuing large-scale demonstration, over the whole of Asia, that the politicians are not only talking technical nonsense, but are ignoring their own proclamations.

They are not the only ones guilty of hypocrisy, as my

good friend Dr. Yash Pal pointed out in these words several years ago:

> "In the drawing rooms of large cities you meet many people who are concerned with the damage that one is going to cause to the integrity of rural India by exposing her to the world outside. After they have lectured you about the dangers of corrupting this innocent, beautiful mass of humanity, they usually turn round and add: 'Well, now that we have a satellite, when are we going to see some American programs?' Of course, they themselves are immune to cultural domination or foreign influences."

When I quoted this at the 1981 UNESCO IPDC meeting in Paris, I added these words:

> "I am afraid that cocktail-party intellectuals are the same everywhere. Because we frequently suffer from the scourge of information pollution, we find it hard to imagine its even deadlier opposite—information starvation. I get very annoyed when I hear arguments, usually from those who have been educated beyond their intelligence, about the virtues of keeping happy, backward peoples in ignorance. Such an attitude seems like that of a fat man preaching the benefits of fasting to a starving beggar.
>
> "And I am not impressed by the attacks on television because of the truly dreadful programs it often carries. Every TV program has some educational content; the cathode tube is a window on the world—indeed, on many worlds. Often it is a very murky window, but I have slowly come to the conclusion that, on balance, even bad TV is better than no TV at all."

Many will disagree with this—and I sympathize with them. Electronic cultural imperialism will sweep away much that is good, as well as much that is bad. Yet it will only accelerate changes which were in any case inevitable; and on the credit side, the new media will preserve for future generations the customs, performing arts and ceremonies of our time, in a way that was never possible in any earlier age.

Of course, there are a great many of our present customs which should *not* be preserved, except as warnings to future generations. Slavery, torture, racial and religious persecution, treatment of women as chattels, mutilation of children because of ancient superstitions, cruelty to animals—the list is endless, and no country can proclaim total innocence. But looming monstrously above all these evils is the ever-present threat of nuclear war.

I wish I could claim that improved communications would lead to peace, but the matter is not as simple as that. Excellent communications—even a common language!—have not brought peace to Northern Ireland, to give but one of many possible examples. Nevertheless, good communications of every type, and at all levels, are essential if we are ever to establish peace on this planet. As the mathematicians would say—they are necessary, but not sufficient.

Perhaps an additional necessity may be the International Monitoring Satellite system proposed by the French government in 1978, and now the subject of a UN report which is being reissued this month (May 1983) at the request of the General Assembly. I refer you to this 123-page document (E.83.IX.3—*The Implications of Establishing an International Satellite Monitoring Agency*) for details; all I need say here is that it considers the potential benefits to mankind if *all* nations had access to the orbital reconnaissance information now available only to the United States and the Soviet Union. Roughly speaking, these powers now have the ability to observe any piece of military equipment larger than a rifle, in clear weather during daylight, and to track surface vessels at *any* time.

You will not be surprised to know that both the United States and the USSR agree in opposing any scheme that will break their joint monopoly on strategic information, and one of their main criticisms of the monitoring satellite system is all too valid. Even if it were established, could it *really* work during a period of international crisis—if more than a hundred nations each had a finger on the ERASE button of the computer that stored the disputed information?

I have a modest proposal. The French, who suggested the IMS in the first place, are about to launch an Earth Resources Satellite (SPOT) whose capabilities in some respects approach those of military reconnaissance satellites. Its images will be available, on a purely commercial basis, to anyone who wants to buy them, at the rate of about 30 cents per square kilometer.

Suppose a small consortium of traditionally neutral countries set up an image-processing and intelligence-evaluating organization. (Sweden, with its Stockholm International Peace Research Institute, is an obvious choice; one could add Switzerland and the Netherlands—perhaps that would be enough!) It would contract with the SPOTimage company for satellite information and analyze it for any country which considered itself threatened—on condition that the results were made available to the whole world.

This would only be a beginning, of course; the next step would be to purchase a SUPERSPOT with much higher resolution. I leave others to work out the details, but none of the problems seems insuperable. And with all respect to the distinguished organization in whose premises we are assembled, three or four nations could have the system running smoothly—*years* before 155 could even agree on its desirability.

Such an institute could well adopt, without irony, the ambiguous slogan of the U.S. Strategic Air Command: "Peace is our profession." And though I wish I could offer the facilities of the Center for Modern Technologies which we hope to set up in Sri Lanka, I fear that it will be quite a while before it would possess the necessary skills and equipment. Yet nothing would be more appropriate, for here in this very building I once heard Prime Minister Sirimavo Bandaranaike make her proposal for an Indian Ocean Zone of Peace. We might take at least one small step toward that goal if everything moving on the face of the Indian Ocean was clearly labeled for all the world to see.

I would like to end this survey of our telecommunications future with one of the most remarkable predictions ever made. In the closing decade of the nineteenth century an electrical engineer, W. E. Ayrton, was lecturing at London's Imperial Institute about the most modern of communications devices, the submarine telegraph cable. He ended with what must, to all his listeners, have seemed the wildest fantasy:

"There is no doubt that the day will come, maybe when you and I are forgotten, when copper wires, gutta-percha coverings and iron sheathings will be relegated to the Museum of Antiquities. Then, when a person wants to telegraph to a friend, he knows not where, he will call in an electro-magnetic voice, which will be heard loud by him who has the electro-magnetic ear, but will be silent to everyone else. He will call 'Where are you?' and the reply will come 'I am at the bottom of the coal-mine' or 'Crossing the Andes' or 'In the middle of the Pacific'; or perhaps no reply will come at all, and he may then conclude that his friend is dead."

This truly astonishing prophecy was made in 1897, long before anyone could imagine how it might be fulfilled. A century later, by 1997, it will be on the verge of achievement, because the wristwatch telephone will be coming into general use. And if you still believe that such a device is unlikely, ask yourself this question: Who could have imagined the personal watch, back in the Middle Ages—when the only clocks were clanking, room-sized mechanisms, the pride and joy of a few cathedrals?

For that matter, many of you carry on your wrists miracles of electronics that would have been beyond belief even twenty years ago. The symbols that flicker across those digital displays now merely give time and date. When the zeros flash up at the end of the century, they will do far more than that. They will give you direct access to most of the human race, through the invisible networks girdling our planet.

The long-heralded global village is almost upon us, but it will last for only a flickering moment in the history of mankind. Before we even realize that it has come, it will be superseded—by the global family.

New Communications and the Developing World

I deeply appreciate the honor His Excellency President Jayewardene has done me in appointing me a delegate of Sri Lanka to this meeting, and it is strange to be back here again, almost sixteen years after addressing the 1965 UNESCO Conference on "Communications in the Space Age." I hope to use that sixteen-year interval as a basis for a still further projection into the future, particularly as it concerns the so-called developing world. (As if there are any parts of

Address to the UNESCO Conference on the International Programme for the Development of Communications (IPDC), Paris, 16 June 1981.

the world which aren't developing, though some portions may well be overdeveloped....)

In many ways, and for many purposes, printed matter—books, newspapers, wallposters—will always be the best and cheapest form of communication. But now electronics has given us tools that can perform miracles impossible to the printed word—and which, of course, can reach millions who are unable to read. The newest and most powerful of these communications devices depend upon space technology, and because this fact is not yet generally realized I shall be concentrating upon it today.

But first, a few basic considerations: What does a country *need* in the way of electronic communications? At the risk of stating the obvious—which is often not a bad idea anyway—I will list them in order of priority.

1. The Telephone

A reliable telephone system must surely have the first priority: it affects every aspect of life—personal, business, government. We have also belatedly realized that it can be a major energy saver, making countless journeys unnecessary. It is also the greatest *lifesaver* ever invented, though often it requires a tragedy to bring that point home. A few years ago, thousands died when a dam burst in an Asian country. The telephone that should have warned them was out of order....

It will be a long time—though not as long as you may think—before everybody has a telephone. But with a telephone in every village, we can have the next best thing. Telegrams can be dictated so that anyone can get a message to anyone else within a few hours, with all the implications this has for business and social life.

2. Radio

There is no need to stress the value of radio, both for spreading information and establishing a national consciousness. If I were dictator of a country so poor that it had to choose between a telephone system and a radio service, I would be tempted to put my money on the the radio—despite everything I've just said about the importance of telephones.

And radio is nowhere near the end of its development. We have seen the transistor revolution of the 1960s merge into the solid state revolution of the 1970s, so that radios are cheaper and smaller and more reliable than anyone could have dreamed, even thirty years ago. I can see at least two more revolutions ahead. First there will be wide scale use of built-in solar cells to generate electricity, so that we won't have to bother about batteries anymore— what a boon that will be in remote places! Second will be the coming of direct-broadcast satellites, so that perfect reception will be possible over all the world, and the horrid cracklings of the short waves will be a thing of the past.

3. Television

Everything that can be said about radio is true of television, squared: so most of my talk will concentrate on this medium.

4. Telex

Telex equipment is still very expensive and limited to commercial and government use. However, recently developments in the home computer field have shown that it could be quite cheap. It will eventually merge into—

5. Data and Computer Networks

Even for highly developed countries, these are still in their infancy, though they undoubtedly represent the wave of the future. It will be a long time before we in the Third World can afford them; of greater importance to us may be what I have named—

6. Electronic Tutors

These will not involve communications links at all; they will be the next generation's equivalent of today's pocket calculators and will be about the same size and cost. They could trigger as big a quantum jump in mass education as did the invention of printing, five centuries ago.

But let me start by going back to 1965, when I was here last. As it happens, that was also the year when the first commercial communications satellite, Early Bird (INTELSAT I) went into orbit. It could carry 240 telephone circuits, or a single television channel.

Fifteen years later, in 1980, INTELSAT V was launched. It carried not 240, but 12,000 simultaneous phone calls—at a fraction of the cost. *And* several TV channels at the same time.

However, we are now reaching the limits of what can be done by purely robot satellites. Comsats as large as tennis courts can just be squeezed into existing launch vehicles, to unfold like glittering metal flowers when they reach space. But in another decade we shall need satellites as big as football fields—ultimately, as large as cities (indeed, some of them will be cities!). They will become possible, thanks to manned transportation systems like the space shuttle, which can carry construction crews and their equipment into orbit.

But why do we need such huge satellites—what have they got to do with the problems of the Third World? The answer may seem paradoxical, even perverse.

In highly developed regions like the United States and much of Europe, communications satellites are a great convenience, but are not absolutely vital. These countries already have excellent cable and microwave links.

To many developing countries, however, satellites are *essential*; they will make it unnecessary to build the elaborate and expensive ground systems required in the past. Indeed, to such countries, satellites could be a matter of life and death. To put it as dramatically as possible, unless major investments are made in space, millions are going to die, or eke out brief and miserable lives. And most of those millions will be in the Third World.

Let me explain this paradox, which is typical of the way in which technology affects modern society—and is why no one without *some* understanding of these matters should be allowed to enter the corridors of power.

Because the first comsats were small and feeble, it was necessary to build huge, multimillion-dollar ground stations, with dishes thirty meters across, to contact them. Thus their sole use was to provide links between national telephone, telex and TV networks—where these existed. They transformed the pattern of world communications but did not directly affect the man in the street—still less the man in the mud hut.

That situation is changing, with explosive speed. When only a few-score earth stations were involved, it made sense—indeed, there was no alternative in the 1960s and 1970s—to put the complexity and expense on the ground. But now that there are larger and more powerful satellites in orbit, ground stations can be much smaller and cheaper. Indeed, for the simplest ones the cost has been reduced a *thousandfold*! All over the United States there are now homes with dishes about three meters across, picking up scores of programs from the communications satellites hovering high in the southern sky. Soon these dishes will be less than a meter across, and everyone who can afford TV at all will have them. This is the beginning of the DBS—*direct-broadcast satellite*—revolution. It means that ultimately a few very large satellites can provide any type of service—telephone, telex, television, data, computing facilities—at extremely low *per capita* cost to every member of the human race.... except for those rather few people who live near the North or South Poles....

I'm not saying that satellites will do everything. In heavily populated areas, fiber-optic cables and short-range radio or infrared broadcasts will often be preferable. But even these local systems will, of course, be linked to the global network through satellites. And *only* satellites can provide every conceivable type of communication cheaply and efficiently over entire continents, and to all moving vehicles on land, sea or in the air.

One of the first persons to realize the implications of this for developing nations was the late Dr. Vikram Sarabhai, whom I first met at the UN Conference on the Peaceful Uses of Outer Space at Vienna in 1968. In the paper he delivered there, he stressed the importance of "leapfrogging" obsolescent technologies and—in some cases at least—going straight to advanced ones. We have seen this happen in transportation; many nations have bypassed the railroad age and gone directly from oxcarts to airplanes.

As you may know, Dr. Sarabhai was the driving force behind the first large-scale attempt to use a communications satellite—the NASA/Fairchild ATS 6—for direct TV broadcasting to rural areas. Unfortunately, he did not live to see even the initiation of that daring experiment which took place in 1975–76. It was brilliantly carried out by his colleagues of the Indian Space Research Organization and the Space Applications Centre at Ahmedabad, headed by Dr. Yash Pal—who I am happy to see will be Secretary General of the next UN space conference in 1982.

Some of the remarks that Dr. Sarabhai made at the 1968 Conference deserve to be repeated now: the intervening years have made them even more timely:

"A developing nation following a step-by-step approach towards progress is landed with units of small size, which do not permit the economic deployment of new technologies. Through undertaking ventures of uneconomic size with obsolete technologies, the race with advanced nations is lost before it is started.... Developing nations such as India have the possibility of effectively using space communications for national needs. Compared to advanced nations ... they have indeed an advantage *through not having an existing major investment in older technologies*" [my italics].

Of course there are problems, and to continue quoting Dr. Sarabhai:

> "We often meet with a lack of self-confidence to pursue major tasks involving complex and unfamiliar technologies... anything which is innovative... is automatically regarded with suspicion. The administrative structure of governments in many nations is dominated at the top not by technocrats but by professional administrators, lawyers or soldiers, who are hardly likely to provide the insights, experience and the first-hand knowledge of science and technology which are necessary at the decision-making level. Moreover, advanced nations often play a negative role in their interaction with the developing countries. There is seduction by their political and commercial salesmen who dangle new gimmicks which they suggest should be imported...."

That last warning of Dr. Sarabhai's is one that I would like to endorse—and amplify. No technology in the history of mankind has ever produced so many hypnotically irresistible gadgets as the electronics business. Radio telephones, visual display units, talking calculators, video recorders—the list is endless. And six months after one device comes on the market, it's superseded by a model twice as good at half the cost.

Thus any developing country wishing to take advantage of all these marvelous new facilities must proceed with great caution. There is, as Dr. Sarabhai warned, always grave danger of becoming locked into an obsolete technology. You must be particularly wary when something is offered you for free—there may be a catch. Even with the best will in the world, and the most expert advice, it's sometimes impossible to avoid bad decisions. The speed of technological development is so swift that the better is the enemy of the good, and the best is the enemy of both.

At this very moment, in the vital field of video recording, such a complex multibillion-dollar battle of standards is raging that a wise buyer will wait to do business with the survivors. We now have three main TV standards—

PAL, SECAM and NTSC. There are three competing videotape systems—Betamax, VHS, Phillips—with rumors
of a much more compact one (longitudinal recording) on
the horizon. Also two incompatible video *disc* systems are
about to come on the market. And in the United States,
CBS has just demonstrated high-definition TV using over
a thousand lines.... If you're not thoroughly confused,
you've not understood what I'm saying.

Fortunately, the development of global networks will
eventually compel some degree of standardization, and
many of the improved systems will still be compatible
with the old ones, as black-and-white TV sets can still
work with color transmissions. Nevertheless, I don't envy
anyone who has to advise his country what to buy—or
to accept as a gift—in the telecommunications field during the next few years. Or, for that matter, for the rest
of the century. By 2001 *everything* we have now will still
be operating somewhere. And it will *all* be obsolescent.

Let us ignore these messy practical problems, which
can and must be solved, and look at the wider view. We
are now entering an era when any conceivable type of
communication or information could be available to any
individual, anywhere on earth, at any time. The only constraints are economic and political, not technical.

Like all technologies, the ability to communicate is
neutral; it can be used for good or for bad. There was an
amusing example of this recently, not a thousand kilometers from Sri Lanka, when the venerable profession
of piracy had a sudden revival. A small ship was forced
to anchor, owing to engine trouble, at a remote Indian
Ocean island—and a flotilla of local canoes promptly descended upon it. In no time, everything that wasn't
screwed down—and many things that were—had been
spirited away, despite the anguished protests of the crew.

How did these latter-day pirates—these unsophisti-
cated islanders—learn so quickly about their windfall?
Simple—they'd all called each other up on their citizen
band radios....

Of course, this doesn't mean that CB radios should be
prohibited any more than one should ban telephones because countless crimes have been committed with their
aid. We must accept the good with the bad, unless we

assume that the invention of speech was a big mistake in the first place.

At this point I would like to draw a distinction between *regulation* and *control* in the field of communications. Regulation of some sort is inevitable and necessary for the good of all users, just as one has to decide whether to drive on the right or the left hand side of the road. Regulation is essential to ensure standardization and because spectrum space is limited; the International Telecommunications Union has been doing this task with considerable success, for over a hundred years.

But *control*—i.e., the management of the *messages*, not the *medium*—that is another matter. It ranges all the way from complete censorship to well-intentioned cultural guidance. Let me quote my friend Dr. Yash Pal on this:

> "In the drawing rooms of large cities you meet many people who are concerned about the damage one is going to cause to the integrity of rural India by exposing her to the world outside. After they have lectured you about the dangers of corrupting this innocent, beautiful mass of humanity, they usually turn around and ask: 'Well, now that we have a satellite, when are we going to see some American programs?' Of course, they themselves are immune to cultural domination or foreign influences."

I'm afraid that cocktail party intellectuals are the same everywhere. Because we frequently suffer from the scourge of information pollution, we find it hard to imagine its even deadlier opposite—information starvation. I get very annoyed when I hear arguments—usually from those who have been educated beyond their intelligence—about the virtues of keeping happy, backward peoples in ignorance. Such an attitude seems like that of a fat man preaching the benefits of fasting to a starving beggar. And I'm not impressed by the attack on television because of the truly dreadful programs it often carries. Every TV program has *some* educational content; the cathode ray tube is a window on the world—indeed, on many worlds. Often it's a very murky window, but I've slowly come to the conclusion that, on balance, even bad TV is preferable to no TV at all.

In this connection, let me quote a testimonial from an unexpected source. During the late 1950s, South Africa was the only wealthy country in the world which did *not* have a television service. The minister in charge of broadcasting adamantly refused to permit one. "Television," he proclaimed, "will mean the end of the white man in Africa."

That was an extremely perceptive remark. From his point of view, the minister was perfectly right. If the pen is mightier than the sword, the camera can be mightier than both.

No wonder that *all* governments, whether they are liberal or not, make some attempt to control what appears on television. Indeed, there is material which virtually everyone would agree should be kept out. Sadistic pornography, incitement to violence against racial or religious minorities are obvious examples.

Back in 1960—five years before INTELSAT I—I published a short story about a plot to brainwash the United States with the help of communications satellites broadcasting pornographic programs. I wrote it with the deliberate intention of making people think about the potential of comsats, both for good and for evil.

There is a vast territory where even men of goodwill may disagree fundamentally on what should, or should not, be presented to the public. Exposures of scandals or political abuses—especially by visiting television teams who go home and make rude documentaries—can be painful, but also very valuable. Many rulers might still be in power—or even alive—had they known what was really happening in their own country. A wise statesman once said: "A free press can give you hell; but it can save your skin." That is even more true of TV reporting—which, thanks to satellites, will soon be transformed out of all recognition.

Last month I had the pleasure of showing my old friend Walter Cronkite around Sri Lanka while we filmed one of his "Universe" programs. I say "filmed," but actually we were using electronic cameras, and it was wonderful to view what we had shot within minutes instead of days.

However, even the electronic cameraman still has to

get his cassettes through an obstacle course of postal authorities and customs officials and censors. But not for much longer; very soon he will need only a small collapsible dish, about the shape and size of a beach umbrella, and he'll be able to beam his pictures up to the nearest satellite, and straight to home. . . .

The implications of this are truly enormous. Just one example: How many soldiers would shoot a cameraman, if they knew that millions of people were watching? And if you think that some countries would not admit TV teams under these conditions—well, as equipment becomes so compact that a single man can carry it, the more difficult it will be to keep him out. And the harder closed societies try, the harder they will have to explain what it is they are so anxious to hide. In the end, they'll give up.

You doubt this? Then let me remind you of one astonishing step which has already occurred in this direction. Could you imagine, twenty years ago, someone in the Pentagon asking his Russian counterpart: "Would you mind if we photograph the Soviet Union from end to end, at such resolution that we can see everything bigger than a football?"

Remember the uproar, back in 1960, when Gary Powers' Lockheed U2 was shot down over Russia, doing precisely this! Yet now it is happening every day, without a murmur of protest from either side. Reconnaissance satellites are of such benefit to both parties that they are accepted by mutual consent.

In the same way, it will have to be recognized that all types of information and communication (with some obvious exceptions) are of benefit to everyone. Truth will out eventually, and those who try to suppress it will be condemned by history, as a recent United States president discovered to his cost.

In the struggle for freedom of information, technology, not politics, will be the ultimate decider. One turning point came several years ago, though few people realized it at the time. With the introduction of IDD (International District Dialing) the power of the state to control news was irrevocably broken. Private individuals could speak to each other across frontiers, and though Big Brother might catch some of them, he couldn't possibly keep track of them all.

But this is just a beginning, for the age of the telephone as a fixed instrument is swiftly passing. One of the main objectives of the very large comsats now being discussed is the provision of mobile, person-to-person communications. The old science-fiction dream of the wristwatch telephone could soon come true, and at a cost of a few dollars—given the determination to achieve it. Can you imagine the impact of this upon societies where, at present, there is only one telephone per thousand people? Sometime during the next century, the human race will become one big, gossiping family.

As the world comes to depend more and more upon satellites not only for all types of communications, but weather forecasting and resources inventories, search and rescue, navigation, etc., etc., the developing countries will be faced with a problem clearly foreseen by Dr. Sarabhai. I quote again from his speech to the 1968 Vienna conference:

> "One of the hardest questions to be faced in adopting a satellite for national needs arises from the fact that many interested nations would not expect in the near future to have an independent capability for placing such a satellite in orbit.... The political implications of a national system depending on foreign agencies for launching a satellite are complex.... Perhaps collaborative participation of nations in the construction and operation of a launching system for the peaceful uses of outer space would be realized in the long run. The military overtones of a launcher development program of course complicate the free transmittal of technology...but knowledge cannot for long be contained within artificial boundaries and one has to learn to share.... Restrictions on the transfer of technologies which are involved in the peaceful uses of outer space merely jeopardize the security of the world through retarding the progress of nations."

Any Third World nation wishing to have its satellite launched will soon have quite a number of options. Currently, the most reliable haulage firms are the United States and the USSR, either of whom will be happy to quote prices...at least to their friends. Many years ago the president of COMSAT remarked to me, in his Washington office: "If the Russians offer me a better deal than NASA, I'll accept." Before long the European Space Agency, China, India and Japan will also be in the market. And there are a couple of dark horses trying to enter the race with cut-price launchers—Lutz Kayser's controversial OTRAG operation, and Gary Hudson's California-based company.

So five years from now there will be no lack of vehicles. I would suggest that a choice be made on purely pragmatic grounds—what insurance premium does Lloyd's quote on the launch? I am not joking—payload insurance is now very big business.

Of course, most developing countries will be concerned neither with building nor launching satellites, but merely renting facilities in them—as they do now. There will be more and more specialized satellites shared by countries in the same geographic region. Even countries which, down on earth, are not very friendly with each other. Radio waves have never respected frontiers, and from an altitude of 36,000 kilometers, national boundaries are singularly inconspicuous. The world of the future will be an open world.

I have time now for only a brief reference to another electronic development which is just about to burst upon us, and which may be at least as important to the Third World as communications satellites.

Little more than ten years ago, pocket calculators came on the market. Instantly, slide rules and mathematical tables became obsolete; engineers, scientists, businessmen—*everyone* who had to work with numbers had their lives transformed. The first calculator cost several hundred dollars: now you can buy far superior models for twenty.

Today, a second and even more momentous revolution is just starting based on the same technology. This is the advent of the electronic *book*—a whole encyclopedia— even a whole library—in the palm of your hand. The pocket translators already on the market just hint at the possibilities; these electronic books will also speak, so that they can, for example, teach a foreign language. Beyond that, they will have plugged-in programs, so that they can provide tutoring in virtually any subject. They will be nothing less than electronic educators—able to work twenty-four hours a day. Of course, no machine can replace a good *human* teacher—but no country ever has enough of those! When they are made in millions, the electronic tutors would cost no more than the pocket calculators of today. Solar powered, they would need no batteries; properly designed, they would never wear out. So their written-down cost would be negligible, and even the poorest countries could afford them, especially when the reforms and improved productivity they stimulate help those countries to boot-strap themselves out of poverty.

The electronic educator was the theme of my first Convocation Address to the University of Moratuwa (and also one of my Vikram Sarabhai lectures at the Physical Research Laboratory, Ahmedabad) and I refer anyone who is interested to the printed paper.*

To sum up—what I have tried to do is to sketch some of the truly astonishing communications possibilities of the next decade. Almost everything I have described will be commonplace by the year 1990—all of it will be available by 2000.

I am well aware that many of these electronic marvels may serve only to increase the sense of frustration in the countries where schools can't even afford blackboards and chalk. But more and more we must think of the human race as a single unit—and mankind can afford anything it wants, especially if it stops squandering its resources on weapons of destruction.

What I have described to you today are the weapons of peace.

*See Electronics and Education.

In the Hall of the Knights

Your Royal Highness, Mrs. Marconi Braga, my kind hosts from Philips, distinguished guests:

My great pleasure in receiving this award is at least doubled by the knowledge that it has already been won by two very good friends, who deserved it far more than I do.

Dr. John Pierce was the first engineer-scientist to publish a detailed technical analysis of communications satellites. Even more important, he was the driving force

Address given on 11 June 1982 at The Hague on presentation of the 8th Marconi International Fellowship Award by Prince Claus of the Netherlands.

behind the pioneering *practical* demonstrations with *Echo* and *Telstar*. He and Dr. Harold Rosen—who played a similar role with the first geostationary comsats—are the true fathers of satellite communications. That title has sometimes been given to me, but honesty compels me to disclaim it. I am not the father of comsats—merely the *god*father....

The other friend, whom I'm delighted to see here today, is my northern neighbor Dr. Yash Pal. I've known Dr. Pal since the early days of the Indian SITE project, which he directed so brilliantly after the untimely death of its founder, Dr. Vikram Sarabhai—whose work he is still continuing as Secretary General of UNISPACE. By a happy chance, I was in Ahmedabad when Dr. Pal received notification of *his* Marconi Award and was wondering how best to utilize it. Yash, I'd like to resume that discussion, just as soon as convenient....

I am not indulging in false modesty—a concept which all my friends would reject with hysterical laughter—when I say that *my* contribution to satellite communications was largely a matter of luck. I happened to be in the right place, at the right time. In the winter of 1944–45, World War II was obviously coming to an end, and one could think once more about the future. Dr. Wernher von Braun—another good friend, whom I miss badly—had demonstrated that big rockets were practical, to the grave detriment of London as target, and The Hague as launchpad. The time was ripe to think about reviving the British Interplanetary Society, which had been in suspended animation during hostilities.

But how could one possibly raise money for such a fantastic enterprise as space travel? Prewar estimates by the BIS had suggested that a lunar expedition might cost the truly astronomical sum of *one million dollars*, and it was ridiculous to imagine that governments would spend such awesome amounts on purely scientific projects. We would have to find the money ourselves; was there any way in which rockets could earn an honest living?

Rocket mail had been suggested, but that seemed a rather limited application, and it might take some time to overcome the poor advance publicity generated by the V.2....

I was pondering these matters in my spare time as an RAF radar officer, while helping to run the Ground Controlled Approach (GCA) system invented by Dr. Luis W. Alvarez and his Radiation Lab team. This operated at the then fantastically high frequency of 10 gigahertz, producing beams a fraction of a degree wide. I can recall, with some embarrassment, using the dear old Mark I to fire single pulses at the rising Moon and waiting for the echo three seconds later. (Obviously, the available power would have been orders of magnitude too low.)

So communications and astronautics were inextricably entangled in my mind, with results that now seem inevitable. If I had not proposed the idea of geostationary relays in my *Wireless World* letter of February 1945, and developed it in more detail the following October, half a dozen other people would have quickly done so. I suspect that my early disclosure may have advanced the cause of space communications by approximately fifteen minutes.

Or perhaps twenty. My efforts to promote and publicize the idea may have been much more important than conceiving it. In 1952, *The Exploration of Space* introduced communications satellites to several hundred thousand people—including John Pierce, whom I first met in May of that year and did my best to turn into a space cadet. (He was already one in secret, but as Director of Electronics Research at Bell Labs he had to conceal such unfortunate aberrations.) When he published his influential "Orbital Radio Relays" in May 1955, he had never even seen my own paper of a decade earlier; but of course he had no need of it—the mere suggestion was enough to an engineer of John's caliber.

From today's vantage point, it's amusing to note that "Orbital Radio Relays" was published in *Jet Propulsion*, the Journal of the American Rocket Society. Not long afterwards, the ARS became the American Institute of Aeronautics and Astronautics; but in 1955 there was not the slightest mention of space flight in the society's by-laws. Even the word "rocket" was avoided as too Buck Rogerish; only "jet propulsion" was respectable....

In complete contrast, the British Interplanetary Society was *only* interested in space travel and would have been quite happy to abandon rockets as soon as someone got round to inventing antigravity. I am not claiming that one viewpoint is superior to the other. The world needs uninhibited thinkers not afraid of far-out speculation; it also needs hard-headed, conservative engineers who can make their dreams come true. They complement each other, and progress is impossible without both. If there had been government—and dare I say industrial?—research establishments in the Stone Age, by now we would have had absolutely superb flint tools. But no one would have invented steel.

Let me end by sharing with you a discovery I've just been delighted to make, by pure luck—or serendipity, to use the now overpopular word derived from the ancient name for Sri Lanka. It links the pioneering days of European astronautics with the great man whose memory we have now gathered to honor.

Back in 1939, the British Interplanetary Society was always alert for publicity, and for several weeks we waged verbal war against skeptics in the dignified pages of the BBC's *The Listener*—until the editor finally declared that "This correspondence is now closed." I had completely forgotten that the controversy was triggered by a radio talk, "Myself and Life," by Dr. W. E. Barnes, then Bishop of Birmingham. It contains words as relevant today as when they were spoken forty-three years ago:

> It cannot be true that the Earth is the only planet on which life exists. . . . On other planets of other stars there must be consciousness; on them there must be beings with minds . . . some far more developed than our own . . . wireless messages from such remote conscious beings must be possible. The only time I met Marconi he told me of his search for such messages. So far we have failed to find them.
> [*The Listener*, 9 February 1939]

Yes, we have failed. But one day we will succeed. And then Marconi's last and greatest dream will have been fulfilled.

To Russia, with Love...

After flying KLM to Amsterdam June 8/9, I was met by my hosts from Philips and taken to the Hotel des Indes in The Hague—which apart from its canals reminded me of Kensington. Here I was greeted by Mrs. Gioia Marconi Braga (Marconi's daughter, and instigator of the award) and her husband George, as well as Dr. Walter Orr Roberts, current secretary of the Fellowship.

On the tenth, after several press conferences, there was lunch at the Italian Embassy (present His Excellency the Ambassador and his wife, the British and Sri Lankan ambassadors, the Bragas, and my host Dr. Pannenborg, Vice-Chairman of Philips). Then we paid a visit to the Frans Hals Museum, followed by a reception at the British Embassy, arranged to finish early so I could get a good night's sleep....

The award ceremony took place on the eleventh in the splendid Hall of the Knights. Philips had arranged a display of radio equipment dating back to Marconi and culminating in a large model of the latest communication satellite. They had installed a dish in the courtyard to receive TV from a European satellite, and the well-known broadcaster Raymond Baxter greeted us from the Goonhilly Downs Earth Station, reminding us that Marconi conducted his famous Atlantic transmission not far from here (also that I was born a little way up the coast, at Minehead....).

There was a welcoming party (the Burgomaster of The Hague, the Chief of Cabinet; Mr. Mili, Secretary General, International Telecommunications Union; Dr. Pannenborg) to meet H.R.H. Prince Claus, who presented me with the truly beautiful trophy; in my speech of thanks I made special mention of the French proposal for an International Monitoring Satellite for the preservation of peace (UN Document A/AC 206/14 of 6 August 1981). I hoped that Sri Lanka would support this project at the forthcoming UNISPACE 82 Conference in Vienna, where I would be one of the country's delegates and would also be delivering one of the four public lectures. I also added that I proposed to apply the $35,000 grant toward the Developing World Communications Centre which the government of Sri Lanka hopes to establish at the University of Moratuwa.

Then my old friend Professor Yash Pal (director of the historic Indian satellite instructional project, SITE, for which he won the Marconi Award in 1980, and now Secretary General of UNISPACE 82) gave an address. One interesting idea he put forward was the suggestion that low-altitude (e.g., two-hour period) satellites could provide cheap telex and similar services to equatorial countries, which need them even more urgently than the voice and TV provided at much greater expense by stationary comsats. When he complained that no one took him seriously, I rallied to his support (even though "Palsats" move in what *he* calls "anti-Clarke orbits").

The day concluded with a lavish dinner at the Hotel des Indes; somewhat to my embarrassment, Philips had put up large notices saying MR. CLARKE KINDLY REQUESTS YOU TO REFRAIN FROM SMOKING, which were received with widespread but not unanimous approval. The main address was given by ITU Secretary Mr. Mili, who stressed the importance of the upcoming World Communication Year, 1983.

The following day (Saturday, 12 June) we all relaxed on a bus trip to the "Floriade," a superb display of trees, shrubs and flowers of every conceivable type, which takes place every ten years. And on Sunday, Simon Welfare and John Fairley (principal perpetrators of "Arthur C. Clarke's Mysterious World") arrived on an arm-twisting expedition from Yorkshire TV, whose results—if any— only time will reveal. . . .

All this, hectic and enjoyable though it was, was a mere prelude to my USSR trip. After saying good-bye to the Bragas and my kind hosts in The Hague, I arrived at Moscow on the evening of the fourteenth, to be met by Counsellor Casie Chetty of the Sri Lanka Embassy and my friend and publisher Vasili Zaharchenko, editor of *Tekhnika Molodezhi* magazine. Also present were Oleg Bitov, translator of my last two books, and my excellent guide and interpreter (*she* called herself "slave-driver"), Svetlana Prokhorova. When I tactlessly announced I'd lunched with the *other* Svetlana (Stalin's daughter) in New York some years ago, she replied cheerfully, "Oh, I'm named after her." Oleg had run into trouble translating *Rendezvous with Rama*. "What," he asked plaintively, "is a *blivet*? I can't find it in any dictionary." I explained it was the same as a gubbins.

Though it was now late evening there was still plenty of light (something I couldn't grow accustomed to after two decades near the equator) so we made a quick trip to Red Square for the usual photos at Lenin's tomb. Then to the huge Ukrania Hotel, where I slept well and woke up to the good news that the Falklands war was over. (Throughout the trip, my trusty Sony ICF 7600—always referred to as my "spy radio"—was invaluable. Despite the amazing—shall we say?—electronic pollution occupying the Soviet ionosphere, I was usually able to get the BBC's English service, though sometimes it wasn't easy....)

June fifteenth was one of the most memorable days of my life. First, Vasili took me to the really stunning display of spacecraft at the Moscow Space Park, with the huge Vostok launcher mounted outside. Then, with Svetlana and our official photographer, we set off for Zvezdny Gorodok ("Star Village") about fifty kilometers from Moscow. Feeling that my camera was an embarrassment, I handed it over before we entered—only to be given it back just as soon as we were inside, so I was able to shoot everything I wanted...

I'd been disappointed to hear that my favorite cosmonaut, General Alexei Leonov (Apollo-Soyuz commander, and the first man to do a spacewalk) would be at Baikonur for the upcoming Soviet–French mission. So I was delighted when I saw him waiting, with TV camera crew, at the entrance to the administrative building. We greeted each other with bear hugs, and he introduced me to two other cosmonauts I'd met before—Vitaliy Sevastyanov and Valery Lyakov, whom I'd recently taken for a spin in my Hovercraft.

Alexei then took me to his commanding officer, General Beregovoy (Soyuz 3 pilot), who gave me an interesting but somewhat unexpected lecture, illustrated by rapid sketches, on the deplorable things man's doing to his environment. (Translating this put quite a strain on Svetlana, who claimed that she not only didn't know any science—she didn't like what she *did* know. Toward the end of the trip, however, she admitted that several of the scientists she'd met seemed quite human.)

Then Alexei led me to his office, and I handed over the various gifts I'd brought—tea, a teak and silver elephant, a set of British Interplanetary Society "space ties," UNDERWATER SAFARI tee-shirts.* I also gave the center a copy of James Oberg's analysis of the Russian Space program, *Red Star in Orbit*, which was soon being rapidly

---

*Pardon the commercial for my Sri Lanka diving company—the spin-off from *The Reefs of Taprobane*, *The Treasure of the Great Reef*, etc.

perused. In return, Alexei gave me the handsome new volume of paintings he has done with his fellow artist Andrei Sokolov, *Life Among Stars*. (Unfortunately I had no time to meet Sokolov, but talked to him briefly over the telephone.)

Next we went to the center's cinema, where I was shown a deeply moving film *Our Yuri*, which I was assured had never been screened elsewhere. It recorded every stage of Gagarin's training as well as his family life; from time to time young Alexei Leonov appeared on the screen, with other cosmonauts (some famous, some dropped from the program, some dead...) and I wondered what memories it evoked in the much-decorated forty-eight-year-old general sitting beside me.

Then, followed by the TV cameras, we visited the Soyuz-Salyut trainers (just vacated by the crew now waiting at Baikonur) and crawled inside for a series of on-the-spot interviews. Since the spacecraft were designed for weightless operation, it wasn't easy to negotiate some of the narrower sections. I was also inserted, with great hilarity, into an EVA suit and then filmed grinning inanely through the visor.

We then left the building and proceeded to the Gagarin memorial a few hundred meters away, where Cosmonaut Sevastyanov demonstrated that he was a very professional TV interviewer. We had almost finished, and Alexei was asking some pointed questions about *Odyssey Two* (we first met at the 1968 premiere of *2001* in Vienna) when the skies opened and we had to run for it.

The next stop was Gagarin's own office, exactly as he had left it, with the clock recording the time of his death. "I heard the crash," Alexei told me somberly. He added that the cause had never been conclusively determined and gave me a memento I shall value as much as the inscribed copy of the autobiography Gagarin himself presented me in 1961—a fragment of the jet trainer in which he was killed. Alexei also gave me another rarity—the handsome medal struck to commemorate the twentieth anniversary of Gagarin's flight.

The last stop was at Alexei's own apartment, where his wife (another Svetlana!) had prepared a meal for us. I also met his engaging little parrot Lolita, who normally perches on his shoulder but occasionally orbits the room uttering shrill cries. And here, between toasts, I revealed that most of the action in *2010: Odyssey Two* takes place aboard the spaceship *Cosmonaut Alexei Leonov*. This obviously delighted Alexei, and now most of the Soviet Union has heard, via TV, his ebullient reaction: "Then it must be a good ship!" (It is.)

I then took a deep breath, and asked *my* Svetlana to translate the next bit very carefully. It was my hope and belief, I said, that *Odyssey Two*—in which seven Russians and three Americans start off as acquaintances and end up as friends (or better) would help to improve understanding between the United States and the USSR. But genuine understanding must be based on honesty, and I would be less than frank if I failed to warn him that there were some aspects of the book that would not be well received in the Soviet Union. In particular, the plasma propulsion system for *Leonov* was being invented right now, by Russia's most famous scientist, whose moving appeals for peace I greatly admired. He has plenty of time on his hands, being exiled in Gorky....*

Alexei gave a wry smile, and we parted affectionately. Then we all drove back to Moscow for dinner at Counsellor Chetty's—and the midnight sleeper to Leningrad, where Vasili and I were ambushed in a bleary condition by TV cameras around 7 A.M., immediately on stepping onto the platform. Among those waiting for us I was delighted to meet Yuri Artsutanov, inventor of the "space elevator" (theme of *The Fountains of Paradise*—my very last book, as I'd been claiming ever since 1977). He seems a shy, modest person, and I hope all the publicity (the

---

*I felt it tactless to spell out in detail that the dedication of *Odyssey Two* would read:

> Dedicated, with respectful admiration, to two great
> Russians, both depicted herein:
> General Alexei Leonov—Cosmonaut, Hero of the Soviet
> Union, Artist
>
> and
>
> Academician Andrei Sakharov—Scientist, Nobel
> Laureate, Humanist.

All concerned have (so far) taken this quite well. When discussing the translation, my Russian publisher, with a polite cough, has said: "You realize, of course...."

cameras invaded his apartment when I was there) hasn't upset his life.

The two days in Leningrad (I now understand why it is called the Venice of the North) passed incredibly swiftly. Highlights were a TV interview in the Gas Dynamics Laboratory Museum, which has a historic display of USSR rocket engine development; showing my Sri Lanka color slides to the local Writers' Union; a surprising chance meeting with an Oak Ridge nuclear physicist in the hotel restaurant; Czar Peter's little country estate, about the size of Versailles, with its famous gilded statues and fountains (inevitably referred to by my colleague as "The Fountains of Paradise"); my excellent and cultured Intourist lady guide; broad daylight at 10 P.M.; and of course the Hermitage. . . .

We spent only an hour there, which is probably about right for a first exposure to its two-million-plus exhibits. As I staggered out, reeling with culture shock, I coined a new passive verb, gleefully adopted by my entourage: to be hermitaged.

In Leningrad there occurred one of those trivial little incidents that do so much to determine a visitor's impressions of a new country. Wherever we went, people were always staring at our official limousine, doubtless wondering what bigwig was riding inside it. I found this rather oppressive, so was delighted when a policeman stopped the car and bawled out the poor driver for no apparent reason. ("He's bored and wants something to do," explained my hosts. "Anyway, it proves we're a democracy." I gladly conceded their point—at *this* level, anyway.)

On the second day, there was time for a full hour's recording in the Leningrad TV studio, later broadcast nationwide, and then Vasili and I were once more on the midnight sleeper back to Moscow, for the final round of official visits.

Friday June 18 saw two important conferences—the first at INTERSPUTNIK with Director General Yuri Krupin and his staff, the second with Deputy Minister Zubarev and staff at the Ministry of Posts and Telecommunications. At each I carefully explained my somewhat anomalous position as a British citizen unofficially assisting Sri Lanka on a private visit arranged by my Russian publisher. I hope it made sense to them; it didn't always to me.

With both Comrades Krupin and Zubarev I left the prospectus for the Sri Lanka Communications Centre and asked for their support. I also mentioned my hope of seeing a serious discussion at UNISPACE of the French control satellite proposal. As I expected, no great enthusiasm was evinced, and someone remarked cynically that perhaps the French wanted to sell the hardware. Unfortunately I didn't think of the right retort: "So what?"

That evening there was a meeting with about twenty science-fiction writers and editors at the Writers' Union; it was end-of-term, and everyone was leaving for the summer holidays, so the place was in a festive mood. After I'd explained some of the problems they might have sanitizing *Odyssey Two*, we went to dinner and I managed to handle all the toasts with the one glass of wine which is my operational limit.

On the nineteenth, to my pleasure and surprise, the Director of the Institute of Space Research, Academician Sagdeyev, brought his top scientists in on a Saturday morning for a two-hour conference. I was particularly interested to meet N. S. Kardashev, author of some of the most fascinating speculations about supercivilizations, and said that I was sorry I'd not been able to make contact with the other best-known astronomer in this field, I. S. Shklovsky (co-author with Carl Sagan of the classic *Intelligent Life in the Universe*). However, I was solemnly informed that putting Nik and Ioseph in the same room might result in a matter—antimatter explosion that could destroy Moscow.

Once again I plugged the Sri Lanka Communications Centre and the International Monitoring Satellite, adding that since both the United States *and* the USSR seemed opposed to it, I thought it was probably a good idea. My reference to "the gentleman in Gorky's" role in *Odyssey Two* also produced some wry smiles.

I was able to pass on a recent report from one of the Jet Propulsion Laboratory teams of inexplicably powerful radio emissions from a point source in Saturn's D-ring. This led to expressions of regret that JPL had now been forced to accept Defense Department contracts to continue its operations. I said I shared that regret—but it was only fair to point out that the Soviet Union's military space effort was *many times* that of the United States. (I've just looked up the figures—*ten* times that of the United States in payload weight, or 300 tons per annum, of which at least 75% is purely military.) Perhaps it was just as well that I did not know—as some of my audience undoubtedly did—that at the very moment the USSR was engaged in an unprecedented salvo of missile tests— one SS20, one submarine launch, several ICBMs— *and* a satellite-killer....

Then I made a quick shopping trip with Svetlana, because my name would be mud if I didn't bring back *some* presents. I never had time to visit any foreign-exchange stores, for the ordinary shops seemed perfectly adequate, with surprisingly low prices.

The final item on Saturday was a meeting with Nina Kubatieva, who'd flown in from Novosibirsk to present me with her university thesis, "The Science Fiction Novels of Arthur C. Clarke." (I wish I could read it; any publisher interested in a translation?) Earlier, I'd also had the pleasure of meeting Larisa Mikhaylova, another longtime correspondent, who gave me *her* candidate thesis on "British and American Science Fiction."

Sunday, June 20, was my last day, and Vasili and Svetlana took me to the apartment of Academician Sergei Kapitza, famous son of Rutherford's *protégé*, the legendary Peter Kapitza.* Here we did a one-hour TV recording for the twice-monthly series Professor Kapitza has been running for many years; except for the fact that he covers a much wider range of subjects, it would not be unfair to call him the Soviet Union's answer to Patrick Moore

---

*Pyotr Kapitza (b. 1894) made great advances in low temperature physics and magnetism while working under nuclear pioneer Ernest Rutherford at the Cavendish Laboratory, Cambridge; he was the first foreigner in 200 years to be elected a Fellow of the Royal Society. When he revisited the Soviet Union in 1934, Stalin took away his passport and made him head of a major science institute, on the quite reasonable (and rapidly justified) grounds that he was needed at home more badly than in the West. When it was clear that he would not be returning to Cambridge, Lord Rutherford arranged for all his science equipment to be shipped to the USSR; they did things differently in those days. Kapitza didn't get back to Cambridge until 1966.

and Carl Sagan (indeed, he is planning a collaboration with Carl). I was particularly interested to learn that he held the country's No. 2 SCUBA license, and we reminisced about spots we'd both dived at along the Great Barrier Reef.

Incidentally, Academician Kapitza was the only Russian I met with no trace of accent; he could pass anywhere as a university-educated Englishman. But then, as he pointed out, he was born in Cambridge—so many Englishmen would consider that he certainly *does* have quite an accent....

When we got back to the hotel I was too exhausted to do anything but go to bed, and was drowsing off when there was a vigorous knocking on the door. Deciding that it was either a reporter, or the bearer of yet another autographed book to add to the two-meter-high pile I'd already acquired (and would have to get the Sri Lankan embassy to ship back), I ignored it. Ditto a phone call, a few minutes later. Now I'm sorry, as someone was trying to tell me that one of my four or five TV programs was on the air; still, I'm not sure I could have stayed awake.

My last evening in Moscow was spent checking my after-word for a book of space-art that Vasili is editing; then I watched one of the finalists in the current Tschaikovsky competition while Svetlana (who disapproved of my "pour-in-and-stir-well" technique) packed my bags. She also gave me a little poem she'd translated, whose sentiments I was now beginning to understand:

> You can't grasp Russia with your mind;
>   Accepted notions here will lead astray.
> Its heart is of a certain kind;
>   Belief in Russia is the only way.
> —Tyutchev

With a twinkle in her eye, she also paid me her ultimate compliment: "You're not a bit like an Englishman."

Around midnight, we were just preparing to leave for the airport to catch the (ugh!) 3 A.M. Aeroflot flight to Sri Lanka when there was a delightful surprise—a call from Alexei Leonov, on his way to the launch site, bidding me "bon voyage." I said I hoped to see him some day in Sri

Lanka, and sent my good wishes for the forthcoming mission (as I write this, I've just heard that the docking has been successful.)

Svetlana, Vasili and Counsellor Chetty got me swiftly through the formalities at the magnificent (and at that ghastly hour almost empty) Sheremetyevo-2 airport. As before, Aeroflot was right on time; I was impressed by the good-natured way in which the stewardesses tolerated in-flight baggage (dolls, knapsacks, etc.) sometimes equal in volume to the people carrying it.

I was lucky enough to get three seats abreast, and though it wasn't as comfortable as the Moscow-Leningrad sleeper, I arrived in Colombo in pretty good shape . . . to confront approximately 200 pieces of mail, including the galleys of *Odyssey Two*—with an editorial request that all corrections be phoned to New York within forty-eight hours.

Life was back to normal, and it was hard to believe that the whole thing hadn't been a dream. . . .

War and Peace
in the
Space Age

We will take no frontiers into space.
Prelude to Space (1951)

Distinguished guests, ladies and gentlemen:
You may well wonder what a talk about
the militarization of space is doing in this
first seminar arranged by our brand-new Institute of Fundamental Studies. To that, I
can only answer that nothing is more *fundamental* than
the prevention of nuclear war. If we fail in this, all else
is irrelevant—science, politics, religion....

Perhaps I should also explain how I got involved with

Address given 11 December 1982 to the First Symposium of the Sri Lanka
Institute of Fundamental Studies, Bandaranaike Memorial International Conference Hall, Colombo.

space militarization, and my qualifications for talking about a subject on which no one without a top-level security clearance can be a real authority. So a brief personal note may be in order.

I became a member of the British Interplanetary Society in 1934, and have been thinking about extraterrestrial activities for rather a long time. These, alas, include warfare; I have just recalled that, as a Royal Air Force trainee, I wrote the space-battle sequence in my novel *Earthlight* (1955) during a lull in the London Blitz, while the buildings around me were still smoking from the impact of primitive iron bombs. Hiroshima was still four years in the future—and Neil Armstrong was only eleven years old....

Since then, either privately or in my capacity as Chairman of the British Interplanetary Society and of various space conferences, I have grown to know most of the leading figures in the field of astronautics. This June, I had the privilege of being hosted at the Gagarin Cosmonaut Training Centre by my friend General Alexei Leonov and his colleagues. In August, I was one of the Sri Lanka delegates to the Second United Nations Conference on the Peaceful Uses of Outer Space (UNISPACE 82); I had also attended the first one in 1968.

It soon became apparent at the 1982 conference that though the subject of space militarization was not on the official agenda—and indeed its inclusion had been opposed by the chief space-faring powers—it was very much on the minds of all the delegates. In their opening addresses, both the Secretary General of the United Nations and the Secretary General of the conference, Dr. Yash Pal, referred to the urgent need to prevent a new arms race beyond the atmosphere. This theme was repeated by almost all the national representatives.

In addition, a sort of parallel conference of "NGOs"—non-government organizations—was taking place half a kilometer away, and discussion here was much less inhibited. Unofficial but often very well-informed speakers—many of whom had come to Vienna at their own expense—expressed deeply felt views on space militarization. The fact that some of them had once made a living in this line of work made their testimony all the more impressive. As has been well said, the best game-keepers are ex-poachers....

On my way back to Sri Lanka from UNISPACE 82, our ambassador in Geneva, His Excellency Tissa Jayakoddy, asked me to address the UN Committee on Disarmament, which I did on August 31. The speech I then gave was subsequently placed in the *Congressional Record* (September 21) by Representative George E. Brown of California (Democrat), who is one of the few congressmen to make a stand against the militarization of space—with surprising courage, since it is the principal industry of his state. The speech I am giving now is an extension of my Geneva address and contains much material which I have been able to acquire since then.

The subject of space warfare graduated abruptly from science fiction to science fact in the summer of 1945, though not many people realized it at the time. The first long-range rocket—the German V.2—had made its appearance only a few months before; it is hard to realize that even while it was being tested, distinguished scientists such as Churchill's advisor Lord Cherwell dismissed the V.2 as a myth, refusing to believe in the existence of rockets with the incredible range of three hundred kilometers. But the V.2, with its warhead of one ton of chemical explosives, had no decisive influence on World War II. Its real implication was not apparent until the arrival of nuclear weapons.

Long before the war—indeed, well before the discovery of uranium fission in 1938—I had amused my friends in the British Interplanetary Society by coining an ominous prediction: "The release of atomic energy will make space travel not only possible—but imperative." Unfortunately, the positive part of this saying has not come true. Nuclear propulsion for spacecraft has proved to be a very difficult problem, and in the United States work on the atomic rocket was abandoned more than a decade ago. So we will have to save our planet, before we can escape from it; we cannot place our trust in nuclear Noah's Arks.

My serious thinking on these matters began in the summer of 1945, when the *Royal Air Force Quarterly* offered an award for the best essay on "The Rocket and the Future of Warfare." The prize of forty pounds—quite a lot of money in those days—was my first major literary income, and it has been a strange experience reading that paper again after thirty-seven years.

I would like to quote the lines of Shelley with which the essay began:

> Cease! Drain not to its dregs the urn
> Of bitter prophecy.
> The world is weary of the past,
> Oh, might it die or rest at last!

Nevertheless, "bitter prophecy" is indeed what we are concerned with today. So first, I must request you—if you have not already done so—to read Jonathan Schell's book *The Fate of the Earth*, which is the most convincing account yet given of the realities of nuclear warfare. It should be required reading for every statesman.

And yet Carl Sagan has summed up the implications of this entire book in a single chilling sentence. In my address to the UN Disarmament Committee I quoted it from memory and made an understandable mistake which only serves to emphasize the appalling—the literally unimaginable—nature of the problem. I quoted Sagan as stating that a full-scale nuclear exchange would be the equivalent of "World War Two once a minute, for the length of a lazy afternoon."

My memory was at fault. The correct quotation is "World War Two *once a second* for the length of a lazy afternoon." I would like those madmen who talk glibly about "protracted nuclear warfare" to think their way slowly through that sentence.

At UNISPACE 82 there was some confusion as to just what is meant by the "militarization of space." There are very few of man's artifacts which cannot be equally well used for peaceful or warlike purposes; what matters is the *intention*. It is impossible to define a class of devices and say, "These must not be developed, because they can be employed offensively."

Let me give an example: few things would seem more

remote from military affairs than the geodetic satellites used to detect minute irregularities in the earth's gravitational field. At first sight, this would seem to be of interest only to scientists; nevertheless, these subtle variations are of vital concern to the designers of intercontinental missiles, because unless the earth's gravitational field is accurately mapped, it is impossible to target a missile with precision. Thus purely scientific satellites, by greatly increasing the accuracy of warheads, can have a major impact on strategy. Yet does anyone suggest that they be prohibited?

Even meteorological satellites, one of the most benign of all applications of space technology, because they have already saved thousands of lives, are of obvious military importance—as was strikingly demonstrated in the recent South Atlantic War. Similarly, communications satellites play an absolutely vital role in military operations; yet neither represents a direct threat to peace.

Just as military helicopters can be used for disaster-relief work, so some military space systems can be positively benign. Indeed, we might not be alive today without the stabilizing influence of the reconnaissance satellites operated by both the United States and the USSR.

Let me remind you of a piece of recent history: in the early 1960s, there was a vigorous campaign in the United States claiming that the USSR was far in advance in the development of intercontinental ballistic missiles. The so-called missile gap was a major theme in the Kennedy-Nixon campaign: millions of words were written urging that the United States start a crash program to overcome the Soviet Union's "enormous" lead.

That missile gap was a total illusion—destroyed when American reconnaissance satellites revealed the true extent of Soviet rocket deployment. President Johnson later remarked that its reconnaissance satellites had saved the United States many times the cost of the space program, by making it unnecessary to build the counterforce originally intended. I would like to quote his exact words, which should be inscribed in letters of gold above the doors of the Pentagon:

"We were doing things we didn't need to do, we were building things we didn't need to build; *we were harboring fears we didn't need to harbor.*" [My italics]

However, in a sense, that information may have come too late. One can picture the feelings of the Soviet military planners when contemplating this American debate. *They* knew they did not have the weapons the United States claimed, so what was the purpose of the exercise? Were the Americans deliberately creating an excuse to rearm? That might have seemed the most plausible assumption—but in fact, ignorance rather than malice was the explanation. In any event, the Soviet Union decided it must produce the missiles which, at that time, existed only in the imagination of the Americans. So the seeds of a space arms race were planted, a quarter of a century ago.

It is possible to play a numbers game with payloads and launchings to prove almost anything. Statistics indicate that the Soviet Union has now launched about twice as many "military" payloads as the United States—by 1981, roughly 860 against 420, and the *numerical* disparity is increasing. Does this mean, as many in the West claim, that the Soviet Union has a more aggressive space program than the United States? Not necessarily, because mere numbers can be very misleading.

Let me quote figures for the vital photographic reconnaissance satellites to clarify this point. In the four years between 1977 and 1981, the United States launched 11. The Soviet Union launched the astonishing number of 175.

However—the giant American Big Birds and KH-11 reconnaissance satellites have operating lifetimes of between half a year and several years; the Soviet satellites (all given the "Cosmos" designation) are designed to function for only two to four *weeks*. Each policy has obvious advantages; the Russian mass-production system clearly scores in cheapness and flexibility. I think we can assume that each side is adequately served.

There is one area, however, in which the Soviet Union is clearly ahead. Photographic or TV reconnaissance is limited by cloud conditions; only radar can give all-weather coverage. And only the USSR has used radar satellites, *powered by nuclear reactors*, to reconnoiter the movements of ships at sea—as was embarrassingly revealed when *Cosmos 954* crashed in Canada in 1978.

At this point it is relevant to mention the Landsats or earth resources satellites, which give superb views of our planet, of enormous value to farmers, industrialists, city-planners, fishermen—in fact, anyone concerned with the use and abuse of Mother Earth. The United States has made its Landsat photographs, which have a ground resolution of roughly eighty meters, available to all nations. Not surprisingly, there has been some concern about the military information that these photographs inevitably contain. That concern will be increased now that Landsat D has started operations with a resolution of thirty meters; I was stunned by the beauty and definition of the first photographs when I saw them at UNISPACE. The French SPOT satellite will have even better resolution (ten to twenty meters), and this is rapidly approaching the area of military importance, although it is nowhere near (by a factor of almost one hundred!) the definition of the best reconnaissance satellites under favorable conditions.

There is a continuous spectrum between the abilities of the earth resources satellites and the reconnaissance satellites, and it is impossible to say that one is military and the other is not. What matters is, again, intention.

One may sum up the situation by saying that although these satellites may be annoying to some nations, they are not aggressive: and that is the essential factor.

More confusion has now been created by the American space shuttle, which has been heavily criticized in the Soviet Union. It is perfectly true that many of the shuttle's missions will be military—yet it is as potentially neutral as any other vehicle.

The one new factor the shuttle does introduce is that, for the first time, it gives a space-faring power the ability to examine, and perhaps to retrieve, satellites belonging to somebody else, thus opening up prospects of "space piracy"—as the Soviet Union has imaginatively put it. I rather like the phrase, but it is of dubious legality—since, by definition, a sovereign state cannot commit acts of piracy. And with all respects to my American friends who are trying to promote free enterprise in space, I very much doubt if it will ever be quite *that* free.

However, one cannot help thinking that fears on this score have been greatly exaggerated. If you do not want anyone to capture your satellite, it is absurdly simple to boobytrap it and thus destroy, with very little trouble, an extremely expensive rival space system.

From past experience, I would venture a prediction in this area. When only the United States possessed reconnaissance satellites, there was a great outcry in the Soviet Union about these "illegal spy devices;" indeed, in 1962 it proposed to the United Nations that they be banned. But it reversed itself only a year later, when it began to develop its own "national means of verification"—to use the formula both sides use when they want to conceal facts perfectly well known to everyone else.

In the same way, when the long-expected Soviet space shuttle is launched, perhaps we will hear no more talk of space piracy . . .

The essential point is that all these systems—communications, meteorological, geodetic, reconnaissance, and the shuttle itself—though they represent some degree of *militarization* of space are still, for the moment, defensive or even benign. Some countries may be upset by certain applications, but they can all live with them, accepting their benefits as well as their disadvantages. The new factor which has now entered the discussion is that of deliberately destructive space systems, i.e., weapons.

It seems to have been forgotten that the first weapons were introduced into space twenty years ago by the United States, which exploded a 1.4-megaton warhead four hundred kilometers above Johnson Island (Operation Dominic) on 8 July 1962 to test a possible antisatellite system. This approach was abandoned when it led to the discovery—only recently *re*discovered, to the consternation of military planners—that a few nuclear blasts in space could disable *all* satellites, simply by the intensity of the radiation pulse.

And not only satellites; when the bomb exploded over Johnson Island, it knocked out street lights and telephones in Hawaii, thirteen hundred kilometers away. Remember, that was twenty years ago; bombs are now bigger and better. A recent study indicates that a single explosion well above the atmosphere could leave an entire continent—the whole of Europe, or the United States—*without power, radio or telephone communications*. Altogether apart from its strategic implications, this means that there would be no neutrals even in a limited nuclear war (if such a thing is possible). It is something quite new in human history when nations thousand of kilometers from the scene of the conflict could be virtually destroyed in a second *without the loss of a single life*. The dying, of course, would start later, with the collapse of the social structure—even before the arrival of the fallout.... I do not know if this fact is fully appreciated by the non-nuclear powers, who may well question the moral right of others to destroy *them*, even in self-defense.

Though a desperate country might blind and cripple all its enemy's satellites—as well as everyone else's—by a few large nuclear explosions above the atmosphere, this lack of discrimination has led to a search for precision weapons. Since as far back as 1968, the Soviet Union has made more than twenty tests of a non-nuclear antisatellite destroyer, or ASAT, which hovers near its victim and explodes in a shower of fragments. On 6 and 18 June 1982 (*Cosmos 1373, 1379*), it tested this satellite system for the first time in conjunction with large-scale ballistic missile launches from silos and submarines.

The interesting question arises—Why are the Russians so concerned with developing an ASAT system, with its obvious destabilizing implications? One can only assume that the Soviet Union, which is able to obtain a great amount of information about the U.S. military establishment by old-fashioned techniques (such as buying trade magazines on the newsstands) realizes that reconnaissance satellites are much more vital to the Americans than to itself.

Predictably, the United States has not been indifferent to this Russian lead. President Reagan has now announced the development of ASAT systems even more advanced than the Soviet satellite-killers; indeed, they introduce a new dimension into space warfare.

One American weapon will be launched not from the ground, but from a high-flying F-15, so that it jumps up out of the atmosphere to home in on a satellite passing overhead. This will make it very flexible and extremely difficult to intercept, as it could operate from anywhere on the Earth at very short notice.

Doubtless, scientists in the Soviet Union are attempting to find a counter to this system, and so the insane escalation of weapons will continue—unless something is done to check it.

Neither the U.S. nor USSR ASAT systems will be operational for some years, so perhaps there is a last chance to prevent the introduction of offensive (as opposed to defensive) systems into space. The importance of halting this arms race before it gets truly under way will be emphasized when one realizes that these planned ASATs are only the primitive precursors of systems now being contemplated. For a horrifying description of the next phase of space warfare, I refer you to the recently published "High Frontier" study directed by General Daniel O. Graham. This envisages building scores of orbital fortresses to intercept oncoming ICBMs before they could reach their targets. Such a system would cost not billions, but *hundreds* of billions of dollars and of course would only be a stepping-stone to something even more expensive.

Which leads us inevitably to the subject of laser and particle-beam weapons. Now that the long-imagined "death-ray" is technically possible, it has been seized upon as a solution to the problem of defense against nuclear missiles. Certainly, a precision weapon which releases its energies at a single point and doesn't harm innocent bystanders is a rather attractive proposition.

A vigorous debate is now in progress over the practicability of high-energy laser weapons, and some scientists believe that though they can certainly be developed for many close applications, the intercontinental ranges needed for an effective missile defense will be unobtainable for decades—and perhaps forever.

Just look at the problems. There are no secrets involved—merely basic principles of physics. If you want to zap a missile soon after launch you've got to hold your beam to an accuracy of centimeters on a target five thousand kilometers away, moving at several kilometers a second. This demands an optically perfect mirror larger than the Mount Palomar reflector—which required years of skilled labor and millions of dollars to make.

That is just the beginning. In addition, the mirror has to be tough enough to handle five or ten thousand horsepower of pure heat, and light enough to flick from target to target in seconds, with accuracy comparable to tracking a tossed dime, a hundred kilometers away.

And then there's the laser itself. The only known type capable of doing the job would be virtually a rocket motor, burning several metric *tons* of fuel a second—almost in the class of the space shuttle itself. I once saw a small one in action (don't ask me where), and the noise and vibration were awesome. Mounting a precision optical-tracking system on such a raging monster would be rather like trying to thread a needle while riding a bucking bronco. And it would require the space shuttle's entire payload to carry up enough laser fuel for only two or three shots!

Remember, too, that a *single* fortress would be useless; because of its rapid orbital movement, it could only patrol a small fraction of near-Earth space at one time. You would need at least a score of them, weaving a basketwork around the planet to keep every danger point under continuous surveillance.

It is easy to "prove" that the whole concept is absurd, and a number of scientists have done just that. However, I am always suspicious of negative judgments: some of you may be familiar with Clarke's First Law, partly inspired by the notorious pronouncement made by the chief American defense scientist Dr. Vannevar Bush in 1945:

"There has been a great deal said about a 3,000-mile high-angle rocket.... I don't think anyone in the world knows how to do such a thing, and I feel confident that it will not be done for a long period of time to come... I think we can leave that out of our thinking. I wish the American public would leave that out of their thinking."

That's exactly what the American public did; and so it was "Sputniked" in 1957.

If a thing is theoretically possible, and someone needs it badly enough, it will be achieved eventually, whatever the cost. And when one side develops a new system, the other will try to outdo it.

However, the answer to the laser-carrying orbital fortress—and indeed *any* complex space-weapons system—is so absurdly cheap and simple that it appears ruled out by economics, rather than by technical feasibility. You don't even need chemical explosives to destroy one—still less nuclear weapons. Let me explain.

Assume that there's an unfriendly object in a two-hour orbit—that's about seventeen hundred kilometers up. To destroy it, you launch your counterweapon into exactly the same orbit—*but in the opposite direction*. And you do it on the other side of the Earth from your target, so you won't be detected.

Your warhead is rather cheap; it's a bucket of nails. However, there's a slight error in your calculations, and you miss by a hundred kilometers. *It doesn't matter*.

Exactly one hour later, going their opposite ways, your slowly expanding cloud of nails encounters the target again, thanks to the inexorable laws of celestial mechanics. Every hour on the hour, your barrage of space shrapnel gets another opportunity; if not today, then tomorrow; if not tomorrow, then next week. Sooner or later, it will do the job. I don't think that anyone really knows what happens when two objects meet at forty thousand kilometers an hour, but it won't be nice. Especially when—as in some scenarios—the target is a tank of laser fuel as big as a jumbo jet, and much more explosive than the *Hindenburg*.

So if space power X wanted to bankrupt space power Y, it should try to persuade Y that it's developing a system of orbiting fortresses—in the hope that its adversary would do just that, and build a Maginot Line in space that could be destroyed for not even one thousandth of its cost.

Perhaps *this* is what's really going on at those mysterious research establishments, like Saryshigan and Semipalatinsk, with which retired generals are continually trying to terrify us....

The two superpowers are both led by intelligent and responsible men, yet they sometimes appear like small boys standing in a pool of gasoline—each trying to acquire more matches than the other, when a single one is more than sufficient.

George Bernard Shaw summed up the matter very well in his play *Man and Superman*. As usual, the Devil has the best lines: if you make a few technological updates, you will find his marvelous diatribe in Act III even more appropriate than when it was written, eighty years ago:

> And is Man any the less destroying himself for all this boasted brain of his? Have you walked up and down upon the Earth lately? I have; and I have examined Man's wonderful inventions. And I tell you that in the arts of life man invents nothing; but in the arts of death he outdoes Nature herself, and produces by chemistry and machinery all the slaughter of plague, pestilence and famine.... When he goes out to slay, he carries a marvel of mechanism that lets loose at the touch of a finger all the hidden molecular energies, and leaves the javelin, the arrow, the blowpipe of his fathers far behind. In the arts of peace Man is a bungler.... I know his clumsy typewriters and bungling locomotives and tedious bicycles; they are toys compared to the Maxim gun, the submarine torpedo boat. There is nothing in Man's industrial machinery but his greed and sloth; his heart is in his weapons.

His heart is in his weapons. That is indeed a chilling indictment, and it is applicable not only to men but to nations; they can share the same pathologies. I once coined the deliberately provocative slogan "Guns are the crutches of the impotent." So are intercontinental ballistic missiles.

It is no longer true that wars begin in the minds of men; they can now start in the circuits of computers. Yet the technologies which could destroy us can also be used for our salvation. From their very nature, space systems are uniquely adapted to provide global facilities, equally beneficial to all nations.

As is now widely known, in 1978 the French government proposed the establishment of an International Satellite Monitoring Agency to help enforce peace treaties and to monitor military activities. This has been the subject of a detailed study by a UN committee, which concluded that such a system could well play a major role in the preservation of peace.

The operational and political difficulties are obviously very great, yet they are trivial when compared with the possible advantages. The expense—one or two billion dollars—is also hardly a valid objection. It has been estimated that its reconnaissance satellites saved the United States the best part of a *trillion* dollars. A global system might be an even better investment; and who can set a cash value on the price of peace?

However, the United States and the Soviet Union, anxious to preserve their joint monopoly of reconnaissance satellites, are strongly opposed to such a scheme. The British government is also lukewarm, to say the least. Nevertheless, we have seen that in matters of great—though lesser—importance, such as international communications, it is possible to have extremely effective cooperation between a hundred or more countries, even with violently opposing ideologies. INTELSAT is a prime example, as on a smaller scale is INTERSPUTNIK; and in the near future ARABSAT will establish its regional space system.

I like the name PEACESAT, and although it has already been preempted by the Pacific Radio Network's ATA 1, I will use the term, with due acknowledgment, for the remainder of this talk.

Reactions at Unispace '82 and elsewhere suggest that the PEACESAT is an idea whose time has come. Those who are skeptical about its practicability should realize that most of its elements are present, at least in rudimentary form, in existing or planned systems. The French SPOT satellite, with a ground resolution of ten to twenty meters, has already been mentioned. Whether the superpowers wish it or not, the facilities of an embryo PEACESAT system will very soon be available to all countries.

May I remind my Russian and American friends that it is wise to cooperate with the inevitable—and wiser still to *exploit* the inevitable. When I visited the Institute of Space Science in Moscow last June, I made a point of stressing the French proposal, and teased my hosts by suggesting that as both the United States and the USSR were against it, it was probably a good idea. Someone then made the cynical remark: "Perhaps the French hope to sell the necessary equipment." I'm sorry I didn't think of the right retort in time: "So what?"

PEACESATS could develop in a noncontroversial manner out of what Howard Kurtz, their long-time advocate, has called the Global Information Cooperative. This could be a consortium of agencies for weather, mapping, search and rescue, resources and pollution monitoring, disaster watch, information retrieval and, of course, communications. No one denies the need for these facilities. If they were provided globally, they would inevitably do much of the work of a PEACESAT system. The only extra element required would be the evaluation and intelligence teams needed to analyze the information obtained.

Since I wrote these words, I am happy to say that the Russian Search and Rescue satellite COSPAS has saved a dozen American and Canadian lives, by detecting the faint radio signals from downed aircraft and wrecked ships (five within two months!). This is just the beginning of a system which we will soon take completely for granted, as we have done ever since the *Titanic* sent out its first distress call seventy years ago.

The organization, financing and operation of a PEACESAT system has been discussed in the UN report, to which I refer you for details. It is not a magic solution to *all* the problems of peace: there is no such thing. But at least it is worthy of serious consideration, as one way of escape from our present predicament—all of us standing in that pool of gasoline, making our Mutual Assured Destruction ever more assured.

I would like to end as I began, with the conclusion of my 1946 essay, "The Rocket and the Future of Warfare":

> The only defence against the weapons of the future is to prevent them ever being used. In other words, the problem is political and not military at all. A country's armed forces can no longer defend it; the most they can promise is the destruction of the attacker. . . .
>
> Upon us, the heirs to all the past and the trustees of a future which our folly can slay before its birth, lies a responsibility no other age has ever known. If we fail in our generation, those who come after us may be too few to rebuild

the world, when the dust of the cities has descended, and the radiation of the rocks has died away.

References

The following sources have proved invaluable in the preparation of this paper:

1. *Space: The High Frontier in Perspective*, by Daniel Deudney (Worldwatch Paper 50, August 1982).
2. *Spaceflight* and the *Journal of the British Interplanetary Society* (27 South Lambeth Rd., London SW8 1SZ, UK).
3. Memoranda from Howard G. Kurtz (War Control Planners, PO Box 19127, Washington, DC 20036).
4. *Outer Space—A New Dimension of the Arms Race*, edited by Bhupendra Jasani (Stockholm International Peace Research Institute, 1982).
5. "Laser Weapons," by Kosta Tsipis (*Scientific American* Vol. 245, No. 6, pp. 35–41, December 1981).
6. "The Strategic Value of Space-Based Laser Weapons," by Barry J. Smernoff (*Air University Review* Vol. XXXIII, No. 3, pp. 2–17, March–April 1982).
7. "Space-Based Lasers," by Wallace D. Henderson (*Astronautics and Aeronautics* Vol. 20, No. 4, pp. 44–53, May 1982).
8. *Spectrum* (IEEE) October 1982.
9. "Nuclear EMP Induced Chaos," by Brian Dance (*Communications International* Vol. 9, No. 9, pp. 45, 49, 51, 52, September 1982).
10. "Study on the Implications of Establishing an International Satellite Monitoring Agency." UN Report A/AC. 206/14, 6 August 1981.

Electronics
and
Education

First of all, I must express my gratitude to His Excellency the President for appointing me the first chancellor of the newly autonomous university. Next to gratitude, my second emotion is that of surprise. I never imagined that I would even *go* to a university, let alone be chancellor of one, when I left Huish's Grammar School, Taunton, at the age of nineteen to enter His Majesty's Exchequer and Audit Department.

Now, as it happened, my very first post was at the old

Chancellor's Address at First Convocation of the University of Moratuwa, 10 December 1979.

Board of Education, in Whitehall itself, and my job was auditing teachers' pensions. Thanks to the fastest slide rule in Westminster, I was able to do my day's work in a couple of hours and spend the rest of the time on the really important business of writing science fiction and dealing with the affairs of the British Interplanetary Society. World War II boosted me out of the civil service, to our mutual benefit, and into the Royal Air Force. I took my slide rule with me, and it was a constant companion until just over ten years ago. . . .

Then occurred one of the swiftest, and most momentous, revolutions in the entire history of technology, whose consequences I wish to discuss this evening. For more than a hundred years, the slide rule had been the essential tool of engineers, scientists—anyone whose work involved extensive calculations. Then, just a decade ago, it was made obsolete almost overnight—and with it, whole libraries of logarithmic and trigonometric tables—by the invention of pocket calculators. There has never been so stupendous an advance in so short a time; there is simply no comparison between the two devices. Not only is the pocket calculator millions of times more accurate and scores of times swifter than the slide rule, but it now actually costs less. To imagine an equal advance in transportation—it's as if we'd jumped overnight from bullock carts to *Concorde* . . . and *Concorde* was cheaper! No wonder the slide-rule manufacturers have gone out of business. If you have a good one, leave it in your will. In a couple of generations, it will be a valuable antique.

Now, pocket calculators are already having a profound effect on the teaching of mathematics, even at the level of elementary arithmetic. But they are about to be succeeded by devices of much greater power and sophistication, which may change the very nature of the educational system.

At this point, many of you remark impatiently: What has technology got to do with education? There's an old saying to the effect that the best educational setup consists of a log with teacher at one end, and pupil at the other. Unfortunately, our modern world is not only woefully short of teachers—it's even running out of logs. But there's *always* been a shortage of teachers, and technology has always been used to alleviate it—a fact which many people tend to forget.

The first great technological aid to education was the book. You don't have to clone teachers to multiply them. The printing press did just that and the mightiest of all educational machines is—the library.

What an astonishing thing a book is, when you stop to think about it! And how baffling it would have appeared to one of our preliterate ancestors! Here's a small object that can be easily held in the hand, but you can't eat it and it's a pretty inefficient weapon—a piece of rock is much better. Yet men devote their lives—and fortunes—making and collecting these fragile artifacts, with their myriads of leaves covered with tiny black marks like squashed insects. . . . Even more mysteriously, they spend hours—days—occasionally much of a lifetime—slowly turning these leaves, often oblivious to their surroundings. What on earth are they doing?

I hope that the mental exercise of trying to think like a Stone Ager helped you to appreciate the everyday miracle of the printed book. That miracle is now about to be surpassed by an even more remarkable one, as astonishing to most of us here today as books would have been to our remote ancestors.

I can still recall my own amazement when, at a NASA conference less than ten years ago, I saw my first "electronic slide rule." It was a prototype of the H/P 35, demonstrated to us by Dr. Bernard Oliver, vice-president of Hewlett-Packard. Though I was awed and impressed, I did not really appreciate that something new and revolutionary had come into the world.

It is indeed quite impossible for even the most farsighted prophet to visualize all the effects of a really major technological development. In *Profiles of the Future* I've quoted some hilarious "failures of imagination" as ghastly warnings; let me repeat a couple of examples.

When Bell invented the telephone, the Chief Engineer of the British Post Office was asked if this amazing new device would ever catch on in the UK. He replied grandly: "No sir. The Americans have need of the telephone, but we do *not*. We have plenty of messenger boys. . . ."

It's pleasant to record that this gentleman—Sir William Preece—subsequently laid the foundations of the British phone system and later backed Marconi with his "wireless" experiments. He was no fool: but he couldn't imagine, when he first heard about it, just what the telephone would do to human affairs.

The second example is perhaps even more surprising—and instructive. When the first motor cars started to run around, it was pointed out that they could only be of use in the cities. Why? *Because there were no roads outside the cities.* At the beginning of this century, even the United States had less than a thousand miles of what we would now call good roads. . . .

The point I am trying to make is that really revolutionary inventions turn the world upside down. And by revolutionary, I mean something that produces a great advance in the satisfaction of some fundamental human need. I'm not referring to such advertising agency breakthroughs as sliced bread, electric can-openers, or striped toothpaste. . . .

The telephone and the motor car produced quantum jumps in communication and transportation; they gave ordinary men a mastery over space which not even kings and emperors had possessed in the past. They changed not only the patterns of everyday life, but even the physical structure of the world—the shapes of our cities, the uses of the land. This all happened in what is, historically, a moment of time . . . and the process is still accelerating. Look how the transistor radio swept across the face of the planet within a single generation.

After these background remarks, let me return to the subject of education. Though they are still of trivial importance compared with books, there has been some penetration into this field by audiovisual aids—film strips, 16-mm projectors, videotape machines. Most of these are still far too expensive for developing countries, and frankly I'm not sure if they are really worth it. Perhaps the most influential of them all is the ordinary TV set, whether intended for education or not. I'd be interested to know what impact the excellent "Sesame Street" has on the relatively few children of a totally different culture from its intended recipients who see it here in Sri Lanka. But *every* TV program has some educational content; the cathode ray tube is a window on the world—indeed, on many worlds. Often it's a very murky window, but I've slowly come to the conclusion that, on balance, even bad TV is preferable to *no* TV.

The unequalled power of TV lies in its ability to show current events, often as they are happening. But for basic educational purposes, the video recorder, with its pre-taped programs which can be shown over and over again, at any convenient time, is much more valuable. Unfortunately, the present chaos of competing systems has prevented standardization and cheap mass production. Video*tape* machines are certainly far too complicated and can never be really cheap or long-lived. Video *discs*, which are just coming on the market, will be much cheaper; but I am sure that they too represent only a transitional stage. Eventually we will have completely solid state memory and storage devices, with *no* moving parts—except laser beams or electric fields. After all, the human brain doesn't have any moving parts, and it can hold quite a lot of information. The electronic memories I'm talking about will be even more compact than the brain—and *very* cheap.

Let me remind you of what has already happened in the very brief history of the machines known popularly—and not inaccurately—as electronic brains. The first models were clumsy giants filling whole rooms, consuming kilowatts of power and costing millions of dollars. Today—thirty-five years later—far greater storage and processing capacity can be packed into a microchip about a quarter of an inch square. *That's* miracle number 1. Miracle number 2 is the cost of that chip—not a couple of million dollars, but about *ten* dollars!

The first great development this would make possible is the portable electronic library—a library not only of books, but of film and music. It would be about the size of a hardcover book and would probably open in the same way. One half would be the screen, with high-definition, full-color display. The other would be the keyboard, much like one of today's computer consoles, with the full alphabet, the digits 0 to 9, basic mathematical functions and a large number of special keys. Because convenience is more important than compactness, and there would have to be about a hundred keys, it wouldn't be as small as some of today's midget calculators, which have to be operated with toothpicks.

In theory, such a device could have enough memory to hold all the books in the world. But we might settle for something more modest, like the *Encyclopaedia Britannica*, Oxford English Dictionary and Roget's *Thesaurus*. (Incidentally, Roget was the inventor of the log-log slide rule.) Whole additional libraries could be inserted, when necessary, by small plug-in modules. All this technology has already been developed, the most skilled exponents of this new art being the designers of video games.

Reading material called up would be displayed as a fixed page—or portion of a page—or else "scrolled" so that it rolled upwards at a comfortable reading rate. Pictures would appear as in an ordinary book; but they might also be displayed as fully three-dimensional holographic images.

Text and pictures could of course be accompanied by the appropriate sound. Today's tape recorders can reproduce a single symphony per cassette. The electronic library might play back the complete works of Beethoven, while simultaneously displaying the score on its screen.

And how nice to be able to call up Lord Clark's "Civilisation" or Bronowski's "Ascent of Man" whenever or wherever you felt like it! (Yes, I know that at the moment these cost about a thousand pounds apiece, unless you are lucky or wicked enough to have a pirate copy. But one day the BBC will have got its money back, and thereafter the price will be peanuts.)

You will appreciate that the possibilities are literally unlimited. But I still haven't touched on the real potential of this technology, for so far I've been talking about a *passive* device—one that merely presents you with information, and can't talk back to you and answer your questions.

But that, I fear, is the case in much conventional education, especially where there are large classes. I recently met a Turkish engineer who said that all *he* ever saw of his professor was a tiny figure up on the platform, above a sea of heads. However, the electronic library would have the enormous advantage that one could extract information from it at any desired rate, stopping or going back at any point. What a boon to slow or handicapped students!

Now, genuine education requires feedback—interaction between pupil and teacher. (Ideally, inspiration as well!) There have been attempts to provide this by programs which allow a student to carry on a dialogue with a computer—asking it questions and answering the questions which it asks him. Computer-aided instruction—CAI—not to be confused with CIA—can be extremely effective. At its best, the pupil may refuse to believe that he is dealing with a computer program, and not another human being.

CAI is now available in many U.S. colleges and high schools; there are consoles with typewriter keyboards which allow the student to "talk" to a central computer at any time of the day or night, going through any particular subject when he feels like it, and at the rate that suits him. The computer, of course, can talk—or type—to hundreds of students simultaneously, giving each one the illusion that *he* is the center of attention. It's infinitely patient—and it's never rude or sarcastic. . . .

However, today's CAI consoles are big and expensive, and they are fixed units usually wired into the college computer. In principle, they could be portable and mobile. Already, there are businessmen traveling round the world with attaché-case-sized consoles which they can plug into the telephone system and talk to their office computer, wherever on the planet it may be. But I'm looking beyond this, to the completely portable and *self-contained* electronic *tutor*—the next step beyond today's pocket calculators.

Its prototype is already here, in the nurseries of the affluent West. The first computer toys, many of them looking as if they'd flown off the screen during a showing of *Star Wars*, invaded the shops last Christmas. They play noughts and crosses (Tic-Tac-Toe), challenge you to repeat simple melodies, ask questions, present elementary calculations and await the answer—making rude noises if you get it wrong. Children love them, when they're able to wrestle them away from their parents. In 1978 they cost fifty dollars; now they're half that. One day they'll be given away with cereal boxes....

Now, these are toys, and are sold as such, but they represent the wave of the future. Much more sophisticated are the pocket electronic translators that first came on to the market in 1979, at about the cost of calculators five years earlier. These have a little alphabetical keyboard into which you can type words and sentences and the translation will appear on a small screen. You change language simply by plugging in a different module.

One of the great advantages of these machines (although their vocabularies are still limited to about a thousand words) is that they can show the translation in the actual script of the country involved—not necessarily in roman letters. You will realize what a boon this would be in Japan, the USSR, Greece, the Arab countries, I don't know if any of them yet speak—but they soon will. Later, they could be superb language teachers—because they could listen to your pronunciation, match it with theirs, and correct you until they were satisfied.

Such a device would be one specific type of the general purpose pocket tutor, which will be the universal student's tool by the end of the century. It is hard to think of a single subject which could not be programmed into it at all levels of complexity, from elementary to advanced. You would change subjects or update courses merely by plugging in different modules or cassettes, exactly as in today's preprogrammable pocket computers.

Now, where does this leave the teacher? I see many of you looking rather nervous...and I think I shook Ivan Ilich, here in this very building, a few months ago with some of these ideas.

Well, if you feel apprehensive about your job—let me quote this dictum:

ANY TEACHER WHO CAN BE REPLACED BY A MACHINE
—*SHOULD* BE!

Back in the Middle Ages, many teachers and scholars regarded printed books with considerable apprehension. They felt that they would destroy the monopoly of knowledge. Worse still, books would permit the unwashed masses to improve their position in society, and perhaps to learn the most cherished secret of all—that no man was better than any other. Those of you who have seen the splendid TV series "Roots," which I hope comes here someday, will recall how the slaves were strictly forbidden to learn reading—and had to pretend that they were illiterate if they had secretly acquired this skill.

Well, the teaching profession survived the invention of books and it should welcome the electronic tutor, because it will remove the sheer drudgery, the tedious repetition, that is unavoidable in so much basic education. Norbert Wiener, the father of cybernetics, called one of his books *The Human Use of Human Beings*. By removing much of the tedium from the teacher's work, and making learning more like play, electronic tutors will—paradoxically—*humanize* education. If you feel threatened by them—you're in the wrong profession.

We need mass education to drag this world out of the Stone Age, and any technology—any machine—that can help to do that is to be welcomed, not feared. The electronic tutor will spread across the planet as swiftly as the transistor radio, with even more momentous consequences. Nothing—no social or political system, no philosophy, no culture, no religion—can withstand a technology whose time has come...however much one may deplore some of the unfortunate side effects—like the blaring tape recorders being carried by pilgrims up Sri Pada. We must take the good with the bad.

When they reach technological maturity, which will be around the end of the century, the electronic tutors will be mass-produced not in millions, but in *hundreds* of millions. They will cost no more than today's pocket calculators; equally important, they will last for years, for no properly designed solid state device need ever wear out. (I'm still using the H/P 35 Dr. Oliver gave me in 1970.) So their written-down cost would be negligible; they might even be *given* away, the users paying only for the programs plugged into them. Even the poorest countries could afford them—especially when the reforms and improved productivity they stimulate help those countries to boot-strap themselves out of poverty.

The question now arises—just where does this leave

the school, and the university? Already, telecommunications are making these ancient institutions independent of space: I'm thinking of TV's "Sunrise Semesters," and the University of the Air. The pocket tutor will complete this process, giving the student total flexibility— complete freedom of choice in space *and* in time.

We will probably continue to need schools of some kind for younger children, to teach them social skills and discipline. But it should be remembered that the educational toys already available are such fun that their young operators sometimes have to be dragged kicking and screaming *away* from their self-imposed classes ...rather a contrast to the usual state of affairs.

At the other end of the spectrum, we'll still need universities for many functions. You can't teach chemistry, physics, engineering without labs, for obvious reasons. And though we'll see the establishment of more and more global classes at the advanced and graduate level, through a video confrontation system involving professors, computers and students scattered over the whole planet, electronics can never completely convey all the nuances of personal interactions. Nor should it attempt to do so, lest we create the pathological societies described by E. M. Forster in *The Machine Stops* and by Isaac Asimov in *The Naked Sun*.

There will be myriads of "Invisible Colleges" operating through the global communications networks; but there will also be nodes or nexuses where campuses still exist and where hundreds or thousands of students and instructors meet in person, as they have done ever since the days of Plato's Academy, twenty-three centuries ago.

I remarked earlier that any teacher who could be replaced by a machine, should be. Perhaps the same verdict should apply to any university, however ivy-covered its walls, if it can be replaced by a global electronic network of computers and satellite links.

What these can *never* replace is something intangible—even spiritual. Graduates of Oxford or Cambridge, or Harvard or Yale—to name only the most obvious and famous examples—will know exactly what I mean. It is best summed up in one word—tradition.

We can scarcely claim that a university that is just

one year old has a very long-established tradition. But it is always exciting to be at the beginning of something; that is why babies are so popular. Vice-Chancellor, Deans, Professors, academic staff—above all, new graduates— I hope that we have now established an institution of which we can all be proud. However swiftly the electronic wave of the future comes rushing into shore, I am confident that the University of Moratuwa will withstand the impact, and will flourish for many years to come.

And I look forward to seeing you all again, a year from now. . . .

A Flash of Golden Fire

His Excellency Ambassador Tissa Jayakoddy

Permanent Mission of Sri Lanka to
      the United Nations, Geneva

18 March 1983

My Dear Ambassador,

Your letter of 18 February 1983, and the speech you recently gave to the United Nations Committee on Disarmament, reached me last month via the diplomatic bag. Since then I have thought of very little else, for you have indeed presented me with a formidable challenge.

I must confess that after I had delivered my own "War and Peace in the Space Age" address to the committee last August, I felt that I had done my duty and could leave Geneva with a clear conscience. The rest was up to the professional skills of you and your colleagues; there was nothing more that *I* could contribute, even on the purely technical side.

But now you ask me to make specific proposals for breaking out of the apparently endless circle of "exploring, discussing, debating" so that you can actually begin "negotiating." Even this would seem a modest enough goal, as negotiation would be years from ratification, and still further from effective enforcement.

You may recall that I began my Geneva speech with these famous lines from Shelley:

> Cease! Drain not to its dregs the urn
>   Of bitter prophecy.
> The world is weary of the past,
>   Oh, might it die, or rest at last!

Perhaps we have already had too many prophecies on the effects of nuclear warfare; however eloquent and necessary, they tend to numb the mind, producing—all too appropriately—a kind of literary overkill. Though every statesman should be compelled to read Jonathan Schell's *The Fate of the Earth*, I have come across two other references that encapsulate the subject of atomic Armageddon so perfectly, and so concisely, that no more need be said.

The first is a single sentence from Carl Sagan's *Cosmos*—which, because I relied on memory, I managed to misquote in Geneva. But the misquotation is so chillingly instructive, and drives home its lesson so unforgettably, that I make no apology for the error. (Repeated, incidentally, when Representative George E. Brown, Jr., read my speech into the *Congressional Record* for 21 September 1982.) The statement I attributed to Dr. Sagan was this: "A full-scale thermonuclear exchange would be the equivalent of World War II once a minute, for the length of a lazy afternoon."

Such a catastrophe is, of course, utterly inconceivable;

yet the truth is much worse. Carl Sagan actually wrote: "World War II once a *second* for the length of a lazy afternoon." I wish that those who talk glibly about "protracted nuclear conflict" would make a mantra of "World War Two once a second." Chanted frequently enough, it might help them to make connection with reality.

My second example is not quantitative, but qualitative: not an unimaginable planetary holocaust, but an idyllic image transformed into horror. It comes from the opening chapter of Robert Scheer's *With Enough Shovels: Reagan, Bush and Nuclear War* and is an eyewitness account of the test, a quarter of a century ago, of a bomb with only *one thousandth* of the power in the largest warheads now available.

The scene is one of classic beauty—the coral island, almost on the equator, discovered by Captain Cook on 24 December 1777, and therefore named after the birthday of Christ.

> The birds were the things we could see all the time. They were superb specimens of life—really quite exquisite. Albatrosses will fly for days, skimming a few inches above the surface of the water.... They are just beautiful creatures. Watching them is a wonder....
>
> We were standing round waiting for this bomb to go off, which we had been told was a very small one, so no one was particularly upset.... No worry....
>
> ...so the countdown came in over the radio, and suddenly I could see all the birds that I'd been watching for days before. They were now suddenly visible through the opaque visor of my helmet...they were sizzling, smoking. Their feathers were on fire. And they were doing cartwheels...they were absorbing such intense radiation that they were being consumed by the heat.... And so far, there had been no shock, none of the blast damage we talk about when we discuss the effects of nuclear weapons...just these smoking, twisting, hideously contorted birds crashing into things....

All this, please remember, from a bomb smaller than that dropped on Hiroshima. I wonder if any of the scientists who had so successfully turned light itself into a deadly weapon recalled how the Ancient Mariner "had done a hellish thing/And it would work them woe" when—

> With his cruel bow he laid full low
> The harmless Albatross.

I am also indebted to the same strange poem for this description of what happened in the sky above Christmas Island: "A flash of golden fire."

And now, while I am actually writing this letter, another piece of news has arrived from this very same spot—something so mysterious, and so ominous, that it chills my blood. I would never have dared to imagine this Reuters dispatch, datelined Washington, March 16:

> More than sixteen million birds have mysteriously vanished from the Pacific atoll of Christmas Island, the first recorded disappearance of an entire island adult bird population.... Thousands of the birds' nestlings had been left behind to die. Dr. Ralph Schreiber (curator of ornithology of the Natural History Museum, Los Angeles) said Christmas Island was teeming with birdlife when he visited it last July, but was virtually deserted on a second visit in November.

What impulse could have triggered this avian hegira? The baffled imagination grasps at fantasy. Some mutation in the irradiated eggs, carried down the generations in the DNA, almost like a delayed cry of warning from those incinerated ancestors? Whatever the answer, creatures who leave their young to die must be desperate indeed.

In any event, the message to us is clear enough. The birds have other islands to which they can fly.

We have no other Earth. Nor will we, for centuries to come.

You asked me for "the scenario that will develop if we sit back and do nothing." An excellent example will be found in the *High Frontier* study conducted under the auspices of the Heritage Foundation by Lt. General Daniel O. Graham. After excoriating the doctrine of Mutual Assured Destruction (MAD) as immoral and militarily bankrupt, it makes a valiant attempt to develop a *defensive, non-nuclear* strategy to counter the threat of Russian ICBMs. This envisages the installation of complex weapon systems in space, beginning with unmanned satellites carrying interceptor vehicles, and leading ultimately to manned battle stations, possibly armed with laser beams.

These ideas are taken much further in "The Coming Weapons," by Allan D. Simon in the November 1982 *Astronautics and Aeronautics*, a journal of the influential American Institute of Aeronautics and Astronautics. To quote from one typical paragraph: "In 2032 at least three of these space battle stations, nuclear-powered, should be in geosynchronous orbit. Each battle station would contain a crew of about 1000 people and sufficient supplies to operate autonomously for a few years."

In an ironic letter which *Astronautics* will be publishing shortly, I congratulated Mr. Simon on his "brilliant parody, which the Crackpot Realists who flourish in the Pentagon and the Kremlin will adore, because it catches to perfection the authentic Strangelovian delight in technological obscenities."

Yet even these nightmares pale into insignificance when compared with a recent study of what can only be called "inner-space" warfare. Did you know that there was a serious proposal to *bury* complete ICBM systems, with their crews, so deeply in the earth that they will have to dig their way back up to the surface with mining machinery after a nuclear war? All this to ensure that a few missiles would still survive to shake up what was left of the rubble.

Even Stanley Kubrick's bloodthirsty General Buck Turgidson never looked that far ahead when he warned the President about the "mine shaft gap." Real life has surpassed the most satirical imagination, and the MAD doctrine has been exponentiated to MAD Squared.

It is possible—though it would be unwise to count on it—that sheer expense will rule out most of the wilder technological fantasies. Thus the "cheap and simple" minimum homing vehicle (MHV) being developed in the United States as an F-15-launched antisatellite weapon has turned out to be neither cheap nor simple. The General Accounting Office now reports that the system could cost "tens of billions of dollars," and has told the Pentagon to go back to the drawing board. As the MHV is indeed just about the minimum possible ASAT, this makes nonsense of the estimates quoted (e.g., in *High Frontier*) for systems hundreds of times more complex. And *all* these systems, even if they were built, could be destroyed at a trivial fraction of their cost, by a surprisingly simple technique based on elementary orbital theory.

However, the past few decades have shown that logic and economics often play little part in the development of military systems: the driving forces are more likely to be fear or its mirror image, aggression. In the hope that men may, after all, learn something from history, let me give two classic examples from the late 1950s.

The first is the notorious "missile gap." A few years after it had been "Sputniked" in 1957, the United States intelligence community (aided by the eager lobbyists of the aerospace industry) managed to convince itself that the Russians were far ahead in the production and deployment of operational ICBMs. A multibillion-dollar crash program was planned to overcome this lead; fortunately for the American taxpayer, reconnaissance satellites proved that it was a complete myth. In fact, the missile gap was in the *other* direction. As President Johnson remarked later: "We were building things we didn't need to build; we were harboring fears we didn't need to harbor."

The second example, now almost forgotten, is equally instructive. A contemporary of the "missile gap" was the giant Russian nuclear-powered airplane, imaginative portraits of which frequently graced the American aerospace journals of the late 1950s (whose advertisements will one day be regarded as the true pornography of our age). A billion dollars were spent in pursuit of this phantom. It must have been one of the most expensive exorcisms on record.

Of course, with the 20:20 vision of hindsight it is easy—and tempting—to apportion blame for these potentially deadly delusions. Though there is enough blame to satisfy everyone, much of it must go to the military-industrial complex, against which General Eisenhower—of all people—warned his countrymen in one of the last speeches of his career. (There is an exact equivalent in the Soviet Union, about which Premier Khrushchev expressed Ikeish sentiments on at least one occasion.) Whether the motivation here is sincere patriotism or cynical, short-sighted greed ("If *we* don't get the contract, it will go to General Tectonics again...") doesn't matter; the end result is the same.

But the military-industrial complex is only the producer, not the *originator* of the hardware that now threatens the planet. The guilt for that lies elsewhere, as Professor Solly Zuckerman (Chief Scientific Advisor to the British Ministry of Defence, 1960–66) has spelled out in his recent *Nuclear Illusion and Reality*. I quote from a review in the International Institute for Strategic Studies *Survival* (Sept/Oct 1982), which refers to his "blistering indictment of weapons technologists, as distinct from either military or civilian strategists, or the political leaders who make the procurement decisions":

> Zuckerman notes several destabilizing nuclear systems which could have been precluded by a ban on testing (MIRV, ERW, cruise), and believes that without negative lobbying from the nuclear technologists, Kennedy and Khrushchev would have been able to reconcile their differences....

This is a serious charge to have on one's conscience; of course, the "nuclear technologists" concerned may retort that Lord Zuckerman doesn't know what he's talking about, since he is a mere zoologist, not a physicist.

One person who certainly should know what he is talking about is George Kennan, author of the postwar "containment" policy. In his recent book *The Nuclear Delusion* he agrees with Zuckerman that the militarization of American policy prevented an accommodation with the Soviet Union in the early Khrushchev years, and now "allows Western alarmists" who are "living in a dreamworld of their own ... to persuade us that a surprise Soviet attack against Western Europe is a serious possibility" when, in fact, "the Soviet leadership has no intention, and has never had any intention, of attacking Western Europe." If this is indeed the case, it is a pity that Mr. Kennan was not able to put it more forcibly when he was in a position of power.

The misreading of one's opponent's intentions is of course a two-way process which, because it involves positive feedback, can rapidly escalate into catastrophe. (The recent South Atlantic War may provide a good example.) In a long and thoughtful comment on my Geneva address, one of your most distinguished colleagues made these points about the rulers of the Soviet Union: "Some of their policies and some of their responses to our initiatives reflect a real misunderstanding of Western attitudes and intentions. They would not be where they are were they not possessed of high intelligence; but they, too, are culture bound. They cannot leap across their own shadow."

Nor, of course, can we; that vivid phrase sums up our mutual dilemma, and explains the lack of progress of your committee, mired for so many years in a morass of suspicion, fear and conflicting interests. There is little that any single individual—except an authoritarian or charismatic head of state!—can do about that, and all *I* can contribute are a few comments on the limited but vital subject of the militarization of space. (Or should I say its *demilitarization*?)

Virtually everyone—except the two principal parties involved—agrees that antisatellite weapons will be destabilizing and will merely add, at enormous expense, to the *insecurity* of all concerned. (See Zuckerman, above, and also the useful Canadian Working Paper to your committee, "Arms Control and Outer Space.") So pressure must be kept up to resume the interrupted negotiations here; I am pleased to note that the declaration of the Warsaw Treaty parties (Prague, 5 January 1983) recommends "opening, without delay, negotiations on a prohibition of the stationing of weapons of any kind in outer space." This, however, does not cover the important case of weapons like the MHV mentioned above, which is earth-launched and *not* stationed in space.

The House of Representatives Joint Resolution 120, recently introduced by Representative Moakley and ninety cosponsors, does make this point, since it asks for a treaty prohibiting "the testing, production, deployment or use of any space-based, air-based, or ground-based weapons system which is designed to damage, destroy, or interfere with the functioning of any spacecraft of any nation."

Prohibition may sometimes be desirable but is a negative, uncreative type of activity which arouses enthusiasm only among gangsters—using that term with the widest possible applications. So I would like to propose some positive measures which would help to build up the trust and cooperation which in the long run are essential for any form of global stability.

The first is based on something that already exists but which has received far less publicity than it merits. (Why, I wonder?) It also has a tragic relevance to Sri Lanka at this very moment. As you well know, our best-known businessman and the head of an entire industrial complex, with several of his colleagues, disappeared recently on a flight from Malaysia to Colombo. Though an enormous search effort has been underway for several weeks, the wreckage of his executive jet has still not been located, and there can now be no hope of any survivors.

Yet in June 1982 the Soviet Union launched a search and rescue satellite (COSPAS) which, by listening out for emergency radio beacons, has already saved many lives (downed planes in Canada and New Mexico, wrecked boats off the Dominican Republic and the New England coast). This is part of an international effort started in 1977 and involving the United States, the Soviet Union, France and Canada; it is virtually the only cooperative space effort to survive recent political strains, thanks to its obvious humanitarian value.

Unfortunately, a single SARSAT can scan only a small portion of the world at any one time; for complete coverage, about half a dozen would be necessary, moving in different orbits so as to weave an invisible basketwork around the globe. When such a system is available, any downed plane or wrecked ship could be pinpointed within minutes. Countless lives could be saved, and even when there were no survivors of a crash, uncertainty would be removed and the vast effort and expenditure on searches (which themselves often cause additional deaths) would be obviated.

I suggest, therefore, that *all* nations be invited to cooperate in this enterprise, so that a global SARSAT system be established as quickly as possible. Hopefully, in the aftermath of UNISPACE 82, some action is being taken on this. And perhaps you can convince your jet-setting colleagues that the lives they save may very well include their own.

My second subject, the International Monitoring Satellite (or PEACESAT) is much more controversial but has moved one small step forward since I raised it at Geneva. You will recall that in 1978 the French delegation to the United Nations submitted a memorandum proposing the establishment of an International Satellite Monitoring Agency (ISMA) for the verification of arms control agreements and for the management of crisis situations. As a result, a group of experts was assembled under the chairmanship of Hubert G. Bortzmeyer and a report was submitted to the Secretary General ("Study on the Implications of Establishing an International Satellite Monitoring Agency." UN Report A/AC.206/14 of 6 August 1981).

The report concluded that it was not only technically feasible, but desirable, to provide the whole world with the facilities now jealously guarded by the United States and the USSR, whose military satellites now have a ground resolution of about 25 centimeters (10 inches) in their "close look" mode. The ISMA, it stated, "would represent a potentially significant step toward developing a climate of international confidence, a prerequisite for any meaningful disarmament measure.... The type of monitoring envisaged would include verification of compliance with cease-fire arrangements; surveillance of demilitarized zones; provision of evidence of border violations or preparations for aggression...." As Representative George Brown has put it (*Congressional Record*, 23 October 1979): "A shared intelligence system... would not make pacifists out of rogues—but it would pin down the rogues in the international forums with hard evidence."

To those who feel a quite understandable distaste toward the idea of orbiting Big Brothers, I would draw a parallel from closer to home. A decade ago there was much opposition to the use of TV cameras so that the police could survey such high-crime areas as subway stations and the more notorious pieces of urban real estate. Now, however, most law-abiding citizens are happy to know that the cameras are benignly watching over them. And let us face the evidence in our daily newspapers:

Planet Earth *is* a high-crime area. I wonder how many of the recent massacres would have been prevented if the perpetrators believed (rightly or wrongly—it would make no difference!) that their atrocities were being observed.

It is easy to think of countless political and economic objections to the ISMA, but they all sink into utter insignificance when compared with its possible benefits. It has been estimated that its reconnaissance satellites saved the United States the best part of a trillion dollars. A global system might be an even better investment; and who can set a cash value on the price of peace?

It is also wise to cooperate with the inevitable; many of the elements that an ISMA would require are present, at least in rudimentary form, in existing or planned systems. The beautiful images from the United States' pioneering Landsat (earth resources satellite) have shown dramatically how well our planet can be surveyed from space. Now the French SPOT (*Système Probatoire d'Observation de la Terre*), due to begin operations in 1984, should produce images of even higher quality. Their resolution (ten to twenty meters) will approach that needed for certain types of military reconnaissance—and they will be sold (for approximately thirty cents per square kilometer!) through a *commercial* company, SPOTimage. So whether the superpowers wish it or not, the facilities of an embryo PEACESAT system will soon be available to all countries in the near future.

This brings back memories of an ironic encounter in Moscow last summer, when I visited the Institute of Space Sciences. As I expected, my gentle advocacy of the international monitoring system was received with a notable lack of enthusiasm. One of the scientists remarked sarcastically: "Perhaps the French hope to sell the equipment." Later, I was sorry not to have answered, "So what?"—but I realize now that an even better retort would have been, "Good for them!" It would be far better for the world if the vigorous French aerospace industry was building SPOTs instead of Mirages and Exocets. Unfortunately, the market for these deadly toys is hundreds of times greater.

Perhaps the best way of getting the International Monitoring Satellite accepted is as one element in a global consortium for weather observation, pollution and disaster watch, information networks, and search and rescue. No one denies the need for these facilities, and the success of INTELSAT, the worldwide communications satellite system, proves that even enemies can cooperate when it is to their mutual benefit.

As all these facts seem to me self-evident, I feel a sense of baffled frustration because they are not equally apparent to everyone else. So before we can make any real progress, or develop the "specific proposals" you request from me, the first order of business must be the education of all concerned. This means the leaders of public opinion in the democracies, and the heads of state and their advisers elsewhere. As H. G. Wells said so long ago, "the future is a race between education and catastrophe."

Fortunately, the prospects for such enlightenment now appear better than they have been for many years; the books already mentioned reflect the growing extent of public concern. Influential voices are speaking out more and more loudly against the madness of present arms policies. In an almost uncanny echo of President Johnson's words of two decades earlier, Senator Barry Goldwater—seldom accused of being a "dove"—recently remarked that it was time to tell the Russians: "We're both in trouble. We're spending too damn much on things we don't need. Let's talk."

With 193 plenary sessions since 1979, you may feel that the talking has already lasted far too long—but when we *stop* talking we will be in yet deeper trouble. So even if I have not provided much in the way of specific proposals, at least I hope to have given you some encouragement and moral support.

Meanwhile, I send greetings from Sri Lanka to you and your distinguished colleagues, especially ambassadors to the United States and the USSR Louis Fields and Viktor Issraelyan, who I enjoyed meeting at our memorable luncheon. May they, and all those associated with the Committee on Disarmament, realize that their true loyalties must now lie with mankind—not with any of its tribal subdivisions that make a fleeting appearance in the pages of history.

*   *   *

With sincere good wishes, and looking forward to our next meeting,

Arthur Clarke

II

Apollo and After

The Eve of Apollo

Half a billion years ago, the Moon summoned life out of its first home, the sea, and led it onto the empty land. For as it drew the tides across the barren continents of primeval Earth, their daily rhythm exposed to sun and air the creatures of the shallows. Most perished—but some adapted to the new and hostile environment. The conquest of the land had begun.

We shall never know when this happened, on the shores of what vanished sea. There were no eyes or cameras to record so obscure, so inconspicuous an event. Now, the Moon calls again—and this time life responds with a roar that shakes earth and sky. When a *Saturn V* soars spaceward on four thousand tons of thrust, it signifies more than a triumph of technology. It opens the next chapter of evolution.

No wonder that the drama of a launch engages our emotions so deeply. The rising rocket appeals to instincts older than reason; the gulf it bridges is not only that between world and world—but the deeper chasm between heart and brain....

These words were written in 1969, just before the first landing on the Moon, to accompany a painting* of the *Apollo 11* crew and some of the men and women who had made their flight possible.

That same momentous week I published a second and longer article in the special souvenir issue of *The New York Times* ("Will Advent of Man Awaken the Sleeping Moon?" 17 July 1969). Both essays looked into a future that had not yet happened, and was still uncertain despite all the skill and genius that had been expended to create it.

A week later, that uncertainty was ended. The year 1969 had become a date that will be remembered, centuries after 1984 is forgotten.

In 1979, ten years after the first lunar landing, *Time* magazine asked me to write a retrospective essay looking back on the previous decade. It was published in the issue for July 16 under the title "The Best is Yet to Come"; I would prefer to call it "Apollo plus Ten."

There is nothing in it that I would wish to change,

*Norman Rockwell: *Look* magazine, 15 July 1969.

and I look forward to writing "Apollo plus Twenty." But I hope that in 1989 *Time* will give me a little more than two days to meet what is, after all, a highly predictable deadline.

The Eve of Apollo

For thousands of years the Moon has signified many things to mankind; a goddess, a beacon in the night sky, a celestial body, an inspiration to lovers, a danger to beleaguered cities, a symbol of inaccessibility—and finally, a goal.

In only ten years, this last image has become dominant, but the change has occurred with such explosive speed that most of the world has not yet made the necessary emotional and mental adjustments. The stunning impact of the first close-up photographs still seems only

Published as "Will Advent of Man Awaken the Sleeping Moon?" *The New York Times*, 17 July 1969.

yesterday; last Christmas, the crew of *Apollo* 8 swept over the far side of the moon and sent greetings back to earth, 240,000 miles distant. Now, even before the wonder of that event has abated, we are preparing to land.

There may be setbacks—perhaps even disasters—in the years ahead; it is unreasonable to suppose that the conquest of a new and strange environment will not demand its toll. But men have never hesitated to pay the price, in blood as well as treasure, of exploration and discovery. Nor will they hesitate now, as they stand, for the second time in a thousand years, on the frontiers of a new world.

Like all human achievements, travel to the Moon will pass through three phases: impossible, difficult, easy. The parallel with the development of commercial aviation will be close, though the time scale may be longer because the challenge is so much greater. But it is naive to imagine that lunar flight must always be an enormously expensive operation and that astronauts will always be highly trained pilots, scientists, or engineers.

If you run your car for a day, the engine does enough work to take you to the Moon; the actual cost of the energy involved for the trip is only about ten dollars. The fact that the present cost is millions of times greater is the measure of our present ignorance and the primitive state of space technology; the time will come, through the use of reusable boosters, orbital refueling, nuclear propulsion and other foreseeable developments, when the cost of a lunar journey may be comparable to that of round-the-world jet flight today.

It is obviously impossible, on the eve of the lunar landing, to predict in detail just what we shall do with an Africa-sized world, the resources of which are still almost entirely unknown. However, the Moon provides such tremendous opportunities for so many types of research that every effort will be made to establish temporary bases there as soon as possible, analogous to those already set up in the Antarctic and those that may be established on the seabed.

Beyond the immediate deployment of small instrument packages that is planned on the Apollo missions, we may eventually expect physics laboratories and astronomical observatories. At first, they will be remote-controlled and visited from time to time by servicing crews; later, they will be permanently manned.

The Moon might have been designed as the ideal site for an astronomical observatory. Its almost total absence of atmosphere means that seeing conditions are always perfect, not only in visible light, but also in the vitally important ultraviolet, X-ray and gamma-ray regions of the spectrum, which are totally blocked by the Earth's atmosphere. The low gravity and absence of wind forces will also greatly simplify the design of large instruments; and the slow rotation means that objects can be kept under continuous observation for two weeks at a time.

These advantages, great though they may be for the optical astronomer, will be even more overwhelming for the radio observer, who can also find another bonus on the Moon. At the center of the far side, he will be permanently shielded from all the electrical noise and interference of civilization by two thousand miles of solid rock. A hundred years from now optical and radio astronomers will find it hard to believe that serious observing was ever possible on Earth.

To the geologist, the Moon represents a bonanza of more value than all the gold mines ever found. Until now, he has had a single example of a planet to study. How much would a biologist know of life if he had been allowed to examine only one specimen of our planet's teeming flora and fauna?

The evolution and geological history of the Moon may be wildly different from that of the Earth; we are not even sure whether the two bodies were once combined or whether the Moon had an independent origin and was later captured. One recent theory suggests that it is a residual "drop," a sort of umbilical fragment left over when the Earth and Mars split asunder from an ancient protoplanet.

Whatever the facts, we can be sure that the Moon will provide many exciting and valuable surprises. Indeed, it has already done so. In the astronomy books of only a decade ago, it was described as a dead, unchanged world. Now we know that there is a good deal of activity there. Orbiter photographs have shown the tracks of rolling rocks, startlingly like footprints, down (and sometimes up) the lunar slopes. There is evidence of immense lava flows, and even what looks like dried-up river valleys. If this is the case, water may still be there, locked in permafrost a few meters underground, where the temperature is constant and far below the freezing point.

The discovery of easily available water or ice would be of the greatest importance to lunar explorers. Electrolyzed, it would provide both oxygen for breathing purposes and fuel for returning spacecraft. Obviously, this last development would not be possible until large-scale engineering operations could be carried out on the Moon. This is not likely for some decades, but eventually it will completely transform the economics of space flight. For a remote comparison, imagine that today's trans-Atlantic aircraft had to carry the fuel they needed for the round trip. The cost of a ticket would be reduced by a factor of perhaps a hundred as soon as it became possible to refuel in Europe. So it will be with lunar operations.

After air and water, the third immediate necessity of life is food. Many plans have been drawn up for growing totally enclosed, or hydroponic, crops on the Moon, using the materials that may be found there. This idea looks particularly promising, now that the Luna and Surveyor spacecraft, in close-up views of the lunar surface, have revealed that it is neither rock nor dust, but nice, crumbly dirt.

Some years ago I suggested that it might be possible to develop plants resembling Earth's with tough, impermeable skins that could grow unprotected on the lunar surface, and I am delighted to discover that the National Aeronautics and Space Administration now has a project investigating this idea. Perhaps a transparent plastic sheet may be necessary to minimize the escape of water vapor; but it is at least conceivable that we may start farming on the Moon without having to build pressure domes and hermetically sealed greenhouses.

The lunar vacuum, so valuable to the astronomers, may turn out to be a much exaggerated hazard to the explorers. The old myth that a man exposed to the vacuum of space will blow up like a deep-sea fish still dies hard; hopefully, the movie *2001: A Space Odyssey* may have spread the news that this is simply not true. Obviously, an unprotected man in space will die from lack of oxygen, but this takes an appreciable time. Animals have survived up to four minutes in a vacuum, and anything an animal can do, a trained and prepared man can do better. There will be many emergencies, in space and on the Moon, where the ten or fifteen seconds of consciousness that a man can expect in vacuum will make the difference between life and death.

Whether the Moon has any indigenous life of its own is a question that may be answered shortly. No one expects to find higher organisms, but microscopic forms of life are a remote possibility. Hence the elaborate precautions of the Lunar Receiving Laboratory, which is intended to establish a quarantine in both directions.

Even if the Moon is sterile, it may be avid for life. Those terrestrial bacteria that have managed to thrive in boiling sulphur springs or at the bottom of oil wells should find the Moon a delightfully benign environment, with consequences that may be annoying to future scientists.

It has been estimated that the combustion products and cabin leakage from only 20 landings of the Apollo type could double the mass of the very tenuous lunar atmosphere. When mining, food-production and similar activities begin, the rate of contamination will be much increased, and though it may seem early to worry about lunar smog, it could be a matter of great concern to the physicists.

At the moment, the Moon's surface provides a vacuum laboratory of unlimited extent. It would be the ideal place for many types of electronic and nuclear experiments. One can even imagine that the great particle accelerators of the future will be wrapped around the Moon, so that the vacuum will be provided automatically, and there will be no need for today's elaborate enclosures and pumps.

This sort of experimenting, which may well revolutionize the many branches of physics concerned with vacuum phenomena, may be possible only in the early stages of lunar occupation. For sooner or later, as industry, commerce and tourism spread across the face of the Moon, it will begin to acquire an atmosphere of its own.

And if it turns out, as some have suggested, that the

expectation of life is considerably increased in low gravitational fields, there will be a move to give the entire Moon a breathable atmosphere, probably by using biological systems to unlock the immense amounts of oxygen (probably about 50 percent by weight) bound up in the crust. The astronomers and physicists will have to move elsewhere in search of ideal conditions, just as on the surface of this planet they have had to retreat from the lights of the cities.

And a century or so after that, as I gloomily predicted in *The Promise of Space*, there will be committees of earnest citizens desperately trying to preserve the last vestiges of the lunar wilderness.

Apollo
plus
Ten

When Neil Armstrong stepped out onto
the Sea of Tranquillity, the science-fiction writers had already been there for
two thousand years. But history is always more imaginative than any
prophet. No one had ever dreamed that the first chapter
of lunar exploration would end after only a dozen men
had walked upon the Moon.

Yet it was not the first time that ambition had outrun
technology. In the Antarctic summer of 1911–12, ten
men reached the South Pole, and five returned. They

Published as "The Best is Yet to Come," *Time* magazine, 16 July 1979, p. 27.

used only the most primitive of tools and energy sources—
snowshoes, dog sleds, their own muscles. Once the pole
had been attained, it was abandoned for nearly half a
century. And then, in the 1957–58 International Geo-
physical Year, men came back with all the resources of
modern technology. Aircraft and snow cats carried the
new explorers swiftly and safely over the frozen hell where
Robert Falcon Scott perished with his companions. For
twenty years now, summer and winter, men and women
have been living at the South Pole.

So it will be with the Moon. When we go there again,
it will be in vehicles that will make the *Saturn 5*—for all
its staggering complexity and its 150 million horsepower—look like a clumsy, inefficient dinosaur of the
early Space Age. And this time, we will stay.

In 1969 the giant multistage rocket, discarded piece-
meal after a single mission, was the only way of doing
the job. That the job should be done was a political decision, made by a handful of men. As William Sims Bainbridge pointed out in his 1976 book *The Spaceflight
Revolution; a Sociological Study*, space travel is a technological mutation that should not really have arrived
until the twenty-first century. But thanks to the ambition
and genius of Wernher von Braun and Sergei Korolev,
and their influence upon individuals as disparate as Kennedy and Khrushchev, the moon—like the South Pole—
was reached half a century ahead of time.

We have bequeathed the solar system to our children,
not our great-grandchildren, and they will be duly thank-
ful. At the very least, this gift will enable them to look
back on such transient crises as energy and material
shortages with amused incredulity.

For the resources of the universe that is now opening
up are, by all human standards, infinite. There are no
limits to growth among the stars. Unfortunately, there is
a tragic mismatch between our present needs and our
capabilities. The conquest of space will not arrive soon
enough to save millions from leading starved and stunted
lives.

Thus it is all the more urgent that we exploit to the
utmost the marvelous tools that space technology has

already given us. Even now, few Americans realize that the skills, materials and instruments their engineers devised on the road to the Moon have paid for themselves many times over, both in hard cash and in human welfare.

Never again will hurricanes smite without warning, after building up their strength unnoticed in the open sea. Every storm that moves upon the face of the globe is now watched by meteorological satellites, to which thousands already owe their lives.

Thanks to communications satellites, the "global village" is no longer a figure of speech. Yet the "comsat" revolution has barely begun. In a few decades it will have solved traffic congestion and rotting cities by making possible a world in which people can live anywhere they please, doing 90 percent of their business electronically, at the speed of light.

From their perches in orbit, Landsats and Seasats allow us to look at our planet with new eyes, surveying instantaneously all its agricultural, mineral and hydrological resources. And, equally important, monitoring their misuse.

The rockets that launched all these systems will soon be replaced by the space shuttle, which will reduce the cost of reaching orbit to a fraction of today's figures. Though the shuttle is only a modest first step, the story of aviation will repeat itself beyond the atmosphere. Many of you now reading these words will be able to buy a ticket to the Moon at a price equivalent to a round-the-world jet flight today.

But the Moon is only the offshore island of Earth. We now know, thanks to our robot explorers, that the other children of the sun are more fantastic places than we had ever dreamed. The Voyager reconnaissance of Jupiter's giant moons has revealed what is virtually a whole new solar system of baffling complexity.

Man has always found a use for new lands, however hostile. A century before Apollo, Secretary of State William Seward was being castigated for wasting $7.2 million to buy a worthless, frozen wilderness. Today, most Americans would consider Alaska quite a bargain, at two cents an acre.

* * *

We will not have to buy the planets from anyone. The main expense will be getting to them. And now there has appeared on the horizon an idea that may ultimately make space transport so cheap that if a million people a day want to commute to the Moon, they can do so.

It is nothing less (don't laugh) than a space elevator. First conceived by a Leningrad engineer, Yuri Artsutanov in 1960, it was reinvented by a group of American scientists a decade later. There is no doubt that, in theory at least, it would work.

Today's comsats demonstrate how an object can remain poised over a fixed spot on the equator by matching its speed to the turning earth, 22,320 miles below. Now imagine a cable, linking the satellite to the ground. Payloads could be hoisted up it by purely mechanical means, reaching orbit without any use of rocket power. The cost of operations could be reduced to a tiny fraction of today's values.

We could not build such a cable today. But materials that could do the job have been produced, though so far only in microscopic quantities—as were the first samples of penicillin, and of plutonium. When anything is needed badly enough, man finds ways of making it.

Ten years ago, it was my privilege to write the epilogue to Armstrong, Aldrin and Collins' own account of their mission, *First on the Moon*. I would like to repeat now the closing words: "It may be that the old astrologers had the truth exactly reversed, when they believed that the stars controlled the destinies of men. The time may come when men control the destinies of stars."

Space Flight—Imagination and Reality

The exploration of space was anticipated for centuries before the reality met the dream. It is not only interesting, but also valuable, to look back on some of those old ideas and speculations, to see what we can learn from their successes as well as their failures. For much that has occurred since the Space Age opened in 1957 was foreseen with remarkable accuracy; yet there were also some stunning surprises. So it will be in the future.

It is somewhat ironic that the first truly *scientific* space

Lecture at the Second United Nations Conference on the Exploration and Peaceful Uses of Outer Space (UNISPACE 82) Vienna, 10 August 1982.

voyage involved supernatural forces. This was the *Somnium* (1643), written by no less a man than Kepler—to whom astronautics owes as much as to Newton himself. The discoverer of the laws governing the motion of planets—and hence of spaceships—was both a scientist and a mystic; his background may be judged by the fact that his own mother barely escaped execution for sorcery.

In the *Somnium*, Kepler employed demons to carry his hero to the Moon, and made the significant remark that as the voyage progressed it would no longer be necessary to use any force for propulsion. His description of the Moon, based on the knowledge revealed by the newly invented telescope, was also as scientifically accurate as was possible at the time—though like many later writers, he assumed the existence of water, air and life.

As is well known, demons are often unreliable servants, though perhaps not as unreliable as some of the early rockets. Other writers have used mysterious mental forces to carry their heroes to other worlds—often at speeds far exceeding the miserable velocity of light. Olaf Stapledon used such a device in his magnificent *Starmaker* (1937), as did C. S. Lewis in *Perelandra* (1944, also known as *Voyage to Venus*). Descending slightly in the literary scale, Edgar Rice Burroughs used the power of the mind to transport his muscular hero, John Carter, to the planet Mars—or Barsoom, as its inhabitants call it. His example had a great influence on Carl Sagan, who has written: "I can remember spending many an hour in my boyhood, arms resolutely outstretched in an empty field, imploring what I believed to be Mars to transport me there. It never worked." From what we now know of conditions on Mars, it was very lucky for Carl that it didn't. . . .

Some early writers who did not approve of trafficking with supernatural powers—transactions in which, however carefully one read the contract, there always seemed to be some unsuspected penalty clause—used natural agencies to convey their heroes away from Earth. This was the case with the ancestor of all space-travel stories, the *Vera Historia* (True History) written by Lucian of Samos in A.D. 160. In this misleadingly entitled tale, a ship sailing in the dangerous and unexplored region beyond the pillars of Hercules was caught up in a whirlwind and deposited on the Moon. It is true that the Bay of Biscay has a bad reputation, but this must have been an unusually rough passage.

About a millennium and a half later, the great Jules Verne improved on this slightly with his *Hector Servadac* (1877), an unlikely tale in which a comet grazes the Earth, scoops up two Frenchmen, and takes them on a trip around the solar system. As they explore the comet they encounter bits of the Earth that it had acquired during the collision—some of them still inhabited. A fragment of the Rock of Gibraltar is discovered, occupied by two Englishmen playing chess and, according to Verne, quite unaware of their predicament. I doubt this: it seems much more likely that they were perfectly well aware of the fact that they were aboard a comet, but had come to a crucial point in their game and, with typically English sangfroid, refused to be distracted by such trivialities.

Perhaps the most ingenious use of natural forces was that employed by Cyrano de Bergerac in his classic *Voyages to the Moon and Sun* (1656). In the first of his several interplanetary voyages, the motive power was provided by vials of dew strapped round his waist—for Cyrano very logically argued that as the sun sucked up the dew in the morning, it would carry him with it....

So much for magic; now for machines.

With the development of the scientific method in the seventeenth and eighteenth centuries, and a fuller understanding of what space travel *really* implied, authors went to greater lengths to give their stories some basis of plausibility, and the first primitive spaceships began to appear in literature. The discovery of explosives and the invention of artillery showed that there was one way of escaping from the earth; and the "spacegun" arrived on the scene.

The most famous version, of course, is that in Jules Verne's *From the Earth to the Moon* (1865), but it was not the first. That dubious honor goes to an obscure Irish writer, Murtagh McDermot, who as early as 1728 wrote *A Trip to the Moon*. Amazingly, he used a spacegun *to come home*, after persuading the Selenites to dig a great hole containing seven thousand barrels of gunpowder.

He placed himself in the middle of ten concentric wooden vessels, "to lessen the shock," and provided himself with wings so that he could glide down to Earth when he arrived.

How did he get to the Moon in the first place? By rocket! Altogether, a remarkable effort for two and a half centuries ago. McDermot was certainly much more far-sighted than many of his successors.

Nearer our own time, it is difficult to say how seriously Verne took his mammoth cannon, because so much of the story is facetiously written, usually at the expense of the Americans. But he went to a great deal of trouble with his astronomical facts and figures; the "Columbiad" was a three-hundred-meter vertical barrel sunk in the Florida soil—not far from Cape Canaveral!—and packed with 200 metric tons of gun-cotton. The projectile itself was made of the newly discovered wonder-metal, aluminum.

Ignoring the slight impossibility of the passengers'— or indeed the vehicle's—surviving the concussion, Verne's projectile must be considered as the first scientifically conceived spacecraft. It had shock absorbers, air conditioning, padded walls with windows set in them, and similar arrangements which we now accept as commonplace in any well-ordered spaceship.

The last—I hope—spacegun was that devised by H. G. Wells for his film *Things to Come* (1936). It was visually spectacular, but of course scientific nonsense, and we members of the three-year-old British Interplanetary Society were quite upset. We wrote Mr. Wells a "more in sorrow than in anger" letter, and received a kind but unrepentant answer.

Because guns are so obviously impractical, there have been many attempts to devise alternative, and less violent, means of escaping from the earth. The American writer Edward E. Hale, author of *The Brick Moon* (1870)—the very first suggestion ever made for an artificial satellite— proposed giant flywheels that could be brought up to speed over a long period of time. At the appropriate moment, the payload would be dropped on the rim and flicked into orbit. I need hardly say that *this* suggestion is even more absurd than a spacegun—as Hale undoubtedly knew, since he was writing with his tongue firmly in his cheek.

If you could make a gun long enough, of course, the initial shock might be reduced to acceptable figures; hence the concept of the launching track. The earliest version of this I have been able to discover is in a story called *The Moon Conquerors* (1930) by a German author, R. H. Romans. In this, a series of giant magnets was used to shoot a spaceship to the Moon, and many later authors have developed the same idea.

But the Earth-based launching track has some fundamental flaws. It would have to be at least a thousand kilometers long, if human passengers were to survive the acceleration, so the cost would be astronomical. It could only do part of the job, though admittedly the most difficult part—the escape from Earth. The spacecraft would still require a self-contained propulsion system, for the landing and return. And as a last fatal defect—any object given the escape velocity of 11.2 kilometers a second near the surface of the Earth would burn up like a meteor in the dense lower atmosphere.

The only way an Earth-based launcher could operate is if it were built in the form of a slowly ascending ramp, the whole width of equatorial Africa or South America, starting from sea level and climbing to a height of say twenty kilometers. I do not know if anyone has ever had the temerity to suggest this, so I cheerfully do so now.

More than thirty years ago ("Electromagnetic Launching as a Major Contribution to Space-Flight," *J.B.I.S.* Vol. 9, No. 6, November 1950) I pointed out that the ideal place for a launcher is the Moon—the low gravity, and absence of atmosphere, makes it the perfect location. Such a launcher could be used for countless purposes, since it could economically project material—and even fragile human passengers—to almost any point in the solar system. This concept, rechristened the "mass launcher," is the basis of the schemes for space-colonization recently popularized by Dr. Gerald O'Neill (*The High Frontier*, 1976).

But you can't build a lunar launcher until you've escaped from the Earth, so it's no use in the pioneering days. Before the possibilities of the rocket were realized, many writers of space-travel stories sought an answer in forces that could overcome gravity. The most famous development of this idea is in H. G. Wells' *The First Men in the Moon* (1901)—still the greatest of all interplanetary stories, despite its inevitable dating.

Wells' "Cavorite" was a substance which blocked gravity, just as a sheet of metal blocks light. You had only to coat a sphere with it, and you would fly away from the Earth. You could steer simply by removing the section of Cavorite facing the body you wished to approach, so that its attraction could act upon you. So much more civilized than those noisy and dangerous rockets!

Is such a thing even theoretically possible? As far as Cavorite is concerned, the answer is a resounding no, as can be very easily proved by a simple "thought experiment."

Imagine a large flywheel, mounted vertically, with a sheet of Cavorite placed beneath one side. By definition, that side would be weightless, while the other half would have normal weight. Thus there would be a continual unbalance, so the wheel would revolve more and more rapidly. It could be a permanent source of energy—a perpetual motion machine, defying the most fundamental law of physics. Q.E.D.

Amusingly enough, Jules Verne pointed this out to the young Mr. Wells in no uncertain terms. "I make use of physics. He invents. I go to the moon in a cannon-ball... he constructs a metal which does away with the law of gravitation.... *Tres joli*—but show me this metal. Let him produce it." Perhaps this justified criticism induced Wells, a third of a century later, to take his retrograde step of using the spacegun in *Things to Come*; but I rather doubt it. Wells was too great an artist to let himself be unduly restricted by mere facts.

Though a *passive* gravity shield of the type imagined by Wells (and many other writers, before and since) is impossible, the laws of physics do not rule out some interesting alternatives. There is no fundamental objection to a substance which is repelled, instead of being attracted, by gravity, just as similar electric charges repel each other. We are hardly likely to discover such a material on Earth, since if it ever occurred naturally it would long ago have shot off into space. But if we could manufacture such an interesting substance, then in principle it could be used to lift a spaceship—though we would have to jettison it to come home, or to land on another planet. The technique of travel with a gravity-repellent material would be rather like old-style hydrogen ballooning. The gas can take you up—but you have to get rid of it when you want to come down again.

Nor is there any objection to an antigravity device *which is driven by some appropriate source of energy*, so that it does not produce something for nothing. I suppose the innumerable "space drives" of science fiction, some of which I have occasionally used myself, come under this heading. They may not defy the law of the conservation of energy—but it is hard to see how they can avoid a conflict with something equally fundamental—Newton's third law, that for every action there is an equal and opposite reaction. *All* motion, without exception, depends upon this law. Even a spaceship must have something to push against; in the case of a rocket, of course, that something is its ejected propellent mass.

During the mid-fifties—just after the announcement of the Vanguard Earth Satellite Program, which may or may not have been a coincidence—there was a rash of reports from the United States about "electro-gravitics." The Princeton Institute for Advanced Studies, Convair, the Glen Martin Company, among others, were involved; Martin actually placed advertisements to recruit scientists "interested in gravity." The whole thing rapidly fizzled out; one cynic told me that it was "much ado about nothing, started by a bunch of engineers who didn't know enough physics." That certainly seems to have been the case. "Electro-gravitics," like exobiology, remains a science without a single specimen for study....

And yet—the subject is not closed, and probably never will be. A few years ago one of the United Kingdom's best-known engineers—Eric Laithwaite, Professor of Heavy Electrical Engineering at Imperial College, London—startled everyone by claiming that a system of two spinning gyroscopes could produce an out-of-balance force; in other words, mechanically produced antigravity.

Interestingly enough, exactly the same conclusion was

once reached by *each* of the great pioneers of astronautics—Tsiolkovski, Goddard, Oberth. As very young men, they all thought that some arrangement of spinning weights could produce a lift, but very quickly discovered a fallacy in their reasoning. Oberth has complained that some inventor approaches him once a month, on the average, with variants of this idea. But Professor Laithwaite is no crackpot inventor, and he proposes to conduct a crucial experiment on *his* system in the weightless environment of the space shuttle. I wish him luck.

If we ever do invent a "space-drive," however, it will surely depend upon some new fundamental discovery in subatomic physics, or the structure of space-time. Until then, we are stuck with rockets—chemical, electric or nuclear.

There is, it is true, one other known alternative, but that is of very limited application. I refer to "solar sailing."

The fact that sunlight produces a tiny—but measurable—pressure when it falls upon a surface has already been used to control the orientation of satellites. Since even a minute force can produce large effects if it operates over a sufficiently long time, small reflecting panels can be used to make a satellite turn around its axis and point in any desired direction. If these panels were large enough—and by large, I mean kilometers on a side—they could produce major orbital changes.

Hence the delightful fantasy—and perhaps one day it may be more than that—of "solar yachts" furling gigantic, gossamer-thin sails as they race from world to world. "Solar sailing" would be the most spectacular sport ever developed; but it will not be a very exciting one, because even the simplest maneuver would take hours or days. And as it is a technology which can only be used in the zero-gravity vacuum of deep space, the use of the sun's radiation pressure for propulsion still depends on the rocket for its initial stages.

Though it was mentioned in passing from time to time—for example, by the ingenious Cyrano de Bergerac—the rocket did not enter the literature of space travel until surprisingly late. Its first serious appearance may have been in Verne's sequel *Round the Moon* (1870), where it was used to change the orbit of the projectile.

Verne—unlike *The New York Times*, in a notorious editorial about Goddard's folly, half a century later—clearly understood that rockets could provide thrust in a vacuum. It is a pity he did not consider them adequate for the whole job; his impossible gun may have set back the conquest of space by years, though hardly by decades.

Popular attention began to be focused on rockets from 1925 onward, with the appearance of serious technical literature and the rise of small experimental groups in Germany, the USSR and elsewhere. For a long time, fact and fiction were inextricably entangled; many of the pioneers were writers, and used their pens to spread the news that space travel need no longer be fantasy. It is hard to believe that this pioneering era is only half a century ago, and that a mere forty years after the flight of the first liquid-fueled rocket in 1926, men were preparing to go to the Moon.

The "Spaceflight Revolution," as Williams Sims Bainbridge called it in his book of that name, was one of the swiftest and most remarkable in human history. Most technological developments arise naturally when some social need is matched by a corresponding invention; the steam engine, the telephone, the automobile are obvious examples. But, to be perfectly honest, no one really *needed* spaceships in the mid-twentieth century, and a lot of people still rather wish they'd go away. Sooner or later, of course, space transportation would have evolved, probably out of high-altitude aviation, but things didn't happen that way. As Bainbridge points out, the imagination and determination of a mere handful of men—of whom the Russian Korolev and the German von Braun were by far the most important—opened up the space frontier decades ahead of any historically plausible scenario.

The full implications of this will not be known for centuries—but let me leave this analogy for you to meditate upon. In 1492 Christopher Columbus did something much more important than merely discovering America—which after all had been known to quite a few people for at least twenty thousand years. He opened up the road between the Old World and the New.

Yet some Renaissance Korolev or von Braun *could* have made that happen fifty—a hundred years—earlier than it actually did; the Vikings almost succeeded. One day we may be very glad that we got to the Moon in 1969, instead of—well, 2001... or even 2051....

And to those who think that the landing on the Moon was merely a technological tour de force of little ultimate importance in human affairs, I offer another lesson from history. One of the early explorers of Australia reported proudly to his mission control, back in Whitehall: "I have now mapped this continent so thoroughly *that no one need ever go there again.*" You may laugh—but as far as space is concerned, there are equally shortsighted people around today.

Among them I would include all those distinguished scientists who keep telling us that the exploration of space can best be carried out by robots. Well, Europe could have waited five hundred years and sent remote-controlled cameras to survey America. Of course, this is a ridiculous analogy—but then the whole debate is ridiculous. Robots are essential as pioneers, and there are environments which only they can penetrate. But there are also missions where it is far more effective—and even cheaper—to have men in the loop, if only to deal with unexpected emergencies. (Remember the Skylab salvage operation, and *Apollo 13.*)

However, cost-effectiveness is not the only criterion. Like all his fellow primates, man is an inquisitive animal and seldom stops to calculate the number of bits per buck. He wants to go and see things for himself. And what he has discovered he never abandons, except temporarily—as in the case of the South Pole between 1912 and 1957, and the Moon between 1972 and 19—??

The science-fiction writers, and the pioneers of astronautics, have imagined human settlements on all the worlds of the solar system—and even in space itself. They have dreamed that we will extend our commerce beyond the atmosphere, into the final frontier (to coin a phrase). And if anyone thinks that this idea is fantastic, let me remind him that half a century ago a single man in the Atlantic sky was headline news. How many thousands are up there at this very moment, dozing through the in-flight movie?

The analogy may be false; perhaps there is nothing in

space to attract more than the occasional scientific mission or asteroid mining consortium. And even if the solar system is full of opportunity, it may be argued that the enormous cost of escaping from the Earth will always place a severe limit on our ability to exploit extraterrestrial resources. Our great airports are already bad enough; even if we could afford it, do we really want a space shuttle taking off from somewhere on Earth every few minutes—and, almost as bad, booming back into the atmosphere?

Well, there is an alternative—and it's not antigravity, which may be impossible even in theory. It's the space elevator, or orbital tower, conceived in 1960 by the Russian engineer Yuri Artsutanov, and since reinvented at least five times.

For those of you who are not familiar with this at-first-sight preposterous idea, let me summarize briefly. It follows from the concept of stationary satellites, which everyone now takes for granted. Clearly, if a satellite can remain poised forever above the same spot on the equator, then in principle it should be possible to lower a cable from orbit to Earth, performing an Indian rope trick 36,000 kilometers high.

And if we can do that, we can go further. We can build an elevator system to send payloads into space without rockets, purely by electrical energy. This would totally transform the economics of spaceflight—as you will appreciate when I tell you that the cost, *in energy*, of carrying a man to the Moon is less than ten dollars.

The engineering problems are, of course, enormous, but extensive studies have found no fundamental flaw in the concept, which is now the basis of a rapidly expanding literature, to which I refer those who would like more details. Much ingenuity has now been applied to extending Artsutanov's basic idea, and it appears—surprisingly—that "Skyhooks" or "Jacob's Ladders" can be built to virtually any altitude, from any spot on the Earth—though at the cost of rather appalling mechanical complexities.

Whether these daring concepts will ever be realized in practice, only the future will tell. But the imagination of the engineers has now opened up wholly new vistas in space and also presents us with a beautiful paradox.

On the small scale, space travel will always be extremely expensive. Yet if—and it's a big if—it can ever be justified on a really massive scale, it could be one of the cheapest forms of transportation ever devised. Exactly as in the case of the familiar terrestrial elevator, a space elevator would require very little energy to run—because the traffic moving downward would lift that on the way up. Of course, the capital cost would be enormous; but a well-designed space elevator could last for centuries and would be an even better long-term investment than that other expensive but highly profitable tourist attraction, the Great Pyramid.

Perhaps you may consider that the space elevator puts too much of a strain on the imagination—but without imagination, nothing is ever achieved, as the history of astronautics amply proves. Yet it is possible to have too much of a good thing; uncontrolled imagination can be an even bigger menace than shortsighted conservatism, because it can lead to much greater disasters.

I would like to conclude with two dreadful, or at least tragicomic, examples of this in our own field of interest. One is history; the other remains a continuing nuisance.

For almost two generations, the planet Mars was central in all discussions of extraterrestrial life, largely owing to the influence of one man, the American astronomer Percival Lowell. His dramatic claim to have discovered a network of apparently artificial "canals" covering the face of the planet generated millions of words of controversy— not to mention whole libraries of fiction.

We now know, thanks to the Mariner and Viking space probes, that the Martian canals are a total illusion, created in the mind's eye from the infinity of detail that can be glimpsed on the planet during the rare moments of good seeing. Yet Lowell—and many other astronomers!—drew them consistently for decades. How could this happen? The explanation, I suspect, runs something like this:

Lowell was so determined to find intelligence on Mars that he created what he was looking for, as we have all done at some time or another. His drawings of Mars became more and more artificial, until eventually they looked like maps of the world's airlines. As an artist can do, he created a style—which was copied by others who were infected by his enthusiasm. More-skeptical astronomers saw merely the natural patterns of light and shade which we now know represent the real Mars. The canals were a—shall we say—*infectious hallucination*, but to Lowell they were perfectly real.

His wealth and prestige—not to mention his considerable literary gifts—enabled him to sustain the illusion. When his very able assistant A. E. Douglass eventually became skeptical—*dis*illusioned—and decided that the canals lay in the eye of the observer, what did Lowell do? He fired him—I am sure with genuine reluctance.

When Lowell died, so did the canals, though slowly. It took the Mariners and Vikings to inflict the final coup de grace.

On a much larger scale, I am now convinced that something like this is responsible for the few UFO sightings that do not have trivial explanations. Let me devote a couple of minutes to the two cases which provided my own "moments of truth" and which closed the subject as far as I am concerned—at least until some fundamentally new evidence comes along, which hasn't happened for twenty years. . . .

In one famous incident, many eyewitnesses saw the classic spaceship, complete with lighted windows, flying a few thousand meters overhead. Some of them thought it had landed not far away. They weren't lying; they had indeed seen something unusual—and we know exactly what it was, without a shadow of doubt.

It was not a spaceship a few kilometers up; it was a reentering satellite at fifty times that altitude, burning up spectacularly in a trail of fire halfway across the sky. But the people who were expecting to see a spaceship, saw one. It was the "Lowell effect" again.

There are so many hundreds of similar—and even more fantastic—misinterpretations, described *ad nauseam* in the literature, that I no longer waste any time on reports of strange things seen in the sky—even by competent observers. I've been fooled too often myself: one of my own half dozen UFOs took weeks to identify. So my philosophy now is very simple, and based on that extremely rare commodity, common sense. Here is Clarke's Rule for dealing with a UFO: even if it does come from Proxima Centauri, but it doesn't stop—there's nothing you can prove one way or the other. So take pity on suffering humanity—*forget* it. Nothing will be lost; when there really *is* a landing, the fact will be established, without a shadow of doubt, within half an hour. We won't still be waving our arms, thirty years later.

Then what about the hundreds of "close encounters," sometimes — though not always — reported by apparently sane and honest people?

Yes, it's the Lowell effect again, in considerably more virulent form. My first glimpse of this obvious truth came when I was sent a book giving an account of a UFO kidnapping, full of drawings showing the spaceship and its occupants. I recognized the ship instantly; I'd known it for thirty years. And so has every American who's spent much time watching the "Late, Late Show."...

Now, it is possible that a superior, space-faring civilization *may* base its designs on 1950 Hollywood movies, but frankly I doubt it. Yet I don't doubt the honesty of the person who drew the sketches; they were no more faked than Lowell's maps of Mars. But they were also no *less* faked....

What clinched the matter, as far as I'm concerned, is the very recent discovery that some people can hallucinate so perfectly that even the electrical patterns in their brains agree with their visions. What this does to our concepts of reality I'm not quite sure. I hope I'm not hallucinating you. Or even worse—that you're hallucinating *me*.

I'm sorry about this rather long digression—but UFOs are such an obstacle to serious discussions of life in space, that perhaps you'll forgive me. And the theme of this talk is, after all, imagination and reality....

I freely admit that I've often used my imagination to do something about reality. And I'd like to give you a couple of examples that are highly relevant to this conference.

Back in 1948, in my first novel, *Prelude to Space*, I coined a slogan that I'd like to leave with you tonight. Here it is:

WE WILL TAKE NO FRONTIERS INTO SPACE

The second example is much nearer in time, and even more directly concerned with this meeting. Back in 1968, one of the non-government organizations who came to UNISPACE 1 was Metro Goldwyn Meyer. MGM used the opportunity to show a little movie my friend Stanley Kubrick had just made.

One of the people who saw it then was Cosmonaut Alexei Leonov, who made quite the nicest comment *anyone* ever made about *2001*: "Now I feel I've been into space *twice*." Since then, of course, he has done just that, when he was commander in the Apollo-Soyuz mission.

Now, I hope it's the worst-kept secret of this conference that I've just completed *2010: Odyssey Two*. (With any luck, the issue of *Playboy* magazine containing the first installment will reach Vienna before we wind up.) Just two months ago at Star Village, I had the pleasure of telling Alexei that most of the action takes place aboard the spaceship *Cosmonaut Alexei Leonov*. When he heard this he exclaimed, "Then it must be a good ship." (It is.)

Still more to the point, it's manned—and womanned—by seven Russians and three Americans, who start off as good friends, and end up as even better ones.

I might also add that a heroic role is played by a spaceship named after the great Chinese rocket engineer Dr. Tsien, one of the original founders of the Jet Propulsion Laboratory.

I apologize for the commercial, but the point I wish to make is that *this* is the sort of future we should aim for. Exciting fantasies like *Star Wars* are all very well; I enjoy them as much as anyone, but with a certain feeling of guilt. This conference may represent mankind's last chance to decide which of the two possible futures in space lies ahead of us. And incidentally the current success of Steven Spielberg's *E.T.—The Extraterrestrial*—the biggest hit in the entire history of movies—may reveal the desire of the American public for peaceful confrontations in space....

So I would like to end by repeating, virtually unchanged, some words I addressed to the British Interplanetary Society in 1950—seven years before the explosive dawn of the Space Age. After surveying the writings of the past, I posed this question: What will happen to tales of interplanetary adventure when space travel actually begins? Will they become extinct—as some foolish critics indeed predicted—the morning after *Sputnik 1*!

This is what I said, thirty-two years ago:

When space travel is achieved, the frontier will merely shift outward, and I think we can rely on the ingenuity of the authors to keep always a few jumps ahead of history. And how much more material they will have on which to base their tales! It should never be forgotten that, without some foundation of reality, science fiction would be impossible, and that therefore exact knowledge is the friend, not the enemy, of imagination and fantasy. It was only possible to write stories about the Martians when science had discovered that a certain moving point of light was a world. By the time that science has proved or disproved the existence of Martians, it will have provided hundreds of other interesting and less accessible worlds for the authors to get busy with.

So perhaps the interplanetary story will never lose its appeal, even if a time should come when all the cosmos has been explored and there are no more universes to beckon men outward across infinity. If our descendants in that age are remotely human, and still indulge in art and science and similar nursery games, I think that they will not altogether abandon the theme of interplanetary flight—though their approach to it will be very different from ours.

To us, the interplanetary story provides a glimpse of the wonders whose dawn we shall see but of whose full glory we can only guess. To them, on the other hand, it will be something achieved, a thing completed and done countless aeons ago. They may sometimes look back, perhaps a little wistfully, to the splendid, dangerous ages when the frontiers were being driven outward across space, when no one knew what marvel or what terror the next returning ship might bring—when, for good or evil, the barriers set between the peoples of the universe were irrevocably breached. With all things achieved, all knowledge safely harvested, what more, indeed, will there be for them to do, as the lights of the last stars sink slowly toward evening, but to go back into history and relive again the great adventures of their remote and legendary past?

Yet we have the better bargain: for all these things still lie ahead of us.

The Discovery of the Solar System

We have been privileged to live through the greatest age of exploration the world has ever known.

The discovery of our own planet took the whole of human history and was completed only during this century—with the aid of space technology. Today, there are earth resources satellites continually surveying the globe, able to detect objects smaller than this building. And the military or reconnaissance satellites can do far better than that; they can

---

Chancellor's Address at University of Moratuwa Convocation, Bandaranaike Memorial International Conference Hall, Colombo, 6 November 1981.

tell what type of car you're driving. There are no hidden places any more on *this* planet.

Yet until a mere twenty years ago—within the lifetime of virtually everyone here!—we were almost totally ignorant of conditions on the worlds around us; even the few facts we *thought* we knew have turned out to be wrong. The first phase of the Discovery of the Solar System occupied, very nearly, the period 1960–1980, and there will now be a slight pause while we consolidate its results and prepare for phase II, which should be well underway in the closing decade of this century.

Let me remind you of our state of ignorance at the dawn of the Space Age (*Sputnik 1,* 1957.) Until then, all our knowledge of the other heavenly bodies was obtained by means of telescopes—and there is a very definite limit to the amount of magnifying power one can use. That limit is set not by optics but by the disturbing effects of the Earth's atmosphere—very obvious when one looks horizontally even a few kilometers.

Let's take a specific case—the Moon, almost 400,000 kilometers away. Under unusually good conditions, and with a large telescope, it is possible to employ a magnification of a thousand—thus bringing the Moon to an apparent distance of four hundred kilometers. Now, if you were poised in space four hundred kilometers above the Earth, how much would you see with the naked eye?

A great deal, of course—but only a minute fraction of what there was to see. And nothing of the multitudinous life forms on the surface—though the larger cities could be made out, especially at night.

By 1960 some three centuries of telescopic observation—mostly by amateur astronomers, because the professionals thought they had more important things to do—had produced maps of the Moon showing everything down to about half a kilometer across. But we were still quite uncertain about the exact nature of the lunar surface; speculation varied all the way from sheets of lava, seas of dust—even ice, believe it or not! There was also a bitter debate about the origin of the lunar craters; some people (mostly the Americans) thought that they were produced by the impact of giant meteorites; others (especially the British) were convinced that they were home-grown—that is, of volcanic origin. Actually, both sides turned out to be partly right—though I regret to say that the Americans were more right than the British. . . .

During a period of little more than ten years, thanks to robot space probes such as Ranger, Surveyor, Lunik and the final triumph of the Apollo landings, the Moon ceased to be a remote object in the sky but became a world whose soil now bears the imprint of human feet.

Even with the Moon—which we thought was a familiar object—there were many surprises. You may have seen the pre-1960 artists' impressions of lunar landscapes; invariably they showed jagged peaks and needles of rock, stabbing into a black sky full of stars—even in the daytime. Well, the lunar hills and mountains are not jagged; they are gently rounded, having been sandblasted smooth by aeons of meteoric impact. And you can't see the stars, at least with the unprotected eye; the glare from the surrounding landscape makes them invisible.

Back in 1950—seven years before the Space Age opened, and when most scientists thought the idea of travel beyond the Earth was utter bilge—I was on the council of the British Astronomical Association. During our monthly meetings, the members would show drawings of the lunar formations, observed through telescopes they had often made themselves. As I looked at those drawings and heard the arguments about their significance, I sometimes daydreamed. I can remember how I used to say to myself: "Some day, friends, all these arguments will be ended—we'll have photographs made on the spot." But I never imagined how soon that day would be—only twenty years in the future. . . .

Let me show you an example that brings that home more vividly than anything else I know. Along the foothills of the lunar Appenines, just inside the great plain known as the Mare Imbrium (Sea of Rains) is a deep winding valley just over a kilometer across. In my own eight-inch telescope, under favorable conditions, it is visible as a fine, meandering hairline. And not even the most powerful telescope in the world can show *very* much more than that.

I have a certain proprietary interest in this region. Back in 1953 I wrote a novel, *Earthlight*, which is set in this general area. When they prepared their maps of the proposed landing site, the *Apollo 15* crew gave this name to a crater about three hundred meters wide. They drove right round it on their second and longest excursion, and sent me the mission map when they returned, autographed "To Arthur Clarke with best personal regards from the crew of *Apollo 15* and many thanks for your visions in space—Dave Scott, Al Worden, Jim Irwin." The map showing "Earthlight" crater is now one of my most valued possessions.

Beyond the Moon, there were only two other planets that gave more than the most fleeting glimpses of surface detail, Mars and Jupiter. And the case of Mars provides a tragicomic example of human credulity and wishful thinking.

The little red planet is about half the size of Earth, and even at its closet, is a hundred times further away than the Moon, so we could hardly expect to see much detail. To make matters worse, we must always observe it fully illuminated because it's further away from the Sun; so there are none of the long shadows that give the Moon such a vivid, three-dimensional appearance. Even the tallest mountains on Mars would be invisible when viewed from the Earth; though this now seems perfectly obvious, it gave rise to the belief that Mars is almost flat. Nothing could be further from the truth.

All that Mars shows through any terrestrial telescope is a little disc, smaller than the Moon to the naked eye, with a few faint smudges and a bright spot at one pole. That's about it; Mars is so disappointing that I never show it to anyone and seldom bother to look myself.

Years of studying those tiny images, plus generous doses of imagination and a touch of eyestrain, convinced some observers that Mars was covered with fine narrow lines—the notorious "canals." *If* they existed, they appeared too regular to be natural, and the immediate assumption was that they were the product of high technology.

Most astronomers were skeptical, even at the height of the canal craze, and one of them—Maunder, at the Greenwich Observatory—conducted a very interesting experiment around the beginning of this century. He made a series of drawings, showing the main patterns of light and shade on Mars, but *no* canals. Then he set them up at a considerable distance from a group of schoolboys, so that the images they saw were the same size as Mars through a telescope—and asked them to draw what they observed. A considerable number inserted canallike features; it seems that the human eye—or mind—has a tendency to link together random features and create order where it doesn't exist.

I recently repeated this experiment for my "Mysterious World" TV series, using some charming young ladies at a Trincomalee school, and got exactly the same result. The canals of Mars simply don't exist.

Now let us look at the real Mars, as shown to us by the United States' Mariner and Viking space probes.

The first photos radioed back (*Mariner 4*, 1965) showed a terrain covered with craters, very much like the Moon—which was quite a surprise, and rather disappointing. It turned out that by bad luck the probe had observed only a limited and rather uncharacteristic sample of Martian terrain, which we now know to contain some most dramatic features.

Not only is Mars anything but flat—it boasts the highest mountains ever discovered. The awesome volcano christened Olympus (by pure coincidence, the name had been applied to the feature long before we knew it was a mountain) is about three times the height of Everest—and would completely bury Sri Lanka.

An equally remarkable feature is the so-called Grand Canyon of Mars, the Mariner Valley. Almost a hundred kilometers wide in places, it is long enough to stretch right across the United States.

The most puzzling—and exciting—features are what appear to be dried-up riverbeds, and evidence of enormous floods. Today, there is no free water on Mars; the atmosphere is so thin—about a hundredth the density of ours—that water can exist there only in the forms of ice or vapor—not liquid.

Does this mean that Mars once had a much denser atmosphere—and perhaps lakes and seas? We don't know, but it seems quite possible.

And what about life? That, of course, is what everyone

hoped to find. Alas, when the Viking lander got down to the surface and looked around, there were no signposts saying "Yankee Go Home." Nothing but a desert that might have been almost anywhere on Earth....

The two Viking landers also carried out elaborate tests looking for chemical indications of life; our own Dr. Cyril Ponnamperuma has been at the forefront of this work. Although the results are still being debated, there is no unambiguous evidence for any biological activity on Mars. But before we pronounce Mars "dead on arrival," remember this—we have investigated only a minute portion of an entire world. Mars has no oceans, so its land area is about the same as Earth's. It's as if we've looked at a couple of football fields in the whole of Africa, Asia, the Americas, the Antarctic.... There may be many surprises, especially around or under the huge ice caps at the poles.

We now possess superb photo-surveys of Mars, with a resolution down to a few hundred meters, showing literally thousands of craters and valleys and mountains. Somebody has to find names for them all....

I gave some thought to this problem in an essay I wrote back in 1958 ("The Men on the Moon" reprinted in *The Challenge of the Spaceship*). To quote:

> As high-definition photographs accumulate from our rocket probes, millions of square miles of hitherto unknown territory will be dumped into the laps of geographers, scientists—and UN delegates. Somewhere in the 1960s, the cartographers will be faced with the biggest job of mapmaking since exploration began.

That has turned out to be quite an understatement. In 1958, I was thinking about the Moon—particularly the unknown Farside. I never dreamed that within twenty years we'd have a couple of dozen new worlds to map, and that it was getting more and more difficult to find suitable names. As I wrote in 1958:

> Let us hope that the experts who must now undertake the task of naming a world do so in the spirit of responsibility and dignity it demands. We do not want to wake up one morning to find that the job has been done in top secrecy by

a Pentagon general who happens to be a baseball fan, or an unimaginative bureaucrat who has stuck pins at random into the Vladivostok telephone directory.

Fortunately, this hasn't happened; names have to be approved by a subcommission of the International Astronomical Union. And I'm happy to say that this body has already put one resident of Ceylon on Mars.

Percy B. Molesworth (1867–1908) was an engineer on the Ceylon railway and a keen amateur astronomer, well-known for his studies of the planets. At the turn of the century he had an observatory in Fort Frederick, Trincomalee; I visited the site a few years ago, and traces of it can still be seen. Crater Molesworth is quite large— 175 kilometers across—and is in the southern hemisphere of Mars at longitude 211, latitude 28. Perhaps someday a researcher with access to local records will dig out the background of this astronomer, who seems to have made a considerable impact in his short life; he was only 41 when he died.

Even though many of our ideas about Mars have turned out to be incorrect, at least we did know *something* about its size, temperature and surface conditions; it was not a completely unknown world. But beyond Mars, our space probes were entering into a region where our ignorance was almost total, which was what made the Pioneer and Voyager missions so exciting. No one knew what to expect among the multitudinous moons of Jupiter and Saturn. Even the largest of these distant worlds appear only as a minute pinhead in the most powerful telescope. We knew their approximate sizes—that was all.

It was reasonable to suppose that they would turn out to be rather like our own Moon—dead, crater-covered globes of no particular interest, once the initial excitement of seeing them in close-up had worn off. But we were in for a big surprise—proving that Nature is infinitely ingenious, and that we can seldom outguess her.

First, Jupiter itself—largest of all the planets, with more than a hundred times the surface area of our world. We knew that it was completely cloud-covered, because any good telescope will show an ever-changing pattern of white and pink clouds, moving in bands parallel to the equator. These can be photographed from Earth fairly easily, but the Voyagers showed them in infinitely greater detail. The meteorology of Jupiter will keep scientists busy for decades: it will also throw much light upon weather processes on Earth, with all the practical consequences that will imply.

The first big surprise of the Jupiter mission was the discovery that, like Saturn, the planet has a system of rings.

But much more exciting discoveries were to come. Jupiter has at least a dozen small moonlets, and four giant ones—the Galilean satellites, so-called because Galileo was the first man to see them, when he pointed his newly invented telescope at the planet in 1609. They are named after four of the participants in the god's rather wide-ranging love life—Io, Europa, Ganymede and Callisto.

Callisto, the outermost of the four, is the only one that didn't produce surprises. It turned out to be covered with craters—like our Moon, only even more so. In fact, it is the most heavily bombarded body in the solar system. Any more craters would simply destroy existing ones.

But when they saw the first pictures of the inner moon Io, the astronomers were completely baffled. They couldn't find a single crater! Yet Io, like all the other bodies in the solar system, must have been bombarded at some time in its history. Where had the craters gone?

The astonishing answer is that Io is in a state of furious volcanic activity: its entire surface is being continually reworked.

It is certainly one of the strangest worlds we have yet encountered. Looking at the photos, one can sympathize with the scientist who remarked, "I don't know what's wrong with Io, but a good dose of penicillin should fix it. . . ."

Europa, next door, is quite different—and even more mysterious. It's covered with canals—like the ones that men once thought they saw on Mars!

And Ganymede, largest of them all, seems to be covered with ploughed fields—except that the furrows are hundreds of meters wide. . . .

What is happening out on these strange worlds? We may know a lot more in about five years' time. The proposed Galileo spaceprobe will go into orbit around the giant planet, looking at *all* the moons in turn, and not merely flashing by for one brief encounter like the Voyagers.

For after their rendezvous with Jupiter, they were deflected—and accelerated by its gravitational field—on to Saturn. Here again they were going into virtually unknown territory and also heading toward two of the most interesting of all satellites. Titan—large enough to be called a world in its own right—is the only satellite on which an atmosphere has been detected; the spectroscope has revealed methane. And Iapetus has the extraordinary characteristic of being almost ten times brighter on one side than on the other.

The first surprise on reaching Saturn was that its beautiful ring system was infinitely more complex than had ever been suspected.

Telescopic observations had revealed at least three rings, and some astronomers had suspected more. But no one dreamed that there would be hundreds—perhaps a thousand—and that some of them would be eccentric and even braided together like a rope!

And the atmosphere of Titan was also a surprise—it turns out to be several times denser than Earth's and to consist mostly of nitrogen. This was a blow to me personally, as in my novel *Imperial Earth* I'd assumed (as was widely believed at the time) that Titan's atmosphere was primarily hydrogen.... Well, you can't win them all....

The other satellites of Saturn also show considerable individuality.

Now *Voyager 1* has gone on to the stars, and *Voyager 2* is heading for a rendezvous with the next outer planet, Uranus. What will it find there? The only thing that will be surprising is that there are no surprises....

I am sorry to keep quoting myself, but I would like to end with the concluding words of a book I wrote about the deep-space probes in 1972, when Voyager was still several years in the future:

> We should build them well, for one day they may be the only evidence that the human race existed. All the works of

man on his own world are ephemeral, seen from the viewpoint of geological time. The winds and the rains which have destroyed mountains will make short work of the Pyramids, those recent experiments in immortality. The most enduring monuments we have yet created stand on the Moon, or circle the Sun; but even these will not last forever.

For when the sun dies, it will not end with a whimper. In its final paroxysm, it will melt the inner planets to slag, and set the frozen outer giants erupting in geysers wider than the continents of Earth. Nothing will be left on, or even near, the world where he was born, of Man and his works.

But hundreds—thousands—of light-years outward from Earth, some of the most exquisite masterpieces of his hand and brain will still be drifting down the corridor of stars. The energies that powered them will have been dead for aeons, and no trace will remain of the patterns of logic that once pulsed through the crystal labyrinths of their minds.

Yet they will still be recognizable, while the Universe endures, as the work of beings who wondered about it long ago, and sought to fathom its secrets.

Viking on the Plain of Gold

I t is pure coincidence that the *Viking 1* Lander made its historic touchdown in a region that astronomers had given the fanciful name *Planitia Chryse*—the plain of gold. No one expected to find gold in Chryse; Viking was looking for something much more valuable than that overrated metal—knowledge.

Yet is it very difficult for the layman, unaware of the way in which the most esoteric scientific discoveries can

Written August 1976 for circulation by the U.S. Information Service. This version was printed in *Spaceflight* Vol. 18, No. 12, December 1976, pp. 429-431.

save millions of lives and create whole new industries, to appreciate the importance of such a project. He is apt to take the short-term view and ask, very reasonably, why the billion dollars spent on Viking could not have been used instead on houses, schools, hospitals, roads, etc.?

It should be admitted at once that all the answers to this question won't be in for a couple of centuries. But it is an act of faith among scientists, based on all past history, that every breakthrough into a new realm of knowledge invariably adds to the total potential—and hence, wealth and happiness—of mankind.

Sometimes the payoff is immediate: from Faraday's first experiments with magnets, to telegraphs and electric motors, was only a few years. Sometimes it takes a little longer; the voyage of Columbus changed the destiny of the human race, but it was several lifetimes before this became apparent.

One can divide the motives behind any voyage of exploration—manned or unmanned—into three main categories: scientific, practical (or commercial), and spiritual (or philosophical-religious). Sometimes it is not easy to separate them, and indeed they are seldom found in isolation, for in the past there have been missionary-scientists and tradesmen-naturalists.

Science first. All men, if their souls are not utterly destroyed by poverty or bad education, have a natural curiosity about the world around them—not only this planet, but any others that may exist. In its purest form, science is simply an expression of this curiosity; any man who is even half-alive must have some interest in conditions on other worlds, even if the knowledge is of no conceivable practical importance.

For over a hundred years, since the development of modern telescopes, Mars has been the center of such interest—though partly for reasons which we now know to be quite erroneous. The reported discovery in 1877 of a network of "canals" inspired millions of words of speculation about Martian civilizations—not to mention countless science fiction stories and movies, of which H.G. Wells' *The War of the Worlds* is the most famous (or most notorious, after it provoked the 1938 radio panic in the United States!).

The canals have turned out to be an illusion, but there was no way of proving this while we were confined to observations from Earth. Viking's precursors, particularly the orbiting *Mariner 9*, which produced the first complete photographic survey of the planet, swept into limbo all the fabled Martian cities and princesses. Instead, they revealed a world almost as fascinating as the fiction—a place of rolling multicolored deserts, of canyons that could swallow those of Arizona and Colorado without trace, and of volcanoes three times as high as Everest.

But even the closest observations from space could not prove or disprove the existence of life on Mars, although they could eliminate many possibilities. Thus there were certainly no extensive areas of vegetation necessary to support animal life as we know it. Such life was in any case ruled out by the almost complete absence of oxygen in the extremely thin Martian atmosphere. Yet for all that *Mariner 9* could tell, there might still be living creatures on the planet, of any size from microbes to elephants, and the only way to settle the matter was by a landing on the surface. Hence Viking, with its pair of electronic cameras and its automated biology lab—an incredible tour de force of technology, containing forty thousand components in the volume of a biscuit tin.

This marvelously compact and versatile type of instrumentation usually, within a very few years, has its impact upon a whole range of down-to-earth applications in medicine, science and industry. Unfortunately, by the time some space-inspired device gets to the general public, its origins are usually forgotten. The shopkeeper or accountant (or for that matter schoolboy or housewife) operating one of the miraculous little electronic calculators that have removed all the drudgery from arithmetic, seldom stops to ask how such a gadget came about. But without the stringent demands of space navigation, these tiny pocket brains would never have been developed. Soon we will find it impossible to imagine how we ever ran our lives without them—and their even more intelligent successors, already on the drawing board.

Perhaps only 10 percent of the world's population can afford pocket calculators, or would know how to use them. But 100 percent of the world requires food, water and the basic necessities of life—and the type of survey equipment carried on space probes has already started to revolutionize the search for these things on Earth. After all, looking for life on Mars, and looking for its prerequisites on our own planet, involves much the same problems.

Quite early in the Space Age, it was discovered that orbiting cameras and other instruments (very similar to those which gave us our first Martian's-eye view from *Viking 1*) could reveal astonishingly detailed information about crops, water supplies, snow cover, ocean fertility, mineral deposits. The list is enormous, and is still growing. As a result, the National Aeronautics and Space Administration has launched two "earth resources satellites," now rechristened Landsats—though Earthsats would have been a better name, because they are doing equally important work on land and sea. Between them, *Landsats 1* and *2* have produced millions of beautiful—and economically priceless—photographs, giving information about our planet that could have been obtained in no other way. This information is available cheaply to any country in the world, and has already enabled some developing nations to produce maps at a fraction of the cost of conventional aerial surveying.

In a very important and fundamental way, when we study Mars we are also studying our own world...and what it may teach us about our planet may one day be a matter of life and death. This may seem surprising, but consider these facts:

For some years it has been known that the Martian atmosphere (mostly carbon dioxide) is so thin that its pressure is about one hundredth of the Earth's. This means that even if it was warm enough (which it seldom is, except near noon on the equator) water cannot exist in the liquid form. There are clouds and snowfields on Mars, but no rivers or lakes, still less oceans. Yet to the astonishment of the scientists, the first good photos of Mars showed vast dried-up riverbeds and huge canyons that seemed to have been cut by torrential rains—on a planet now more desert than the Sahara.

What has happened to the lost lakes—and perhaps oceans—of Mars? Is the same process occurring on Earth? There has been tragic evidence, in the past few years, that profound changes are taking place in the weather patterns of our planet. Mars may tell us what is happening here—and perhaps what to do about it. Few discoveries would be more important than unraveling the forces which control climate, and while we have only a single planet for study, our chance of understanding this process is small. We urgently need the tools of space to save our own world, midway, it would seem, in the evolutionary sequence between cold, low-pressure Mars and red-hot, high-pressure Venus.

During the last decade, we have learned more about our cosmic neighbors than in the whole of previous history. We now have robot scouts reporting steadily from the Moon and Mars, and have obtained close-ups of Mercury and Jupiter. We have even received a couple of hours of observation from the surface of Venus, before the hellish conditions there destroyed the instruments. For the first time, therefore, we are beginning to develop a real science of the planets.

Why is that important? Because when we understand how our own Earth works, we will know where to look for its mineral deposits, how to anticipate earthquakes and major changes in climate—and, perhaps, how to prevent them. Such knowledge may one day save millions of lives and create billions of dollars of wealth.

The engineer-visionary Buckminster Fuller once remarked that the most important thing about Spaceship Earth is that it comes without an operating manual; hence many of our present troubles. Today's space explorers are helping us to write that manual.

Even if Mars had been known to be as lifeless as the Moon, most of Viking's instruments and objectives would have been unchanged. But understandably, public interest has focused on the life-detecting experiment. And rightly so, because the discovery of even simple microbes on Mars would have the most profound implications not only to science, but to philosophy and even to religion.

After centuries of fruitless speculation, Viking gave us the first opportunity of settling that ancient question: "Is there life beyond the Earth?" True, it represented a gamble against very long odds, and many scientists considered that the biology experiments were a waste of money.

They argued that conditions on Mars were so severe that life was impossible—or that if it did exist, we wouldn't know it when we saw it. But one has to start looking somewhere, and Viking's designers assumed that any life forms must eat and excrete certain basic chemicals, so that even if they were invisibly small, their presence could still be detected. The cameras, of course, would quickly spot anything comparable to plants or trees, though probably not animals, unless they were very slow-moving. For technical reasons, Viking takes many minutes to scan the whole Martian panorama; thus even a tortoise would only appear as a streak on its pictures.

The first question which we would want to ask of anything that crawls, hops, burrows or walks within range of Viking is rather surprising and may even appear simpleminded. Whether it has three heads or four eyes or six tentacles, we would still want to know of any passing Martian: "Are you identical with us?"

One of the most profound discoveries of the past generation is that, despite all appearances, there is in a sense only a single life form on the planet Earth. "We men, we microbes, we cabbages, we sharks..." to paraphrase Dr. Carl Sagan. The infinite diversity of the living world is an illusion. Deep down, we are all variations of the same very few biochemical themes. It is as if every creature on Earth was built from one huge organic Meccano set, with only a few basic components. It would be impossible to tell, purely from the disassembled fragments, what any original model was like. This fact, incidentally, is a far more conclusive proof of life's evolution from a single origin than the relatively superficial resemblances between men and apes which helped to launch Darwin's theory.

The great unanswered question which Viking may settle is this: Must all life, everywhere, depend on the same handful of reactions as it does on Earth? If we find that Martian life forms have just the same chemical themes as we men, we microbes, etc., that will suggest that no other arrangement is possible.

If, on the other hand, it turns out that Martian life has a fundamentally different chemistry—or, to continue our analogy, that the Mars Meccano set has quite different components—that would open up whole new vistas in biology and, ultimately, medicine. Remember how many of the drugs in the doctors' armory were discovered by travelers to strange places on this planet. On a much more sophisticated level, this situation may be repeated in space.

And beyond the sheer excitement and practical importance of finding life elsewhere, there are philosophical implications which may change the patterns of human thinking until the end of time. A single Martian microbe would prove that life will arise on any world where it has the slightest chance of survival. We will look up to the stars with new emotions, in the virtual certainty that we are not alone, and that scattered across the Milky Way galaxy of more than a hundred thousand million suns there must be civilizations which could make us look like savages. Perhaps that knowledge may be just what we need—to stop us from behaving like savages.

And even if there is no life on Mars today—sometime in the next century, there will be. Next to the Moon, Mars is the new frontier for manned exploration—and, one day, settlement—using the tools of future science to tame a world whose opportunities and challenges are as yet almost wholly unknown.

Space Facts
and
Space
Fallacies

It is now more than fifty years since I started thinking seriously about space travel, and in that time I have seen it go through the three phases characteristic of any new and revolutionary idea. They can be summed up by this set of quotations:

1. "It's crazy—don't waste my time."
2. "It's possible—but it's not worth doing."
3. "I *said* it was a good idea, all along..."

Chancellor's Address at Convocation of University of Moratuwa, Bandaranaike Memorial International Conference Hall, Colombo, 31 March 1983.

The speed with which distinguished scientists can sometimes proceed from stage 1 to stage 3 never ceases to amaze me. However, let us not be too critical. So many ideas that sound crazy are indeed crazy, and if a busy man paid equal attention to all of them he would never get anything done. The test of a truly first-rate mind is its readiness to correct mistakes and even to change course completely—when the facts merit it.

One of the best examples I can give of this is based on my own experience, and I feel free to pass it on to you as the scientist concerned has been dead for many years.

In 1953—four years before the launching of the first Earth satellite, *Sputnik 1*, New York's Hayden Planetarium asked me to arrange a symposium on spaceflight. Among the experts I invited was the chief scientist of the U.S. Weather Bureau; I wrote to him asking if he would give us a talk about the possible value of artificial satellites to meteorology. I was flabbergasted by his answer: satellites wouldn't be any use for weather research or forecasting. . . .

When the initial shock had worn off, I returned to the attack. I pointed out that we space cadets had been saying for years that satellites *would* be useful to meteorologists; if we were talking nonsense, it was his duty—as one of the leaders in the field—to explain exactly why we were wrong.

To his great credit, the scientist accepted my challenge and started to look into the subject. In the course of writing his paper, he converted himself from a skeptic to a wild enthusiast. A few years later, he was directing the United States meteorological satellite program, and he ran it until his untimely death.

This is not a bad example of the way one should treat a new and revolutionary idea. Be skeptical at first, but if it has possibilities—look into it carefully. And if it is *really* valuable—adopt it enthusiastically.

Unfortunately, few people have the mental flexibility needed to do this. This is particularly true when they have, after long study and effort, become "experts" on some particular subject. Beware of experts, even though they are right 99 percent of the time—or they wouldn't stay in business. But that remaining 1 percent, when they are quite wrong, may be what really matters.

I tried to sum this up in what is now fairly well known as Clarke's first law, viz:

"When a distinguished but elderly scientist says that something is possible, he is almost certainly right. When he says it is impossible, he is very probably wrong."

The history of spaceflight is full of such examples, and in a moment I look forward to giving some choice specimens of ignorance and stupidity I've encountered both at the expert and nonexpert levels. But some of the best I've discovered only recently, because the full story could not emerge until wartime security had lapsed—and the principal culprits were safely dead.

The ancestor of today's giant rockets was the German V. (or A.4) designed by Dr. Wernher von Braun's team at Peenemunde, and test-flown successfully for the first time on 3 October 1942. With a takeoff weight of twelve tons and a range of two hundred miles, it was far in advance of anything else that existed at the time; so much so, in fact, that many of Prime Minister Churchill's wartime advisers refused to believe in its existence. Now that our rockets can go round the world in ninety minutes, and have traveled thousands of millions of miles into outer space, it's hard to realize that only forty years ago distinguished scientists were arguing that a two-hundred mile range was impossible. And the head of the most famous British fireworks firm stated categorically: "My family has been making rockets for more than a century. I can assure you that no rocket will ever cross the English Channel."

The whole story—which would be funny if its implications had not been so tragic—will be found in Professor R. V. Jones' history of British scientific intelligence (or lack of it) during the 1939–45 period, *Most Secret War* (Hamish Hamilton, 1978).

To quote from Jones: "The *naïveté* of our 'experts' was incredible. They were all eminent, some very eminent, in particular fields of science or technology, and yet they were completely out of their depth when dealing with the rocket. I can remember a Fellow of the Royal Society...saying that he was amazed at the accuracy with which the Germans would have to set the rocket before launching it.... What he had calculated, quite possibly correctly, was the trajectory of a rocket fired, as on 5th November, with a stick attached, and launched in the familiar way from a bottle... we knew that the Germans were using gyroscopic control, with information... transmitted to rudders in the main jet.... As we explained the system, our scientist looked Heaven-wards and said, 'Ah, yes, gyroscopes! I hadn't thought of them!' And that was about the level of the better contributions from the experts."

It seems equally incredible that one of the reasons the "experts"—led by Churchill's chief scientific advisor, Lord Cherwell (Professor Lindemann)—refused to believe in long-range rockets was that they thought only in terms of such solid propellants as cordite. Yet liquid fuels had been known and tested for years, particularly by Robert Goddard in the United States, and almost all the literature of spaceflight was devoted to them. Despite this, it took months to convince the "experts" that liquid fuels might make long-range rockets possible. To quote Jones again: "I can remember at one meeting Sir Robert Robinson saying, 'Ah, yes, liquid fuel!' and several others taking up the chorus as though the realization that the fuel could be liquid instead of solid completely exonerated them from their previous failure." It was the gyroscope story again....

But at least even these pathetic "experts" were not ignorant of one basic fact about rockets—that, unlike all other prime movers, they could operate in the airless vacuum of space. How many times, in the 1930s, we would-be astronauts heard the argument that "the rocket won't work in a vacuum, because there's nothing for the exhaust to push against."

Even in those days, it was hard to stomach the sheer Olympian conceit of the critics who brought forward this argument. Apparently they believed that *they* were the very first to wonder if a rocket could work in a vacuum—even though scientists had been thinking about spaceflight for several generations.

Fallacies are always amusing and are often extremely instructive, for it is by exposing them that one can get a better understanding of the facts that they conceal. One argument that used to be employed against spaceflight by professional pessimists about fifty years ago ran something like this: "It takes 20 million foot-pounds of energy to lift one pound out of the Earth's gravitational field. The most powerful propellant combination contains only a quarter of this—5 million foot-pounds of energy per pound. Therefore no propellant can even lift itself, let alone anything else, out of the Earth's gravitational field. Therefore spaceflight is impossible. Q.E.D."

It is surprising how a few figures, quoted with a show of authority, can "prove" a case. (There is no need for the figures to be right as long as there is no one around who can contradict them.) In the example above, the figures were correct—at least approximately—but the interpretation was hopelessly wrong.

The propellants a rocket carries obviously do not have to lift themselves out of the Earth's gravitational field. If they are burned while the rocket is still close to the Earth— say just above the atmosphere—they impart nearly all their energy to the vehicle and waste little of it lifting their own mass against gravity.

The most extraordinary suggestion I have ever seen concerning rockets, however, was made in perfect seriousness in an old astronautical journal by a gentleman for whom Sir Isaac Newton had obviously lived in vain. He proposed catching the exhaust gases, by means of a funnel behind the rocket motor, and using them over again. This scheme reminds me irresistibly of those cartoons of becalmed yachtsmen blowing furiously at their limp sails with a pair of bellows and forgetting the unfortunate equality of action and reaction.

A rather more sophisticated piece of spurious reasoning appeared about forty years ago in, I am sorry to say, the leading physics journal of a country not very far from here. The author put forward the curious argument that it is impossible for a body to exceed the velocity of sound in the material of which it is made. As the velocity of escape from the Earth is seven miles a second, and the velocity of sound in most metals barely half of that, we would never be able to build rockets that could leave the Earth. . . .

It is not surprising that some of the most interesting space fallacies have involved gravity. We will not discuss here the whole range of fictional "antigravity" devices, many of which have their own built-in contradictions, but will concern ourselves with some proposals which at first sight seem quite sound and reasonable.

One of the first involves the question of jumping on a planet of low gravity, such as the Moon. On Earth, the record for the high jump is about seven and a half feet. So at first sight it would seem that on the Moon, where gravity is a sixth of Earth's, an Olympic champion should be able to clear a bar at $6 \times 7\frac{1}{2}$, or an impressive forty-five feet.

This isn't true, for a number of reasons. First of all, when a man jumps seven and a half feet on Earth, he's already starting with his center of gravity about three and a half feet from the ground—so he's only lifting it an extra four feet or so. Assuming that he could put forth the same effort on the Moon, therefore, he could lift his C.G. about twenty-four feet. So the lunar high-jump record couldn't possibly be more than about twenty-seven feet—still impressive, but a long way from forty-five.

And I doubt if it would be anything like this, even inside a pressurized dome where the athlete was not encumbered with a spacesuit. It is very difficult to run on the Moon—or even walk naturally—so I'm not sure what sort of takeoff speed could be attained.

Many years ago I read a science-fiction serial in which one of the characters jumped off Phobos, the inner moon of Mars, and was in danger of falling onto the planet below. This involves a fallacy to which I'll return later, and it can be said at once that Phobos (diameter about fifteen miles) is too large a body to permit human beings to escape by muscle power alone. However, there is no doubt that a man could jump off some of the smaller asteroids. The limiting diameter, for one made of ordinary rock, is about four miles, and this raises interesting possibilities for future athletic contests. Interplanetary high jumping, however, would be almost as boring to watch as cricket, since it would be many hours before the slowly rising contestants had sorted themselves out into those who had achieved escape velocity and those who were falling back again....

If anyone did succeed in jumping off Phobos—even

if he jumped directly toward Mars—there would be no possibility whatsoever of his falling on to the planet, as he would still possess the satellite's orbital velocity, which is almost 5,000 miles an hour. All that his jump would have done would be to compound this speed with the very few miles an hour which his own muscles could provide. His velocity vector would therefore be virtually unchanged, and he would still be a satellite of Mars, moving in an orbit very slightly different from that of Phobos. At the most, he would recede a few miles from Phobos—and if he waited three hours and fifty minutes (half a revolution) the two orbits would intersect again and he would return to the surface of the little moon!

Many years ago I wrote a story based on this idea— "Jupiter V"—published in *Reach for Tomorrow*, and I refer you to that if you want to know more about high jumping on small worlds.

A number of writers have fallen into another gravitational trap by proposing that space travelers should use asteroids or comets to give them free rides. Some asteroids, they point out, have passed within a few hundred thousand miles of the Earth and then gone on to cut across the orbits of the other planets. Why not hop aboard such a body as it makes its closest approach to Earth and then jump off at a convenient moment when passing Mars? In this way your spaceship would only have to cover a fraction of the total distance: the asteroid would do all the real work. . . .

The fallacy arises, of course, from thinking of an asteroid as a kind of a bus or escalator. Any asteroid whose path took it close to Earth would be moving at a very high speed relative to us, so that a spaceship which tried to reach and actually land on it would need to use a great deal of fuel. And once it had matched speed with the asteroid it would follow the asteroid's orbit whether the asteroid was there or not. There are no circumstances, in fact, where making such a rendezvous would have any effect except that of increasing fuel consumption and adding to the hazards of the voyage. Even if there was any advantage in such a scheme, one might have to wait several hundred years before there was a chance for a return trip. No, interplanetary hitchhiking will not work. . . .

The commonest of all gravitational fallacies is that enshrined in the words "How high must you go before you get beyond the pull of gravity?" In the public mind, the idea of weightlessness is inseparably tied up with escaping from the gravitational field of the Earth. It is extremely hard to explain in understandable language (a) that one can never "get beyond the pull of gravity"—because it extends to infinity—and (b) that one can be completely weightless while still in a powerful gravitational field—if one is in free fall.

Perhaps the most complete misunderstanding of conditions in space I have ever encountered was shown by a cartoon-strip artist who depicted two spaceships being coupled together by suction pads. Presumably he had grown a little tired of magnets, and had tried to think of something original.

Though this is not a fallacy in the sense that it can be easily disproved by logic, it seems fairly certain that the fate which would befall the human body when exposed to the vacuum of space has been greatly exaggerated. Certainly there is no question of the body being severely damaged—or even exploding, as some writers have gruesomely imagined. Men have been safely subjected, in explosive decompression tests, to greater pressure changes than would be experienced in a spaceship whose cabin walls were ruptured.

If a man is suddenly plunged into a vacuum, he will of course quickly lose consciousness owing to lack of oxygen. The time quoted for this to happen is about fifteen seconds, but there is little doubt that this could be greatly extended if there was time to make suitable preparations. Divers, by breathing deeply and so flushing out their lungs with air, can hold their breath for three or four minutes. As far as lack of oxygen is concerned, therefore, a man could certainly survive in space for at least a minute.

After a certain length of time, the absence of pressure would cause his blood to vaporize, though at body temperature, so the word "boiling" is rather misleading. This would be quite a slow process since the veins and arteries are tough enough to provide considerable internal pressure, and the latent heat needed for the boiling process would have to come from somewhere. It seems plausible to assume, therefore, the short excursions into space could be tolerated, at least for emergencies—as Stanley Kubrick showed in *2001: A Space Odyssey*.

Somebody once suggested to me that when a spaceship was under power, the resultant acceleration would cause the air inside the ship to be compressed at one end so that the people "at the top" might suffocate. Fortunately, this novel danger doesn't bear serious analysis. The atmosphere inside a spaceship under one gravity acceleration would have exactly the same pressure gradient as it would on Earth. I've never heard of anyone suffocating while walking upstairs, though a sufficiently sensitive barometer would show that the pressure in the bedroom is slightly lower than in the kitchen....

Designers of the five-mile-long interstellar spaceships launched by the more ambitious science-fiction writers would certainly have to allow for this effect, since the atmospheric pressure difference between the prow and stern of such a vessel would be as great as that between the base and summit of Everest. However, one fancies that this would be among the very least of their problems.

Another astronautical fallacy that still persists is the idea that on the Moon, or in space, the stars are brilliantly visible at all times. Old science-fiction drawings invariably showed lunar landscapes beneath a sky full of stars, with the sun's corona stretching outward in a glorious mantle of milky radiance. So, usually, do science-fiction films....

The truth is rather different. When a large amount of light enters it, as is normally the case during the daytime, the human eye automatically cuts down its sensitivity. At night, after a period of minutes, it becomes about a thousand times as sensitive as during the day. It loses that sensitivity at once when it is flooded with light again—as any motorist who has been blinded by an approaching car will testify. During daylight, on the Moon, the eye is constantly picking up the glare from the surrounding landscape. It never has a chance of switching over to its "high-sensitivity" range, and the stars thus remain invisible. Only if the eye is shielded from all other light sources will the stars slowly appear in the black sky.

You can put this to the test quite easily by standing well back from the window in a brilliantly lit room one night, and seeing how many stars you can observe in the sky outside. Then remember that the light reflected from the walls around is only a fraction of the glare that the lunar rocks would throw back.

This situation poses a dilemma to the artist attempting to illustrate lunar scenes. Should he put in the stars or not? After all, they are there and can be seen if you look for them in the right way. Besides, everybody expects to see them in the picture.... I am afraid one has to cheat and put them in—as indeed Kubrick and I did in 2001. The same argument applies to the beautiful solar corona: it is impossible to look anywhere near the Sun without dark glasses, so although the corona is there you can't see it, unless you contrive an artificial eclipse and block out the Sun's light completely.

For quite different reasons, the human eye will never see many of the gorgeous colors shown in the magnificent photographs of spiral and gaseous nebulae produced by today's great telescopes. The colors are real enough, but they are so faint that it takes minutes—or hours—of exposure to reveal them. They are below the threshold of vision, just as the colors of our familiar world are, under even the brightest of full moons.

I would like to end by discussing what is not only the most fascinating, but also the most important, of all the facts—or fallacies—about space. And this is the existence of extraterrestrial intelligence.

There was a time when we believed that we were alone in the universe—but, perhaps, for the not-insignificant exception of God. Then the planets were discovered to be other worlds, and imagination quickly peopled them with inhabitants. From about the seventeenth century onward, the concept of the "plurality of worlds" has been taken almost for granted. So has the idea that, out there in this immense cosmos of billions upon billions of stars, there *must* be races much superior to mankind.

The invention of the space rocket, and still more the radio telescope, added a new dimension to this argument. For the first time there was a means—in theory at least— of discovering extraterrestrial intelligence, and perhaps communicating with it. No wonder that there is now great public interest in SETI and the even more ambitious CETI (Search for and Contact with Extraterrestrial Intelligence). Undoubtedly Carl Sagan's splendid "Cosmos" television series, and such movies as *E.T.* and *Close Encounters of the Third Kind* have been largely responsible for this state of affairs, though unfortunately they have also spawned such pathological by-products as flying saucer cults.

Now there has been a reaction—a scientific backlash. Because our very limited investigations over a mere few decades have produced not the slightest hard evidence for the existence of extraterrestrials, some scientists have gone to the other extreme. They argue that intelligent life outside this planet may be so exceedingly rare that we will never be able to discover its existence. Some have even suggested that we may be unique—the only intelligence in the whole of creation!

This point of view has been put most forcibly by the American mathematical physicist Dr. Frank Tipler. One of his most interesting arguments runs something like this:

We have started to build robot space explorers, and in the very near future—after a century or so at the most—will be able to make far more sophisticated ones which when they reach new planets *can reproduce themselves from local materials*. Such "van Neumann machines," as the class of self-replicating automata is called, would obey the old Biblical command "be fruitful and multiply," in a kind of cosmic chain reaction, until they had filled the galaxy.

This would take only a few millions of years, and the galaxy is a thousand times older. So it should have happened long ago—*if* there ever were intelligent and inquisitive creatures out among the stars. But it hasn't . . . at least, we don't think it has. Therefore, ours must be the first technological civilization to make its appearance in this galaxy, and perhaps in the whole of space.

Of course, Tipler's argument is considerably more sophisticated than this, and I haven't done it justice. One can think of many possible refutations—and people like Carl Sagan are busily doing just that. It's now become almost a theological issue, and the tantalizing thing is that if Tipler is right, we'll never know. It would be possible to prove that extraterrestrials exist by meeting them; it won't be possible to prove that they don't exist—without exploring the whole of space and time. For as has been wittily said: "Absence of evidence is not evidence of absence."

So—what is fact, and what is fallacy, in this most fascinating, and most portentous, of all cosmological debates? *Do we have neighbors?*

We may never know....

We may get an answer a thousand years from now....

Or it may be the only headline in tomorrow's newspapers.

Predictions

Many years ago, in the opening words of *Profiles of the Future*, I stated: "It is impossible to predict the future, and all attempts to do so in any detail appear ludicrous within a very few years."

Strictly speaking, the very concept of prediction is logical nonsense, because it's a statement about the future—and how can one make any meaningful assertions about something that doesn't exist? (What color are a unicorn's eyes?) The best that can be done—and sometimes even

---

Reprinted from *The Book of Predictions*, edited by David Wallechinsky, Amy Wallace and Irving Wallace (New York: William Morrow, 1980).

this is a very poor best—is to outline the entire spectrum of possible futures and to assign probabilities to each item. This is not *prediction* but projection, or *extrapolation*; there is a profound difference between the two, which many people find hard to understand. Let me give an example.

If I said that the population of the United States on 1 January 2001 would be 236,453,328, that would be a *prediction*—and it would be wrong (barring fantastic luck!). However, a statistician might say that the population of the United States at that date has a 90 percent *chance* of being between 220 million and 240 million. That would be an *extrapolation*, and if he were good at his job, he'd have a fair chance of being right. He would have taken the existing birth, death, immigration and emigration rates; made reasonable guesses about their future values; and done some arithmetic. But this procedure assumes that history won't produce any surprises, which it invariably does. The population of the United States in 2001 might be only a couple of million, if there had been a nuclear war. And if you think there's *no* possibility of a similar error in the other direction, consider this science-fiction scenario: When the King (!) orders the multiple cloning of everyone named Kennedy, the population jumps in one year from 230 million to 1 billion-plus.

So, having proved the impossibility of prediction, here are my extrapolations, in the areas where I feel I can speak with any authority. I have given dates only to the nearest five years; anything else would be to convey a misleading impression of accuracy.

Most of the headings are self-explanatory, and I have omitted the two most important of all—the detection of extraterrestrial life and the detection of extraterrestrial intelligence. Either could happen tomorrow—or a thousand years from now. We have no hard facts on which to base even a guess, still less a *reasonable* extrapolation.

1985

- Permanent space station similar to Skylab, but in a higher orbit; carries five to ten men.

- Electronic tutors. These will be the erudite descendants of today's computer toys—completely portable, cheap, capable of giving programmed instruction in almost any subject at any level of difficulty. They could trigger an educational explosion (particularly in developing countries) which could boost mankind out of the Stone Age.

1990

- Return to the Moon.

- Wrist telephones. These will become possible with the construction of very large communications satellites and will start a social-economic revolution as great as that produced by the telephone itself a century earlier.

1995

- Lunar base established. The beginning of planetary colonization—the main theme of the twenty-first century.

2000

- Commercial fusion power. Era of cheap energy dawns.

2005

- Manned flight to Mars.

2010

- Space cities.

2020

- Mars base.

2030

- Manned exploration of the solar system. First robot interstellar probes.

III

The Literary Scene

Of
Sand
and
Stars

Forty miles to the east, the Sun has just climbed above the Sacred Mountain which for so long has haunted my imagination. Another quarter turn of the planet, and it will bring a cold winter dawn to the English seaside town where I was born sixty-five years ago this morning.

So it is already a little late in the day to consider *why* I became an author, or to wonder if there was ever any real alternative; that may have been as genetically determined as the color of my eyes or the shape of my head. But the *kind* of author I became is another matter: here,

First printed in the *New York Times Book Review*, 6 March 1983.

I suspect, both chance and environment played decisive roles.

The fact that I was born half a mile from the sea—or at least an arm of the Bristol Channel which to a child seemed positively oceanic—has certainly colored all my life. As usual, A. E. Housman expressed it perfectly, in the poem from which I took the title of my first novel:

> Smooth between sea and land
> Is laid the yellow sand,
> And here through summer days
> The seed of Adam plays.

Much of my youth was spent on the Minehead beach, exploring rock-pools and building wave-defying battlements. Even now, I feel completely relaxed only by the edge of the sea—or, better still, hovering weightless beneath it, over the populous and polychromatic landscape of my favorite reef.

So in an earlier age, I would probably have written stories about the sea. However, I was born at the time when men were first thinking seriously of escaping from their planetary cradle, and so my imagination was deflected into space.

Yet first I made a curious detour, which is obviously of great importance because it involves virtually the only memory I have of my father—a shadowy figure who has left no other mark, even though I was over thirteen when he died.

The date would have been around 1925; we were riding together in a small pony cart near the Somerset farm into which First Lieutenant Charles Wright Clarke had sunk what was left of his army gratuity, after an earlier and still more disastrous adventure as a gentleman farmer. As he opened a pack of cigarettes, he handed me the card inside; it was one of a series illustrating prehistoric animals. From that moment, I became hooked on dinosaurs, collected all the cards I could on the subject, and used them in class to illustrate little adventure stories I told the other children in the village school. These must have been my first ventures into fiction—and the schoolmistress who encouraged them celebrated *her* birthday a week ago. Sorry I forgot to send a card, Maud Hanks—

I'll make a special point of it for your ninety-fifth....

There is a certain irony in the fact that the tobacco trade (one of the few professions where I consider the mandatory death penalty is justified) had such a decisive and indeed beneficial impact on my career. To this day I retain my fascination with dinosaurs and eagerly look forward to the time when the genetic engineers will re-create *Tyrannosaurus rex*.

For a couple of years I collected fossils, and at one time even acquired a mammoth's tooth, until the main focus of my interest shifted rather abruptly from the past to the future. Once again—significantly—I can recall exactly how this happened, though almost all the other events of my childhood seem irretrievably lost.

There were three separate crucial incidents, all of equal importance, and I can even date them with some precision. The earliest must have been in 1929, when at the age of twelve I saw my first science-fiction magazine, the November 1928 *Amazing Stories*.

The cover is in front of me at the moment—and it really *is* amazing, for a reason which neither editor Hugo Gernsback nor artist Frank Paul could ever have guessed.

A spaceship looking like a farm silo with picture windows is disgorging its exuberant passengers onto a tropical beach, above which floats the orange ball of Jupiter, filling half the sky. The foreground is, alas, improbable, because the temperature of the Jovian satellites is around − 150 degrees Centigrade. But the giant planet is painted with such stunning accuracy that one could use this cover to make a very good case for precognition; Paul has shown turbulent cloud formations, cyclonic patterns and enigmatic white structures like Earth-sized amoebae which were not revealed until the Voyager missions over fifty years later. *How did he know?*

Young readers of today, born into a world when science-fiction magazines, books and movies are part of everyday life, cannot possibly imagine the impact of such garish pulps as that old *Amazing* and its colleagues *Astounding* and *Wonder*. Of course, the literary standards were usually abysmal—but the stories brimmed with ideas, and amply evoked that sense of wonder which is (or should be) one of the goals of the best fiction. No less a critic than C. S. Lewis has described the ravenous addiction that these magazines inspired; the same phenomenon has led me to call science fiction the only genuine consciousness-expanding drug.

During my lunch hour from school I used to haunt the local Woolworth's in search of my fix, which cost threepence a shot—roughly a quarter, at today's prices. Much of the hard-earned money my widowed mother had saved for my food went on these magazines, and I set myself the goal of acquiring complete runs. By 1940 I had almost succeeded—but, alas, all my beloved pulps disappeared during the war years. That collection would now be worth thousands of dollars.

In 1930 I came under the spell of a considerably more literate influence, when I discovered W. Olaf Stapledon's just-published *Last and First Men* in the Minehead Public Library. No book before or since ever had such an impact on my imagination; the Stapledonian vistas of millions and hundreds of millions of years, the rise and fall of civilizations and entire races of men, changed my whole outlook on the universe and has influenced much of my writing ever since. Twenty years later, as Chairman of the British Interplanetary Society, I persuaded Stapledon to give us an address on the social and biological aspects of space exploration, which he entitled "Interplanetary Man." His was the noblest and most civilized mind I have ever encountered; I am delighted to see a revival of interest in his work and have just contributed a preface to a new collection of his writings.

By the time I encountered Stapledon I had begun my secondary (U.S. = high school) education in the nearby town of Taunton, making the ten-mile round trip by bicycle every day *after* sorting the local mail in the small hours of the morning and then delivering it (another five or so miles). It was at Huish's Grammar School—now Richard Huish College—that I began to write sketches and short stories for the school magazine.

I can still recall those editorial sessions, fifty years ago. About once a week, after class, our English master Captain E. B. Mitford (who was actually a fiery Welshman) would gather his schoolboy staff together, and we would all sit around a table on which there was a large bag of assorted toffees. Bright ideas were rewarded instantly; "Mitty" invented positive reinforcement years before B. F. Skinner. He also employed a heavy meter rule for *negative* reinforcement, but this was used only in class—never, so far as I recall, at editorial conferences.

My very first printed words thus appeared in the *Huish Magazine*, and from the beginning my science-fictional tendencies were obvious. Although this Christmas 1933 message purports to come from "Ex-Sixth Former" stationed at a torrid and high-altitude Outpost of Empire (Vrying Pan, British Malaria) its true locale is at least a quarter of a million miles further away:

> The precautions we have to take to preserve our lives are extraordinary. Our houses are built on the principle of the Dewar vacuum flask, to keep out the heat, and the outsides are silvered to reflect the sunlight. . . . We have to take great care to avoid cutting ourselves in any way, for if this happens our blood soon boils and evaporates.

Such attention to technical detail shows that even at sixteen I was already a hard-core science-fiction (as opposed to fantasy) writer. Credit for this must go to the book which had almost as great an impact on me as Stapledon's epic—and which illustrates rather well the fundamental distinction between art and science. No one else could ever have created *Last and First Men*—but if David Lasser had not written *The Conquest of Space* in 1931, someone similar would certainly have appeared in a very few years. The time was ripe.

Although there was already considerable German and Russian literature on the subject, *The Conquest of Space* was the very first book in the English language to discuss the possibility of flight to the Moon and planets, and to describe the experiments and dreams (mostly the latter) of the early rocket pioneers. Only a few hundred copies of the British edition were sold, but chance brought one of them to a bookstore a few yards from my birthplace. I saw it in the window, knew instinctively that I *had* to read it and persuaded my good-natured Aunt Nellie—who was looking after me while Mother struggled to run the farm and raise my three siblings—to buy it on the spot. And so I learned, for the first time, that space travel was not merely delightful fiction. *One day it could really happen*. Soon afterward I discovered the existence of the British Interplanetary Society, and my fate was sealed.

When he wrote *The Conquest of Space*, the twenty-eight-year-old David Lasser was editor of a whole group of Gernsback magazines, including *Wonder Stories*. Later he became a labor organizer and was denounced in Congress—not only as a dangerous radical but also as a madman, because he believed that we would one day fly to the Moon. . . . When I met him in Los Angeles just a couple of weeks ago, he told me he was working on a new book; a good title might be *Lasser's Last Laugh*.

Despite all these influences, I was well over thirty before writing graduated from a pleasant and occasionally profitable hobby to a profession. The Civil Service, the Royal Air Force and editorship of a scientific abstracting journal provided my bread and butter until 1950. By that time I had published numerous stories and articles, and a slim technical book, *Interplanetary Flight*. The modest success of this volume led me to seek a wider public with *The Exploration of Space*, which the Book-of-the-Month Club, in a moment of wild abandon, made a dual selection in 1952. To allay the alarm of its anxious readership, Clifton Fadiman explained in the BOM newsletter that *The Exploration of Space* was no crazy fantasy but a serious and level-headed work because "Mr. Clarke does not appear to be a very imaginative man." I've never quite forgiven him, and my agent Scott Meredith has never forgotten my plaintive query: "What *is* the Book-of-the-Month Club?"

This stroke of luck—repeated exactly thirty years later with *2010: Odyssey Two*, so I can claim it wasn't a fluke—encouraged me to give up my editorial job and become a full-time writer. It was not a very daring or heroic decision: if all else failed, I could always go back to the farm.

I was lucky; unlike most of the writers I know, I had very few setbacks or disappointments, and my rare rejection slips were doubtless thoroughly justified. And because every author is unique, the only advice I have ever been able to pass on to would-be writers is incorporated in a few lines on the notorious form letter which Archie, my word processor, spits out at all hopeful correspondents at the drop of a floppy disk: "Read at least one book a day, and write as much as you can. Study the memoirs of authors who interest you. (Somerset Maugham's *A Writer's Notebooks* is a good example.) Correspondence courses, writer's schools, etc., are probably useful—but all the authors I know were self-taught. There is no substitute for living; as Hemingway wisely remarked, "Writing is not a full-time occupation."

Nor is reading—though it would have to be, if I tried to keep up with the avalanche of science fiction now being published. I estimate that almost as much is printed each *day* as appeared every year when I was a boy.

Today's readers are indeed fortunate; this really is the Golden Age of science fiction. There are dozens of authors at work today who can match all but the giants of the past. (And probably one who can do even that, despite the handicap of being translated from Polish....) Yet I do not really envy the young men and women who first encounter science fiction as the days shorten toward 1984, for we old-timers were able to accomplish something that was unique:

Ours was the last generation that was able to read *everything*. No one will ever do that again.

Last and First Books

Though more than fifty years have passed, I can still visualize the very shelf (it was just below knee level) in the Minehead Public Library where I discovered *Last and First Men*. No other book had a greater influence on my life.

Olaf Stapledon's most famous work was published in 1930, to considerable applause from a wide range of reviewers. "As original as the solar system," said Hugh Walpole, while Arnold Bennett commended the author's

Foreword to *Nebula Maker and Four Encounters: Olaf Stapledon*, an anthology of Olaf Stapledon's shorter pieces (New York: Dodd, Mead, 1983).

"tremendous and beautiful imagination." It was also praised by a failed politician, then earning a living by his pen—one Winston S. Churchill. Almost at once it became one of those works that define a genre—which is somewhat ironic in view of the fact that Stapledon had never even heard of "science fiction" when he was writing his "story of the near and far future."

Last and First Men and its successor *Star Maker* (1937) are the twin summits of a literary career which began just before World War I, ended soon after World War II, and was profoundly influenced by both conflicts. One touching proof of that lies on my desk at this moment.

It is with an awe approaching reverence that I now hold in my hands the slim volume *Latter-Day Psalms* (Liverpool, England: Henry Young & Sons, Limited, 1914) and read the inscription: "Miss H. M. Barnard, with the author's compliments. Christmas 1914." Tucked inside is a letter to the recipient, on a single folded sheet with the embossed heading "Annery, Caldy, West Kirby. (Telephone 215 Hoylake)." It is written in a copper-plate which later became the most minute but legible script I have ever encountered, and is dated 22 December 1914—four months after the guns of August started to thunder across Europe.

"My dear Miss Barnard," it begins. "Will you please accept the enclosed small token of affection and respect, with best wishes for Christmas and the New Year. Let us hope for peace before the close of 1915...."

This first book by "Wm. Olaf Stapledon," as he signs himself (though the W is omitted on the title page) was what would now be called a vanity edition. "Father has got it published for me, which is very good of him, as of course I could not have financed it." This admission of dependency seems a little surprising for a man who was, after all, past his twenty-eighth birthday.

The letter continues with an intriguing remark: "I am in the midst of another and larger effort, but the war distracts one; and anyhow I cannot get it done before April, when at latest I am going to take a commission." I wonder what that "effort" could have been; Stapledon's next book (*A Modern Theory of Ethics*) did not appear for another fifteen years.

Miss Barnard was apparently a Quaker, because the letter expresses the view that the war "must be very terrible for such fervent peace lovers as the Friends. I think I shall be as fervent before I have done." This proved to be the case; Stapledon spent three years with the Friends' Ambulance Unit.

The rest of the short letter concerns family matters, and contains a wistful reference to "the girls from Adelaide." (Soon after the war, Stapledon married an Australian girl, Agnes Miller.) "I am longing for news. Yet I have no desire to see my cousin again till I have had my share of the war. Then we will begin a new age."

A new age was indeed beginning, though it was hardly an improvement on the old one. And yet another was starting when an older and sadder Stapledon wrote *Four Encounters*, which can be dated to late 1945 or early 1946 by its reference to the atomic bomb and "prisoners of war, demolishing an old air-raid shelter."

Stapledon was probably still working on *Four Encounters* when I had *my* only personal encounter with him, in 1948. The British Interplanetary Society had invited him to London to give a talk, "Interplanetary Man" (*J.B.I.S.*, November 1948; reprinted in *The Coming of the Space Age*, Meredith Press, and Gollancz, 1967). With shame and incredulity I confess that I recall nothing of that meeting—even though I opened the discussion and had dinner with our speaker after his talk.

But I do remember the impact of Stapledon's personality; the two words which always come to mind when I think of him are "gentleness" and "nobility." Though he has always had many devoted followers, in his own time and for thirty years after his death he was shamefully neglected—and even misrepresented. Now he speaks to us more clearly than he could ever address his contemporaries.

They cannot be blamed for their failure to share his vision; the Space Age had to dawn before the world could understand Stapledon's thoughts and look through his eyes. It is sad that he died too soon to see the first journeys beyond the atmosphere; had he lived as long as H. G. Wells (who, aged eighty, predeceased him by only four years), he would have witnessed the birth of Apollo.

I do not know if Wells and Stapledon ever met in the flesh, but they certainly did in spirit. So it seems appropriate to end this tribute to Stapledon with his great percursor's most famous words, which surely express the hopes and fears of both men:

> For Mankind it is the Universe—or nothing.

Which shall it be?

The
Poetry
of
Space

From time immemorial, the starry heavens have provided inspiration to artists of all kinds, but to poets in particular. Until the rise of modern astronomy, most of the poems they wrote were purely descriptive, as indeed many of them still are today. But after the invention of the telescope, at the beginning of the seventeenth century, man's attitude toward the starry sky began to undergo a transformation. Its natural beauty was unchanged, but its grandeur was immeasurably increased as the time scale of the universe

Chancellor's Address, University of Moratuwa Convocation, Bandaranaike Memorial International Hall, Colombo, 16 January 1981.

became apparent. No longer was this world the only world; it was one of many—perhaps an infinite number.

No sensitive or intelligent man could be unaffected by the new knowledge. In English poetry, we see the change very clearly in the work of our two giants, Shakespeare and Milton. Shakespeare was obsessed by time; indeed, that is the theme of the *Sonnets*—but he shows no consciousness of Space as we think of it today, with a capital S. That is hardly surprising: he retired to Stratford-on-Avon in 1610, the very year that Galileo first opened up the heavens with his "optic tube."

But Milton was only two years old when Galileo made his great discoveries, and grew up with the "new astronomy." Indeed, he visited Galileo, then an aging prisoner of the Inquisition, and may even have looked through one of the now blind scientist's telescopes. So the universe of *Paradise Lost*, though still medieval in some respects, is one that we can recognize. As Marjorie Nicolson points out in *Science and Imagination*, Milton was well aware of the possible existence of other worlds than ours—although he made his Angel warn Adam:

> Dream not of other worlds, what creatures there
> Live, in what state, condition or degree....
> (*Paradise Lost* 8. 175–6)

That reminds me of the old cliche so familiar in bad science fiction movies: "Such knowledge was not meant for man...."

Now, we live in an age which has some close parallels with the time of Milton and Galileo. The telescope expanded mental horizons then as never before in the history of mankind. In this century, the dawning Space Age has produced a physical expansion, equally unprecedented. No matter that only a handful of men have reached the Moon, a few dozen probes, the planets. The frontier has opened, and it can never be closed....

Any literature that reflects our age must, if it is to be of any validity, take note of its greatest technological achievement. (Or perhaps its second greatest, after the release of atomic energy.) Perhaps it is too soon to expect **great poetry inspired by the conquest of space. Poetry has** been described as "emotion recollected in tranquillity," and the key word here is "recollected." There has not been enough time, as yet, to absorb the implications of our first faltering steps beyond the cradle of this Earth.

But let us go back a little, and start with astronomy rather than astronautics. One poet fascinated by the starry sky was Alfred, Lord Tennyson, and among the most famous lines he ever wrote are:

> Many a night from yonder ivied casement, ere I went to rest,
> Did I look on great Orion sloping slowly to the West.
> Many a night I saw the Pleiads, rising through the mellow shade,
> Glitter like a swarm of fireflies tangled in a silver braid.

The same poem, "Locksley Hall," contains the even more celebrated lines:

> For I dipt into the future, far as human eye could see,
> Saw the Vision of the world, and all the wonder that would be;
> Saw the heavens filled with commerce, argosies of magic sails,
> Pilots of the purple twilight, dropping down with costly bales.

Those lines predict the conquest of the air, but they could equally well refer to the conquest of space. "Saw the heavens filled with commerce, argosies of magic sails"—what a beautiful description of the unmanned freighters, driven by radiation pressure on "solar sails" many kilometers across, which some engineers believe may be used to carry payloads cheaply between the inner planets.

But back to the Pleiades. That description "glitter like a swarm of fireflies, tangled in a silver braid" is not only poetically beautiful, but also scientifically accurate. We now know that the stars of the Pleiades cluster are enmeshed in a huge nebulosity—as even the smallest telescope will show.

Tennyson's coupling of the Pleiades with "great Orion sloping slowly to the west" has a striking—and probably quite conscious echo in a poem of our own century, one

of the most perfect expressions of unrequited love in the
English language.

> The rainy pleiads wester
>   Orion plunges prone;
> The stroke of midnight ceases
>   And I lie down alone.

> The rainy pleiads wester
>   And seek beyond the sea,
> The head that I shall dream of
>   That will not dream of me.
>   (*More Poems:* XI)

Anyone who has read *A Shropshire Lad* will recognize
the authentic voice of A. E. Housman; these lines are
taken from *More Poems*. Now, Housman, one of the greatest classical scholars of his time, knew almost as much
about astronomy as about Latin. He spent the greater
part of his career editing the five volumes of the Roman
poet Manilius, (first century A.D.) author of an unfinished
five-volume epic, *Astronomica*.

I have never read any Manilius, even in translation . . . which is the only way I could read it, because like
Ben Jonson's Shakespeare I have little Latin and less
Greek. It appears that Manilius was not a very good poet,
but according to the *Encyclopaedia Britannica* he had
"an amazing ability for versifying astronomical calcula-
tion." As Housman himself puts it, his great talent was
"doing sums in poetry."

This must certainly be a rare talent, and you might
think it a singularly useless one. However, I've just remembered that there are long poems in Sanskrit—I think
it may have been Dr. Sarabhai himself who told me this—
that are nothing less than versified instructions for cal-
culating eclipses. Such "poetic algorithms" must be
astonishing feats of virtuosity—computer programs
rendered into verse so that they can be more easily remembered and handed down from generation to generation!*

---

*I am much indebted to Prof. P. R. Pisharoty, P.R.L., Ahamadabad, for con-
firming this and bringing my attention to the Surya-Siddhanta.

If this Hindu tradition of combining poetry and astronomy had flourished
elsewhere, we would never have been threatened by the "Two Cultures."

Before we leave Housman and his old Roman astronomer, I'd like to quote a verse he inscribed on a copy of *Manilius* when presenting it to a friend. It's always amused me because we have disobeyed it as thoroughly as Adam disobeyed the orders that Milton's Angel gave him about "not dreaming of other worlds."

> Here are the skies, the planets
>   seven,
> And all the starry train:
> Content you with the mimic heaven,
> And on the earth remain.
> (*Additional Poems:* V)

The planets *seven*? Of course, the only planets known to the ancients were Mercury, Venus, Mars, Jupiter and Saturn—a mere five. The extra two were presumably the Sun and Moon, which we would no longer include—though we would add the Earth, Uranus, Neptune and Pluto to make a grand total of nine.

Obviously, we can't expect poets to anticipate advances in scientific knowledge, but at least they should avoid blatant mistakes, perhaps the most famous astronomical error in English poetry is in Coleridge's notorious lines from *The Rime of the Ancient Mariner*:

> Till clomb above the eastern bar
> The hornèd Moon, with one bright star
> Within the nether tip.

A man as intelligent as Coleridge must have known that a star couldn't possibly shine against the darkened face of the Moon. But something very similar can be seen on rare occasions, when Venus is occulted by the almost new moon. If the brilliant planet appears close to the darkened disc, it requires only a little imagination—not even that of a poet!—to perceive it as shining inside the arms of the thin crescent.

And now that we are on the subject of astronomical error, here is a much less culpable one, in a minor but charming poem by Lord Dunsany, *The Traveller*:

> Beautiful when the world lies dreaming
>   Are the light from the Evening Star's

Oceans of pale blue water gleaming,
And the tawny deserts of Mars.

Alas—with the discovery that the surface of Venus is as hot as a blast furnace, those oceans have well and truly evaporated. But even when Lord Dunsany wrote that poem half a century ago, it was known that we could observe only the dazzling top of the Venus cloudscape. Indeed, if we had been able to see an oceanic surface, the planet would have been much less brilliant, because water is a poor reflector. Look at the photos of Earth from space, if you want proof of that.

But Dunsany was right on target with Mars—"tawny deserts" is a pretty good description. So let us now listen to the whole poem, because its basic message is still perfectly valid—as must be the case with all true poetry, however much the natural world, and our knowledge of it, may change.

Beautiful when the world lies dreaming
    Are the lights from the Evening Star's
Oceans of pale blue water gleaming,
    And the tawny deserts of Mars.

Alas, that they lie beyond our reaches,
    Our sisters sidereal,
And never an earth-ship touches the beaches
    Of any one of them all.

Yet far journeys we can adventure,
    From mind to mind there lie,
Spaces of apathy, doubting and censure,
    Through which our thoughts scarce fly.

And whoever bridges the gap between us,
    We being lonely as stars,
Is well on his way to Jupiter, Venus,
    Mercury, Saturn and Mars.

At this point I would like to mention that Lord Dunsany's delightful and deservedly popular fantasies had a great influence on me, and I was privileged to meet their author in the late 1940s; we also had an extensive correspondence, which may one day be published. He wrote several tongue-in-cheek stories about space travel; one of my favorites is about a man who flies to Mars and discovers, among other wonders, a herd of *very* small elephants. He brings one back to Earth with him, but unfortunately it escapes. The only evidence he has to prove his story is the broken matchbox out of which it battered its way.... Yes, Martian elephants are *very* small indeed.

Lord Dunsany also wrote a beautiful poem about Farside—the Moon's hidden hemisphere, totally unknown to man until the first probes of the Space Age revealed its features. He called it "At the Time of the Full Moon." Here it is:

> It is dark tonight in moon country
>   On the far side of its girth,
> It is all dark in the valleys,
>   Where none seeth Earth.
>
> The sun with his day-long dawning
>   Tomorrow in that land
> Will rise with a golden anger
>   On the old rocks and the sand:
>
> But they never see, there, Earth's splendour
>   Lift like a silver hill
> Monstrously over the sea-beds
>   That no waters fill.
>
> Gleaming with eerie beauty,
>   Continents bright, and the seas
> Lucid as palest sapphires
>   Sold by the Sinhalese:
>
> With the long shadows lying
>   Black, in a land alight
> With a more luminous wonder
>   Than ever comes to our night.
>
> They never see Earth float ever
>   Whoever they be;
> And they know no hint of her purpose,
>   Neither do we.

Now, this is a beautiful poem, but it contains one phrase which is at least ambiguous and, if taken literally, dead wrong. On the far side of the moon, says Dunsany:

> They never see, there, Earth's splendour
>   Lift like a silver hill

Lift like a silver hill—a lovely phrase, but it surely implies that the Earth can rise on this side of the Moon, which, of course, is nonsense. Apart from tracing out a small ellipse due to libration, it stays fixed in the lunar sky. The only kind of "Earthrise" ever possible is that witnessed by the Apollo astronauts, when they orbited the Moon. Perhaps it would be better to rewrite the lines:

> They never see, there, Earth's splendour
> Float like a silver hill

From nonexistent Earthrise on the Moon it is only one small step to familiar Moonrise on the Earth. My favorite description of this is in a poem by A. E. Housman's lesser-known brother Laurence:

> Then out of the east in a paling mist,
> The dead-faced moon came up to be kissed.
> Slow and solemn, we watched her rise,
> A face of wonder, with cavernous eyes.
>
> There life is changeless, and time without worth,
> There nothing dies or is brought to birth;
>
> Her day is done, she is filled with dearth;
> Old she looks to the young green Earth,
> Old as the foam on a frozen shore,
> Old—for nothing can age her more.
>
> Oh young green Earth, go down into night,
> Rejoice in thy youth, till its days are o'er;
> Time speeds, life spends; therein is delight
> Till youth and the years can age no more.
> (*The Heart of Peace*)

The vastness and emptiness of space has often had a depressing influence on poets, as indeed it has had on philosophers at least since the time of Pascal. The best evocation I know of the immensity of the universe comes from John Masefield's sonnet sequence *Lollington Downs*, and it is probably no coincidence that Masefield spent his early life at sea; there is an oceanic grandeur about these lines:

I could not sleep for thinking of the sky,
The unending sky, with all its million suns
Which turn their planets everlastingly
In nothing, where the fire-haired comet runs.
If I could sail that nothing, I should cross
Silence and emptiness, with dark stars passing;
Then, in the darkness, see a point of gloss
Burn to a glow, and glare, and keep amassing,
And rage into a sun, with wandering planets,
And drop behind; and then, as I proceed,
See his last light upon his last moon's granites
Die to a night that would be night indeed:
Night, where my soul might sail a million years
In nothing, not even Death, not even tears.

Masefield's closing lines echo thoughts which Tennyson had expressed many years before in one of his later poems, *Lucretius*:

> . . . The Gods, who haunt
> The lucid interspace of world and world,
> Where never creeps a cloud, or moves a wind,
> Nor ever falls the least white star of snow,
> Nor ever lowest roll of thunder moans,
> Nor sound of human sorrow mounts to mar
> Their sacred everlasting calm;

That "everlasting calm" we now know to be an illusion—at least to beings capable of perceiving more than the tiny fraction of the spectrum detectable to human senses. The Gods of *Lucretius* would have been subjected to a ceaseless bombardment of radiations of all wavelengths and energies, from the longest radio waves up to the shortest gammas. To the modern mind the eternal *tumult* of the infinite spaces is at least as terrifying as was the eternal silence to Pascal.

The vastness, complexity and beauty of the universe had, of course, inspired religious as well as poetical thoughts, and often they have been combined. One of the most famous, and certainly most forcible, expressions of this is the much-quoted (in the Victorian era, anyway) *dictum* of Edward Young's: "The undevout astronomer is mad."

This is all that anyone remembers from the ten thousand lines of *Night Thoughts*, written between 1742 and 1745. Alexander Pope remarked of Young that he possessed genius—but no common sense, so that his poetry often degenerated into bombast. One writer who would agree with this is the author of the next poem—much the longest, and certainly the funniest, of all those I am inflicting on you today.

The name of Aldous Huxley is familiar to every student of modern English literature—and to every reader of science fiction through his classic anti-utopia, *Brave New World*. Not so well known is the fact that his biologist brother Julian, the first Director General of UNESCO, among many other distinctions, including one I am happy to share with him, the Kalinga Prize, was equally talented. He produced an enormous amount of popular-science writing, including one book in collaboration with H. G. Wells, and a science-fiction story, *The Tissue Cultured King* (*Amazing Stories*, August 1927) on the now highly topical subject of cloning.

And he was also a pretty good poet—or at least versifier. I think you will agree that "Undevout Astronomers" makes mincemeat of poor Edward Young....

Undevout Astronomers

'The undevout astronomer is mad.'
  Thus Young declared a century ago.
Today we'd like to know what right he had,
  To dogmatise and lay the law down so.

Theology's anthropomorph projection,
  Has now become a little out of date.
Night thoughts are often queer and need correction,
  In light of mornings' sunny postulate.

For the starry heavens today
  Things seem quite the other way.
It's really lucky Young is dead,
  Or he'd be eating what he said.

A fiver to a row of beans,
  I'd bet him, after reading Jeans
(or Eddington) that he'd reverse
  His judgement on the universe.

1984: Spring

Inevitably he'd transfer
  (Madness from the astronomer)
(Whether devout or otherwise)
  And find it fragrant in the skies.

To earlier man the sky had been
  A kind of cosy soup-tureen,
Spangled with stellar decorations,
  Performing orderly gyrations,
Kept going only by the intervention
  of the Almighty's personal attention.

But now the heavens' single face
Is all dissolved in frightful space.
Each twinkler is a monstrous sun
Which a portentous race must run,
From aimless formless infancy
Of star-dust nebulosity

Though a billion years of aimless shining,
And a billion years of slow declining,
And a billion more of growing old,
To perish, hard and dark and cold,
  And stars are moved upon their courses
By quite ordinary forces,
Such as made the apple drop
On to Newton's cranium's top.

Yes, and once upon a time
Heaven's spheres seemed to sublime
That blemish or decay or change
Could not come within their range—
Change, corruption, death and birth
Were only to be found on earth.

But this unchangeable perfection
Alas! will hardly bear inspection:
For now we're certain, sure enough,
That everything's the self-same stuff—
Just matter—in the heavenly host
Or in a piece of buttered toast;
In Sirius and Betelgueuse,
Or in the dirt upon your shoes;
In mud and sun, dishwater, planet, flame,
Matter, we find, is always just the same.
And heavenly matter
Is had as a hatter—
Just atoms daemonic
A dance electonic

That cannot keep still
An endless quadrille
Or breathless fandango
Which turns to a tango
Or runs to a trot
Of fox or what not
Or senseless garotte
—The pace is so hot
Within this micro-dervishes' tornado
I really cannot keep it up as they do.
Phew, what a ceaseless crazy superfluity
Of motion without any continuity!

   Modern astronomy
(A mad Deuteronomy)
Restates all the laws
Of Time, Space and Cause.
   See reason out-reason

Herself and play treason
To sense, till you feel
Your cerebrum reel
And your logic go blank
With Einstein and Planck!

So how could you expect today,
My honest Young, how could you, pray
Astronomers to be devout
When all their world is inside-out?
When science with its spectroscope
Has quite abolished cosmic hope?
When, all because of mathematics,
Full of bats are heaven's attics?
And starry songs are merely jazz—
As you were, and as it was,
So will they be, jazzing dumb
(For there's no band) till Kingdom come. . . .
. . . Young pricks his ears: God's Kingdom then,
Where He is justified to men.

No Young! For as the facts turn out
Even the end is undevout—
Merely a coma of the skies,
Of which the very matter dies,
With human spirit long before
Frozen out of Times' back door
And life become, on Earths' cold ember,
A memory—with none to remember.

Your pious and poetical flight
Was but a Thought that passed in the night
The world was floated
Undevoted;
Its every motion
Is undevotion;
And undevout
It all fades out.

One English poet who did not regard the universe as undevout was Alfred Noyes (1880–1958). He was much influenced by science, and wrote a trilogy, *The Torch-bearers*, which has as its theme the progress of science through the ages. Unfortunately, I don't find him very poetical, though he does have some good descriptive passages:

I see beyond this island universe,
Beyond our sun, and all those other suns
That throng the Milky Way, far, far beyond,
A thousand little wisps, faint nebulae,
Luminous fans and milky streaks of fire;
Some like soft brushes of electric mist
Streaming from one bright point....

These lines are taken from "William Herschel Conducts"; before he became an astronomer, Herschel was a professional musician, and Noyes has tried to imagine his thoughts during a concert. However, the phrase, "island universe," is an anachronism; it did not come into use until our own day, and in fact discovery that such extragalactic nebulae as M 31 in Andromeda *are* separate star systems like our own Milky Way was not made until well into this century. But Herschel had correctly surmised it long before.

Another poem of Noyes' is of interest because it is the only one I know by a poet in the literary mainstream which touches not merely on astronomy but on *astronautics*—though that word was not invented when Noyes wrote *The Last of the Books*.

The Last of the Books

Is it too strange to think
That, when all life at last from earth is gone,

And round the sun's pale blink
  Our desolate planet wheels its ice and stone,
Housed among storm-proof walls may yet abide
  Defying long the venoms of decay,
A still dark throng of books, dumb books of song
  And tenderest fancies born of youth and may.

A quiet remembering host,
  Outliving the poor dust that gave them birth,
Unvisited by even a wandering ghost,
  But treasuring still the music of our earth.
In fading hieroglyphics they shall bear
  Through death and night, the legend of our Spring,
And how the lilac scented the bright air
  When hearts throbbed warm, and lips could kiss and sing.

And, ere that record fail,
  Strange voyagers from a mightier planet come
On winged ships that through the void can sail
  And gently light upon our ancient home;
Strange voices echo, and strange flares explore,
  Lift the brown volumes to the light once more.
  And bear their stranger secrets through the stars.

A poet who looked at astronomers with a more jaun-
diced eye than Alfred Noyes was America's unofficial lau-
reate, Walt Whitman. Perhaps he was just unlucky on
some occasion; I'm sure we have all experienced the emotions Walt recalls in the following lines—though perhaps
at lectures on other subjects than astronomy:

When I heard the learn'd astronomer,
When the proofs, the figures, were ranged in columns before
    me.
When I was shown the charts and diagrams, to add, divide
    and measure them,
When I sitting heard the astronomer where he
  lectured with much applause in the lecture-room,
How soon unaccountable I became tired and sick,
Till rising and gliding out I wandered off by myself,
In the mystical moist night-air, and from time to time,
Look'd up in perfect silence at the stars.

I trust that no one in this audience has yet become
"tired and sick," or feels like "rising and gliding out." This

poem has always annoyed me, because it tends to widen the gulf between the "Two Cultures,"—that great divide which is a modern invention and a modern problem. It is a pernicious fallacy to imagine that the more we learn about the real nature of the universe, the less we can appreciate its beauty. The exact reverse is true—or *should* be.

For Walt Whitman has a point, which should be taken to heart by every educator. The wrong kind of teaching can, all too easily, destroy a student's interest in even the most fascinating subject. I can give an example from my own experience.

After I had taken my degree at King's, I went to another London college to do postgraduate astronomy. At least, that is what I'd intended, but it didn't turn out that way. I fell into the hands of an elderly professor whose main interest was instrumental defects. He spent his entire lecture time deriving long equations showing how all the possible errors in azimuth, right ascension, elevation, declination, latitude and longitude were related and how one could correct for them....

Now, I loved astronomy and mathematics (and still do) but this sort of thing, important though it might be to the few specialists who really need it, perfectly fitted G. H. Hardy's description of those branches of applied mathematics that are "repulsively ugly and intolerably dull." Luckily I escaped after a single term; but it took me a long time to get over the experience.

Yet perhaps my professor knew exactly what he was doing; this may have been his way of separating the men from the boys. For unless my memory plays me false, one of my classmates went on to become one of the most celebrated of contemporary British astronomers.

I'd like to end this address with a short poem and a shorter quotation—the first comic, the second solemn. Yet they both evoke, perhaps better than prose can do, emotions that we can all share when we look up at the the starry heavens.

The first poem I've just discovered in Kingsley Amis' *New Oxford Book of Light Verse*; it's by one B. L. Taylor and was probably written around the turn of the century, so the astronomy is slightly out of date. Rigel would have been a better example than the star that the poet chose—it's even further away, and much more luminous. But it wouldn't have given the nice rhyme in the opening verse. . . .

> When quacks with pills political would dope us,
>   When politics absorbs the livelong day,
> I like to think about the star Canopus,
>   So far, so far away.
>
> Greatest of visioned suns, they say who list 'em;
>   To weigh it science always must despair.
> Its shell would hold our own darned solar system,
>   Nor ever know 'twas there.
>
> When temporary chairmen utter speeches,
>   And frenzied henchmen howl their battle hymns,
> My thoughts float out across the cosmic reaches
>   To where Canopus swims.
>
> When men are calling names and making faces,
>   And all the world's a jangle and ajar,
> I meditate on interstellar spaces
>   And smoke a mild cigar.
>
> For after one has had about a week of
>   The arguments of friends as well as foes,
> A star that has no parallax to speak of
>   Conduces to repose.

I'm sure that anyone who spends much time on government committees and university boards will agree with those sentiments. . . .

Finally, on a more serious note. . . .

At the base of the thirty-one-inch reflector of the Allegheny Observatory, Pittsburgh, is a small white-tiled crypt, containing the ashes of the astronomer and lens-maker John Brashear. It carries an inscription from an otherwise forgotten poem, "The Old Astronomer to his Pupil." Like Edward Young, Sarah Williams is remembered for a single line: yet that is enough to ensure her immortality:

We have loved the stars too fondly to be fearful of the night.

Shaw
and the
Sound
Barrier

There seem very few subjects in which Shaw was not interested, and fewer still on which he was not prepared to express his opinion. Nevertheless, it may surprise most people to learn that toward the end of his life the ubiquitous playwright concerned himself with such advanced ideas as space travel and supersonic flight. It happened in this manner.

During the summer of 1946 I wrote a paper entitled "The Challenge of the Spaceship"—yes, I had been reading Toynbee—which was an attempt to evaluate the ef-

First printed in the *Virginia Quarterly Review* Vol. 36, No. 1, Winter 1960.

fects of interplanetary travel upon human thought and society. After I had presented it as a lecture to the British Interplanetary Society in London, it was published in that organization's journal, and later in a number of books and periodicals all over the world (such as, for example, the UNESCO magazine *Impact*). Most of the basic ideas in this paper have now reached a considerably larger audience by being incorporated in the closing chapters of *The Exploration of Space*, and I shall not attempt to repeat them here. My main thesis was that the crossing of space would not merely be an exciting scientific stunt, but would have profound cultural repercussions affecting philosophy, art, religion and indeed every aspect of our society. I drew a parallel—which has now become something of a cliché—between the Renaissance and the coming age of space exploration, suggesting that the Moon and planets might play a role during the next century not unlike that of the Americas in the fifteenth and sixteenth centuries.

In the paper I made a passing reference to Shaw, and soon afterward I came across the magnificent speech with which Lilith closes the play *Back to Methuselah*: "Of life only there is no end; and though of its million starry mansions many are empty and many still unbuilt, and though its vast domain is as yet unbearably desert, my seed shall one day fill it and master its matter to its uttermost confines. . . ." This, I thought, showed a considerable sympathy with the ideals of astronautics, so I sent Shaw a copy of the British Interplanetary Society's Journal containing my lecture—not in the least expecting a reply.

Much was my surprise when one of the famous pink postcards arrived, completely covered with shaky but perfectly legible handwriting:

> Ayot Saint Lawrence, Welwyn, Herts.
> 25 Jan 1947
>
> FROM BERNARD SHAW
>
> Many thanks for the very interesting lecture to the B.I.S. How does one become a member, or at least subscribe to the Journal?

When de Haviland [sic] perished here the other day it seemed clear to me that he must have reached the speed at which the air resistance balanced the engine power and brought him to a standstill.

Then he accelerated, and found out what happens when an irresistible force encounters an immovable obstacle.

Nobody has as yet dealt with this obvious limit to aeronautic speed as far as I have read.

G. B. S.

The reference is to a tragic event of a few months earlier. On 27 September 1946, Geoffrey de Havilland had been testing the experimental DH 108 jet plane over the Thames, making the last run before a forthcoming attack on the world speed record. He put the plane into a dive, reached the highest speed then attained by man— and was killed instantly when the tremendous forces encountered in going through the sonic barrier tore the aircraft to pieces.

What I did not realize at the time—and indeed have discovered only recently—was that Shaw was a close neighbor of de Havilland's and knew the young test pilot quite well. This helps to explain one of the points in his second letter.

The receipt of this card filled me with mixed feelings. I am naturally flattered by the response, and was also surprised to discover that at the age of ninety-one Shaw was willing to join an organization with aims as advanced as ours. (Back in 1947, anyone who talked about such things as artificial satellites and long-range rockets was still regarded as a little touched. Vanguard, Atlas and Titan were still hidden in the mists of the future.) At the same time, I did not know exactly how to reply—for the main point of his letter was complete nonsense. It did not require any knowledge of aeronautics to appreciate this; it was a matter of common sense. *If* de Havilland's plane had reached the speed at which the engine power balanced the air resistance, it would continue at that speed like a motor car that is flat-out. It would certainly not be "brought to a standstill," and the last thing the pilot could do would be to accelerate, since by definition he had no excess power with which to increase his speed any further.

After some thought, I sent Shaw the following tactful reply, hoping to put him right without hurting his feelings:

Kings College
London.
27 Jan 1947

Dear Mr Shaw,

I am very gratified by your interest in my article and in this Society, and have great pleasure in enclosing further details, as well as our latest publication. I hope that "Astronautics and Poetry" amuses you.

Although the precise cause of de Havilland's death is still unknown, it seems likely that the accident was due to some structural failure. As you say, the limit of speed is set when air resistance equals engine thrust. But the latter can always be increased with more powerful motors, so there is no absolute limit—only a limit for any particular type of machine. V.2, for example, had more than a dozen times the thrust of de Havilland's machine, and a number of rocket-propelled aircraft are nearing completion which will have speeds in the 1,000 m.p.h. range.

In the vacuum of space, of course, where the rocket works at maximum efficiency, there is no resistance and no speed limit at all. A motor of any power could build up any speed as long as its fuel supply could be maintained.

Purists may object to my oversimplification; there is, in fact, a natural limit of speed—that of the velocity of light. However, as light travels almost a million times as fast as sound, I felt justified in ignoring this complication in the (vain) hope that Shaw would do likewise.

We know now that it was supersonic flutter, produced when the DH 108 traveled too fast at too low an altitude, which broke up the plane. And there is a sinister little story about the aircraft's wreckage which, as far as I am aware, has never been told elsewhere. After the crash, all the pieces that could be found were dredged out of the Thames and brought back to the factory for examination. It was here, late one night, that the engineers working on the cause of the accident were startled—to say the least—by the sound of something moving inside the mass of twisted metal. It was a loud scratching noise, traveling with some determination from place to place. The engineers were perhaps more relieved than they would care to admit when, a few minutes later, one of the broken combustion chambers disgorged a small crab.

Shaw wasted no time in answering my letter. Back by return of post came his check, application for membership to the B.I.S.—and this time not a card but a two-page letter. I have since read it a good many times, and it remains one of the most baffling communications I have ever received:

31 Jan 1947

I am not convinced about de Haviland. It is necessary mathematically to have a zero to count from to infinity, positive or negative, Fahrenheit or Centigrade; but the zero is not a physical fact: it is only a convention: and infinity means only the limit to human counting. I approach the subject, being a dramatist, first from my knowledge of the man, and my conviction that he would accelerate to the utmost of his machine if air resistance stopped him. And this would smash his machine as it actually did smash, in spite of all assumptions that speed cannot exceed the velocity of light and that above the stratosphere is sheer vacuum, both of them mathematical conventions and not scientific facts.

Besides, what proof is there that he was above the stratosphere when his machine broke up?

However, this may be only my ignorant crudity; so do not bother to reply.

G. B. S.

Despite the polite brushoff in the last paragraph, I felt that it was impossible to let such hopeless confusion go quite unchallenged, so after some thought I replied as follows:

8 Feb 1947

Dear Mr Shaw,

Thank you for your letter. I am so glad that you have decided to join our Society.

I am afraid that my comments on de Havilland may not

have been quite clear. He was actually at a relatively low altitude when the accident occurred, and my point is that whatever limit may exist to speeds *in* the atmosphere there can be none to speeds outside it. This has been proved experimentally by V.2 which traveled six times as fast as de Havilland's plane (reaching England from Germany [sic] in five minutes and attaining a maximum speed of 3,600 m.p.h.). At heights of more than thirty miles the German scientists were unable to detect any appreciable air resistance, even at this extremely high speed.

This concluded, perhaps none too soon, the Clarke-Shaw correspondence. But Shaw continued to be a member of the British Interplanetary Society until his death three years later; he still holds the record as the oldest member we ever had.

Today, when men have flown at two thousand miles an hour and are preparing to travel twice as fast, this echo from the early days of supersonic flight (all of ten years ago!) seems somewhat quaint and old-fashioned. It may even be a little unkind to preserve what some might consider the words of genius in its dotage. Though it is true that Shaw never hesitated to lay down the law on any subject, even one about which he knew nothing whatsoever, the younger G. B. S. would surely have produced a less eccentric letter than that of 31 January 1947.

Yet whatever one may think of the old man's aeronautical confusion, it is hard not to admire his efforts to keep abreast of the times. How many of us will do as well at the age of ninety-one?

Richard
Jefferies

I do not know how many people are still familiar with the name of Richard Jefferies (1848–87), but I am happy to see that the new *Encyclopaedia Britannica* devotes half a column to him, describing him as a "naturalist, novelist, essayist whose prophetic vision was unappreciated in his own Victorian age but has been increasingly recognized and admired since his death." His best-known books were the autobiographical *The Story of My Heart, Bevis* and one of the earliest of postcatastrophe novels, *After London*.

By what struck me at the time as a most peculiar

First printed in *The Field*, May 1948, p. 494.

coincidence, I came across a bundle of Jefferies' letters on the very first day of his centennial year—1948. They were tucked inside a copy of his book *Red Deer*, which had probably been lying unnoticed around our Somerset farmhouse since I was a boy. I have no idea what impulse prompted me to open it on January 1.

Jefferies visited Exmoor in 1882 to collect material for his book, which was published two years later by Longmans. At that time the Huntsman of the Devon and Somerset Staghounds was my great-grandfather, Arthur Heal; he died at the age of one hundred in 1916, the year before I was born. Though I don't approve of hunting, I am proud to be named after him; when I realize that he was still riding horseback at the age I shall be in 2010, my hopes of flying in the space shuttle brighten appreciably. His wife Mary was a keen amateur astronomer, and I wonder. . . .

Much of Jefferies' information about the beautiful and majestic red deer was obtained from Arthur Heal and his second son Fred. The book that came into my hands sixty-four years later bears the inscription "Fred G Heal Esq. From the author, Jan 10, 1884." I was amused to discover that when Jefferies requested more copies from his publisher, Longman replied rather testily that he'd already had sixteen, and couldn't his friends buy them? This may have been one of the extra six (over the author's standard ten free copies) that provoked this not unreasonable reaction.

On discovering these letters, I incorporated them in a short article which was published in *The Field* (May 1948, page 494) under the title "A Link With Jefferies." Unfortunately, book and letters no longer exist: they were loaned to a journalist friend who lost all his papers (and many of the Clarke family's) in a disastrous fire.

Here—except for three opening paragraphs of introduction—which have been incorporated in the text above—is the rest of the article from *The Field*.

These letters probably form part of a more extensive series, and though they are largely concerned with staghunting, they throw a considerable light on Jefferies' personality and show that his long fight against ill health had destroyed neither his kindliness nor his range of interests.

Two of the letters do not bear the full date but are merely headed "Aug. 5th" and "Sept. 9th." However, they were probably written in 1883 or 1884, and both are addressed from "Savernake," Lorna Road, West Brighton.

Aug. 5th.

Dear Mr. Heal,

I did not forget the book I offered you, but I have been so pressed with business that everything else has had to be put aside. I looked at a Fly-book for you but it seemed to me that you knew all the flies in it so that it would be like sending coals to Newcastle. So I have sent you a complete edition of Tennyson's poems; the Northern Farmer may amuse you, whose horses' hoofs said "Property, Property." I still hope to see something of the stag-hunting (*two words illegible*) this month: should I come I will write to you. Remember me to Arthur and give the hound Sovereign an extra biscuit for me; he is a yellow hound.

Faithfully yours,
Richard Jefferies.

"Arthur" is, of course, Arthur Heal, who is frequently referred to indirectly in *Red Deer*.

On September 9 Jefferies raises a technical query which suggests that at the date of writing he was working on his book.

Sept. 9th.

Dear Mr. Heal,

I have just read in *The Field* that you have had two runs in the Quantocks, the hunt being through the places I was visiting before I came on to Exford. Will you answer the following enquiry?—we have had some disputes and arguments as to the number of points a stag should bear to be runnable, and on reference to old books (one of them 300 years old), I find that a difference of opinion has always prevailed, some saying that a stag at five years bears so many points, and some another number. There seems to be great difference of opinion among the authorities, and also among sportsmen. The question is this, How many points must the

antlers of a young stag bear before he becomes runnable?
Or to put it in other words, How many points does a stag
usually bear at five years? I am sure you will understand
what I mean and if you can find time to reply I shall feel
obliged.

My stag's skin is stretched out on the floor of the room
here in which I am writing—Everyone admires it.

> I remain, Faithfully yours,
> Richard Jefferies.

It would be interesting to know Mr. Heal's reply to
this query, for the answer is not a straightforward one.

A third letter, dated 10 January 1884, also comes from
West Brighton.

> Jan. 10th, 1884.

Dear Mr. Heal,

I have written a little book about the Red Deer—it is just
published and I send you a copy by this post. When you have
read it write and tell me how you like it. The idea of the book
is to introduce the red deer and the fine old sport of stag-
hunting to the great numbers of people who have scarcely
heard of it, and who will scarcely believe it when they do.

My health was so bad in September that I was quite unable to come down; indeed I am still very unwell indeed.

Please remember me to "Arthur" (which is more his name
than any other) and to your kind Mother.

> I remain, Faithfully yours,
> Richard Jefferies.

What is certainly the last of the four letters is dated 16
September 1884. It is addressed "14, Victoria Road, El-
tham, Kent," and the writing is noticeably poorer. Perhaps
it is the last letter Mr. Heal ever received from Jefferies.

> Sept. 16th, 1884.

Dear Mr. Heal,

I should like to hear how the stag-hunting gets on this
season, I see notices in the papers occasionally but rather
bald and should like to hear from you. I have left Brighton,
it was considered that to live inland would be better for me
and so I came here. Though close to London it is quite coun-

try, fields, trees and so on. I still remain so weak that it is impossible for me to enjoy any sport but my interest is as keen as ever, and if I should ultimately recover I shall certainly revisit Somerset. I hope you are all well at home.

> I remain, Faithfully yours,
> Richard Jefferies.

The hopes expressed in this last letter were never to be fulfilled: Jefferies' health had now broken completely, and after a long and painful illness he died in 1887. He was less than thirty-nine years of age.

Who's Afraid
of
Leonard Woolf?

I n October 1904, I sailed from Tilbury Docks in the P & O *Syria* for Ceylon... when we disembarked... I went to the G.O.H., the Grand Oriental Hotel, which in those days was indeed both grand and oriental...."

So Leonard Woolf records in the opening chapters of *Growing: An autobiography of the years 1904 to 1911.* Almost exactly fifty years later I followed the same route in the P & O *Himalaya* when she sailed from Tilbury in

December 1954, though owing to a slight detour to Australia's Great Barrier Reef, I did not actually check into the G.O.H. (now, as the Hotel Taprobane, even less G and O) until 1956. Somewhat incredibly, Woolf himself was back again four years later, at the age of eighty, on a final, triumphal tour of Ceylon, and I am sorry to have missed him. Not until 1979—ten years after his death—did I finally make his acquaintance. More than that; for a couple of days, I *became* him.

But first, back to 1904....

In seven years of energetic overachievement, the conscientious young Cambridge graduate rose from a humble cadet in the Ceylon Civil Service to Assistant Government Agent. By the age of twenty-eight he had so impressed the Governor General that he was put in charge of a major area along the south coast of the island; to quote from a letter he wrote to Lytton Strachey on 2 October 1908 he was

> on my own in my district which is about 1,000 square miles with 100,000 people in it... I live at the Hambantota Residency.... 26 miles away on one side are two Europeans a judge and a Supt. of Police and 20 miles away on the other is another an Irrigation Engineer.

The young A.G.A. loved Ceylon and its people but administered his mini-empire with an honesty and impartiality that did not always endear him to his subjects. When he returned to England for a year's leave in 1911, he had decided that even the most benevolent imperialism, for all the good that it undoubtedly brought in terms of peace, justice and improved standards of health and education, could not be morally justified. He had also fallen in love with Virginia Stephen, and the combination of these two factors was more powerful than the claims of the Colonial Office. So he resigned, married Virginia, founded the Hogarth Press, and helped to launch one of today's major growth industries, the Bloomsbury business.

But Ceylon continued to haunt him, even when he was courting Virginia and resuming acquaintance with Strachey, Maynard Keynes, Duncan Grant, the Bells and the other luminaries of his Cambridge days. He had been back only six months when he started to write *The Village in the Jungle*, which was published two years later (1913) by the Hogarth Press.

Though much less well known than *A Passage to India* (which, incidentally, might never have been completed without Woolf's encouragement) many consider it the better book. It is certainly an astonishing feat of sympathetic imagination for a young colonial administrator to enter so completely into the minds of Sinhalese peasants that his novel has now become a classic in their own language.

> The village was called Beddagama, which means the village in the jungle.... All jungles are evil, but no jungle is more evil than that which lay about the village of Beddagama.... The trees are stunted and twisted by the drought, by the thin sandy soil, by the dry wind. They are scabrous, thorny trees, with grey leaves whitened by the clouds of dust which the wind perpetually sweeps over them; their trunks are grey with hanging, stringy lichen. And there are enormous cactuses, evil-looking and obscene, with their great fleshy green slabs, which put out immense needle-like spines. More evil-looking still are the great leafless trees, which look like a tangle of gigantic spiders' legs—smooth, bright green, jointed together—from which, when they are broken, oozes out a milky, viscous fluid.

Such is the stage upon which Woolf's villagers pass lives as twisted and stunted as the trees around them. The book is an unrelieved tragedy; one by one, its characters are destroyed by disease, starvation and the malice of their fellows. At its end, the village itself has been overwhelmed by the jungle, and only Punchi Menika, "a very old woman before she was forty," remains in its ruins, to meet a fate as unforgettable as any in literature:

> The perpetual hunger wasted her slowly, and when the rains came she lay shivering with fever in the hut. At last the time came when her strength failed her; she lay in the hut unable to drag herself out to search for food....
> ... When the end was close upon her a great black shadow glided into the doorway. Two little eyes twinkled at her steadily, two immense white tusks curled up gleaming against the

darkness. She sat up, fear came upon her, the fear of the jungle, blind agonising fear.

"Appochchi, Appochchi!" she screamed. "He has come, the devil from the bush. He has come for me as you said. Aiyo! save me, save me! Appochchi!"

As she fell back, the great boar grunted softly, and glided like a shadow towards her into the hut.

Stories of such inspissated gloom, however superbly crafted, do not normally appeal to movie makers. But for many years, Sri Lanka's most eminent director, Lester James Peries, had set his heart upon filming *Village*, and after somewhat Byzantine negotiations had managed to obtain the rights. Still more remarkably, he had raised sufficient money for the production and early in 1979 announced that filming would soon commence in the actual setting of the novel, the Hambantota district.

Sixteen years earlier, as described in *The Treasure of the Great Reef*, I had spent a good deal of time in this region, for Hambantota is the last reasonably safe harbor along the south coast of the island. Only twenty miles further east lie the treacherous rocks of the Great Basses Reef, where in 1961 my associate Mike Wilson was foolish enough to discover a wreck containing at least a ton of beautiful silver rupees, all bearing the date 1113 A.H. (1702–3 A.D.). During our salvage operations, we sometimes stayed at the Hambantota Resthouse, literally next door to the little District Court where Leonard Woolf had presided half a century earlier.

The site is one of the most splendid in the whole of Sri Lanka, on a headland overlooking miles of curving beach. Although Hambantota is only six degrees north of the equator, it is never excessively hot, because there is always a steady breeze from the sea. And the sea dominates the life of the little town, for as Woolf writes in *Growing*:

> . . . continually, at regular intervals a wave, not very high but unbroken two miles long (would) lift itself up very slowly, wearily, poise itself for a moment in sudden complete silence, and then fall with a great thud upon the sand. . . . It was the last thing I heard as I fell asleep at night, the first thing I heard when I woke in the morning—the moment of silence,

the heavy thud; the moment of silence, the heavy thud—the rhythm of the sea, the rhythm of Hambantota.

That rhythm was somewhat disrupted one weekend in July 1979, when Lester's film unit descended upon the little town. The shooting in which I was involved had to be done during the weekend, because only then was the District Court available; come Monday, the defendants in the dock would be genuine ones, not actors.... Luckily, the only change necessary was the removal of the Seal of the Republic of Sri Lanka, and its temporary replacement with the Royal Crest. Nothing else had altered since Leonard Woolf's time.

But the world around had certainly changed. The very evening I arrived, gliding in the air-conditioned comfort of my Mercedes-Benz over the road along which Woolf had jolted in bullock carts for a couple of dusty days, I had to address a science-fiction convention in Washington. The Rest House telephone was tied up for an hour while my words winged their way via the local microwave beam to the earth station near Colombo, and thence to the satellite 22,000 miles overhead. So it is amusing to discover that Woolf wrote in his diary for 23 September 1908: "Personally I hate machinery in this country. Very few natives can be got to understand it; in fact in Hambantota itself it has been found impossible to keep an ordinary village pump working at the wells for more than a few days." Needless to say, the satellite station I was using was being run by the local "natives."

Next morning, I was dressed in my Edwardian colonial garb and patiently thatched by the makeup man, who restored all the hair that had unaccountably disappeared over the past few decades; the result was sufficiently judicial to terrify the innocent, let alone the guilty. But as I had never done any acting in my life—and had seen the script only two days earlier—there was no way of predicting the outcome when I finally appeared before the camera. "The next couple of hours," I told Lester, "will decide whether you're filming *Village in the Jungle* or *Carry On, Judge*."

Fortunately, my worst fears proved groundless, and everything went very smoothly. There was no danger of forgetting my lines, for I had them concealed in my legal papers—which I had a perfect right to consult whenever I wished. In any event, all I had to say was in the form of brief questions put to the defendants through the court interpreter. Only one phrase was in Sinhalese, *"Mata umbagena kanagatui"* ("I am sorry for you"), when I sentenced the principal accused to six months hard labor. The verdict was given with reluctance. ("There is almost certainly something behind this case that has not come out, but I have to go by the evidence. . . .") The evidence was, in fact, entirely fabricated; the accused was quite innocent of the robbery with which he had been charged.

As I sat on the bench in my borrowed judicial robes, I was not in the least conscious of acting a role; even the camera and lights did not break the spell. The courtroom was a time machine that had carried me back to the beginning of the century:

> . . . At one end was the bench, a raised dais, with a wooden balustrade round it. There were a table and chair upon the dais. In the centre of the room was a large table with chairs round it for the bar and the more respectable witnesses. At the further end of the room was the dock, a sort of narrow oblong cage made of a wooden fence with a gate in it. Silundu and Babun were locked up in this cage, and a court peon stood by the gate in charge of them. There was no other furniture in the room except the witness box, a small wooden platform surrounded by a wooden balustrade on three of its sides.

If Leonard Woolf could have looked through my eyes, as I sat on the dais he had occupied so many times, he could not have told that seventy years had passed. Any doubts would have been resolved by a glance outside:

> The judge, as he sat upon the bench, looked out through the great open doors opposite him, down upon the blue waters of the bay, the red roofs of the houses, and then the interminable jungle, the grey jungle stretching out to the horizon and the faint line of the hills. And throughout the case this vast view, framed like a picture in the heavy wooden doorway, was continually before the eyes of the accused. Their eyes wandered from the bare room to the boats and the canoes,

bobbing up and down on the bay, to the group of little figures on the shore hauling in the great nets under the blazing sun, to the dust storms sweeping over the jungle, miles away where they lived.

Sixteen years earlier, my own little boat, the cantankerous and ill-fated *Ran Muthu*, had been "bobbing up and down" in that same bay, as she prepared to carry me to the greatest adventure of my life. During the intervals between takes, while cameraman Willie Blake was changing lenses and magazines, my eyes strayed continually to that magnificent view, and I kept wondering how many had seen it for the last time, before they were taken to the jail—or the gallows. One of Woolf's duties, which doubtless encouraged his ultimate resignation, was that of seeing that hangings were properly carried out.

By working steadily all through Sunday, we managed to finish shooting at dusk. The Royal Arms were taken down, and the court was handed back to the Republic of Sri Lanka for its normal operations. The following morning, half our Bar would still be here—because they were real lawyers, not actors. I was never sure which was which, and the genuine items returned the compliment by saying that *they* couldn't tell I wasn't a real judge. I certainly felt like one as I interrogated the prisoners—even though one of them was an old friend of twenty years' standing.

Monday was our day in the jungle, and for the first time in my life I wore a solar topee. To my surprise it was extemely light and comfortable; I am sure it would still be popular if it didn't look so hopelessly Colonial-Kiplingesque. Only fifty years ago, the superstitious Europeans were convinced that anyone who ventured outdoors without a topee would be instantly smitten by that wholly mythical malady, sunstroke.

For the purposes of the movie, two Beddegamas had been constructed—one Before, and one After. The first was a reasonably prosperous and well-populated village, at which I arrived by bullock cart with a set of census forms; and accompanied by a uniformed official, the Rate (pronounced 'Ratay') Mahatmaya, or local district supervisor. This was the opportunity for a delightful and completely authentic bit of dialogue:

1984: Spring

L. W.: This rinderpest business is terrible. But the villagers won't take any precautions—they blame it all on Halley's Comet.

R. M.: Another evil they blame on the comet, sir, is a very strict Government Agent.

In 1910, the year of the comet, the villagers did indeed compare Leonard Woolf unfavorably to his kind-hearted predecessor. Also in that year, the dreadful cattle disease rinderpest wiped out whole herds in the Hambantota district; having to shoot stray cattle did not add to Woolf's popularity. His own reaction to the most famous of celestial visitors is, to say the least, unusual:

> The head of the comet was just above the horizon, the tail flamed up the sky until the end of it was almost above our heads...it was a superb spectacle; as a work of art, magnificent. And I suppose it is what is called awe-inspiring. But there is something about these spectacular displays of nature, about the heavenly bodies and the majestic firmament which, while I admire them as works of art, also irritates me. From my point of view—the human point of view—there is something ridiculous about the universe—these absurd comets racing round the sun and the absurd suns flaming away at impossible speeds through illimitable empty space. Such futility is sinister in its silliness.... [*Growing*, Chapter 4]

That certainly puts the universe in its place, as a rather ill-managed extension of Bloomsbury. When Halley's Comet again blazes above the Hambantota Rest House early in 1986, I hope I shall be there to see it.

Beddegama No. 2 was merely a single ruined hut, at the sight of which I had to exclaim, "Is *this* all that is left? I remember it well...." Followed, of course, by our old friend Flashback, as my wire-rimmed spectacles go out of focus and we move back into the past.

Both of the village sequences were shot in a single day, despite poor cooperation from the weather. For my weekend's work, Lester insisted on paying me union rates, and I later handed over the check to the Prime Minister. It will go into a fund for indigent actors; I hope that no one accuses me of trying to safeguard my own future.

As for the movie, it will make its European appearance

at the 1980 Cannes Film Festival. Having seen the rushes, I am convinced that it will receive wide acclaim... and I can't help doing a little daydreaming....

Ten years ago, bravely hiding my tears, I left the Dorothy Chandler Pavilion carrying one of the best *undelivered* speeches of acceptance in the history of the Academy of Motion Picture Arts and Sciences. (I still stick pins in wax statues of Mel Brooks.) Maybe next time—

"For best supporting actor in a foreign language film, this year's Oscar goes to—"

Postscript: *The Village in the Jungle* rapidly proved itself to be the first Sinhalese film to make much of an impact on the outside world. It has been dubbed into several languages and has appeared on TV channels in the United States, England, Germany, Japan and elsewhere.

With Brendan Behan

Before we get any further, I had better admit that I never met Brendan Behan in my life, though I still don't understand how I managed to miss him. To make matters worse, my image of him is irrevocably colored by Peter Sellers' "In a Free State" (recorded on EMI PMC 1111, 1959). In this brilliant parody—at least, I *thought* it was a parody before I read this book—the temperamental Irish playwright Brendan Behan eventually strangles his hapless BBC interviewer when he discovers that

---

Foreword to *With Brendan Behan: A Personal Memoir*, by Peter Arthurs (New York: St. Martin's Press, 1981).

the studio carafe contains (ugh) water. ("What's this filthy stuff doing here? A man could die o' thirst....")

So what am I doing here? It's a long story and begins in the mid-1950s, when I first discovered the Hotel Chelsea and its unique fauna. For almost a quarter of a century, the Chelsea was my second home—the base from which I ventured out on lecture tours, flew to Cape Canaveral for Moon shots and even managed to do some work, despite the surrounding distractions. Thus the novel *2001: A Space Odyssey* was written—several times— up on the tenth floor.

One of the many reasons I felt at home in the Chelsea was its totally democratic, easygoing atmosphere; about the only house rule was "Bring out your own dead." As a natural-born slob who hates ties even more than socks (I must be the only person ever to attend an IBM banquet wearing a sarong—which I hasten to add is purely *male* attire here in Sri Lanka), I was happy to wander round the lobby and echoing stairway in whatever I grabbed first from the clothes closet. At least that is my recollection; but another resident suggests that my wardrobe must have contained a few conventional items:

> The Chelsea, a seedy, run-down, part residential, part transient, past-its-prime hotel, has long been a home for notorious writers like Thomas Wolfe, Brendan Behan, Dylan Thomas and Clifford Irving. More recently it has become a mecca for way-out British rock-and-roll groups "on the road" in the United States. But though Clarke loved the free and easy atmosphere of the Chelsea, he couldn't quite go along with it all the way. He continued to rise at 7 A.M., don his customary English suit, vest and tie, and, with attaché case in hand, venture into the totally deserted corridors and elevators still pervaded with the stale marijuana smoke of the up-till-dawn Chelsea clientele.

Thus Dr. Jerry Grey, in his lively book about the space shuttle (*Enterprise*, William Morrow, 1979). He must have caught me on my way to the CBS-TV studios, or on my first (but not second) day at the Time-Life Books division. In any event, Jerry's independent assessment of the Chelsea's ambience will prove that I am not exaggerating.

Looking back on those years, it seems to me that most of the friends and acquaintances I made in the United States were first encountered at the Chelsea. Among them was an Irish seaman and ex-boxer named Peter Arthurs, who disappeared from time to time into gigantic oil tankers and then emerged, in a crippled condition, to sue the owners for negligence. When he was not hobbling between the Seaman's Union, his lawyer and the hotel, Peter had plenty of time for conversations and socializing, so it was inevitable that we should meet sooner or later in the lobby or the immediately adjacent bar. And it is typical of the stimulating way in which the Chelsea's social and professional crosscurrents mix people of entirely different interests and walks of life that it was through Peter—and not the other way around—that I got to meet such writers as Arthur Miller, Charles (*Lost Weekend*) Jackson and Norman Mailer. They were already friends of his.

Like most Irishmen, drunk, sober or half-and-half, Peter was a good talker and was full of stories about his old buddy Brendan. When, by the mid-1960s, I'd heard these for the seventh or eighth time, I finally said in exasperation: "Why don't you write them down?" It was obvious that Peter had a great deal of unique information about Brendan, which might be of interest to a wide public. I also thought (and hoped) that the discipline of writing would (a) keep Peter away from the gargle (q.v.) and (b) provide the psychotherapy which, as we sane, well-balanced English are much too polite to mention, all refugees from Erin badly need to overcome environmental handicaps.

After a lot of prodding, and sundry emotional and financial crises, Peter bought a stack of paper and started to write down everything he remembered about Brendan. When he could no longer afford to live at the Chelsea, he holed up in a downtown loft, where his manuscript was in permanent danger of being eaten by cockroaches. (Peter ran no small risk himself, if they ever caught him when he couldn't fight back.) I met him whenever I was in town, made sure that he had at least one good meal at El Quijote or the Angry Squire and provided any other assistance that seemed necessary. This was not always easy to decide; it is fatal to throw too many life belts to struggling writers.

When, to my pleased surprise, Peter had produced some hundred thousand words of reminiscences, I sent him to meet Jack Scovil, vice-president of the Scott Meredith Agency, which has represented me for (good heavens!) more than thirty years. Although Norman Mailer, Arthur Miller and I all played roles as midwives—or godfathers—of this book, Jack deserves the credit for finding the brawling infant a home.

Now, having just completed my first reading of the whole manuscript only a few hours ago, I am still slightly punch-drunk. My sense of syntax is partly paralyzed, and it will take me some time to unscramble my vocabulary. I don't envy Peter's editors (there *must* be more than one—no single person could stay the course) but I sincerely hope that there will be the minimum of tampering with the original text. Much of it reminds me of James Joyce—except that Peter's meaning is always perfectly clear, however unorthodox his use of words.

I congratulate him on performing an extraordinary feat of literary reincarnation. His book, unlike many in the marketplace today, delivers exactly what its title promises. When you turn these pages you will be, whether you like it or not, With Brendan Behan.

Colombo, Sri Lanka
7 June 1980

The
Science Fiction
Hall of Fame

A cynic might argue that no art form can now be taken seriously unless it is honored by awards and award ceremonies so that the public can be reassured by some official certificate of excellence. ("And the name in this envelope is—LEONARDO DA VINCI! Better luck next time, Michelangelo!") In the science fiction and fantasy fields, we have the Galaxy, Jupiter, John W. Camp-

Introduction to *The Science Fiction Hall of Fame, Volume III*, edited by Arthur C. Clarke and George W. Proctor, (New York: Avon, 1982).

bell, and International Fantasy awards; but the best-known and undoubtedly most prestigious are the Hugo and Nebula.

The Hugo is named after Hugo Gernsback (1884–1967), alternately praised and reviled as the father of magazine science fiction. Though many of his authors would have preferred the title Godfather, he was a great man and genuinely loved the medium; it wasn't his fault that he sometimes couldn't find the half-cent per word his rapacious writers demanded.

The Hugo Award is a finned, streamlined torpedo in the shape of a classic pre-Space Age spaceship. (I once had the challenging problem of carrying one aboard an airplane during a bomb scare.) It is presented annually at the World Science Fiction Convention, after a prolonged period of balloting and voting by the "fans." *Vox populi, vox dei*; Hugo is the customers' token of gratitude to the books, short stories and dramatic works that have given them the greatest pleasure.

The Nebula, on the other hand, is the tribute of the professionals, to their peers. Titles are nominated and voted upon by the members of the Science Fiction Writers of America. It is thus the precise equivalent of the Oscar in the movie world, but is considerably more beautiful. (Sour grapes, perhaps; it's a harrowing experience to slink out of the Dorothy Chandler Pavilion with your undelivered speech of acceptance. I've never forgiven Mel what's-his-name for beating *2001* with *The Producers*.)

The Nebula is a block of transparent plastic, wherein are cunningly embedded various crystals and minerals to give it an astronomical motif; it puts on quite a display when you shine a laser into it. I am now the proud possessor of three (who was the criminologist who said, "Once is an accident, twice is a coincidence but three times is a conspiracy"?) and won't be in the running for any more, so I can regard the entire Nebula voting system with detached complacency. Over the years the award has been the subject of heated debate by the members of the Science Fiction Writers of America, some of whom have suggested its abolition altogether. They argue that it's meaningless to talk about a "best" in any category, and that no one can possibly read all the titles nominated in the final ballot.

They have a point. On checking the preliminary ballot for the 1979 awards, I'm depressed to discover that I've read only six of the twenty-three novels nominated—and this includes one I'd written myself. In the other categories my record is even more deplorable: two of the eight novellas (17,500–40,000 words) and none of the twenty novelettes (7,500–17,500 words) or twenty-six short stories. No wonder I had to disqualify myself from voting....

Incidentally, the problem with the Oscars is even worse, except for anyone who lives in Hollywood. The Academy of Motion Picture Arts and Sciences used to send me lists of several hundred movies; I resigned the year I'd not seen even *one*.

I'd be surprised if even half the people who vote for the Nebulas have read a quarter of the stories nominated; most of them are too busy writing their own. But does it matter? Perfection is impossible in this world, and the laws of statistics usually even matters out. Rough justice is eventually done, and a really poor story seldom makes it to the finals.

And perhaps the most important function of the Nebulas is precisely that claimed for the Oscars. However worthy or unworthy the winners may be, the general ballyhoo (when will the Nebula dinners be televised?) creates interest and excitement that is good for the *genre*, as well as the writers, publishers, editors, agents, readers, and sales. Despite the tears and heartbreak (how many Kleenexes did Isaac use up before he finally made it?), *everyone* gains in the long run.

On looking at the contents of this volume, I'm happy to discover that I've met every one of the authors, and with a single exception, all are still very much alive. They and their stories can speak for themselves and need no words of introduction from me. Instead, let me talk about Richard McKenna (1913–64).

Last night by a weird coincidence, his name flashed on the ship's TV as we steamed through the waters he knew half a century ago. There was a screening aboard of the excellent movie made from his only novel, *The*

Sand Pebbles (1962). To the five hundred students of our floating campus, this saga of U.S. gunboat diplomacy in a vanished China must have seemed as remote as the Civil War. (I wondered, too, what our all-Chinese crew, from the captain on down, thought when they saw Steve McQueen patiently explain the mysteries of steam power to their primitive countrymen.)

Dick McKenna spent twenty years below decks in the U.S. Navy, then took his B.A. in literature at the University of North Carolina. Though his academic training must have been valuable, the magic of "The Secret Place" could have come only from his own subconscious. There are lines in this story that make my skin crawl; the voters for the 1966 Nebula knew what they were doing. But by then, the author was already dead.

I met him and his wife Eva at the Milford Science Fiction Writers' Workshop in 1958. Though it was our only encounter, I have never forgotten the impression of quiet power and integrity that he radiated.

There are many lessons to be learned from Richard McKenna's tragically brief career. He showed that a writer of real talent can emerge from any environment. In our own time, Alex Haley has also used the U.S. Navy as a launching pad, against even greater odds.

But perhaps the most important lesson McKenna can teach us is one that we are only just beginning to learn. Science fiction *is* different from "mainstream" literature—but there are no barriers between them.

S.S. *Universe*
Krakatoa to Gt Basses Reef
October, 1980

My
Four Feet
on the
Ground

It was very unsporting of Gerald Durrell to preempt the title my mother really needed for this book. *My Family, and Other Animals*. She thought of using it anyway, and the heck with the lawyer— but then decided that wouldn't be fair to all the millions of people who would buy Durrell's book under the impression that they were getting this one...

The Somerset that Mother remembers already seems to belong to another world—a world where motor cars and telephones were rare novelties, cinema and radio still

Introduction to *My Four Feet on the Ground* by Nora Clarke (London: Rocket Publishing Co., Ltd., 1978).

undreamed of. In many respects, the way of life on the farms and estates had not changed for centuries; there may still be some who look back on it with nostalgia. For the few percent who had wealth, position and continuous good health, that vanished age was indeed a golden one: but I do not think that the average man, if he could be miraculously transported back to the last days of the Victorian era, would care to stay after he had felt the first twinge of toothache.

Yet despite all the changes, much of the West of England is still largely unspoilt, and long may it remain so. The rising interest in the countryside, in animals and in ecology may help to preserve what is best in the past; we should not grieve for the rest, but reading about it will give us a better historical perspective—and a better appreciation of our own age.

With the appearance of this book, we now have three authors in the family, since my brother Fred's *Small Pipe Central Heating* is a standard reference in its own field. However, sister Mary has shown no signs of dabbling in literature, having her hands full with her children, her husband and his stable of unemployed polo ponies... But my youngest brother, Michael, when not building Hovercraft and running the family farm, has written and produced numerous sketches for local talent. He shows a comic genius that must be discouraged at all costs; I await with apprehension his threatened horror epic, *THAT—Son of IT*.

Perhaps some word of explanation is due to those many authors who, over the years, have written to me begging piteously for introductions to *their* books. I have always refused such requests, as a matter of policy, and I hope they will understand why I have made an exception in this case. A mother has, of course, unique opportunities for blackmail; and I am writing these words in return for a promise that chapers 2, 3, 4, 5 and 6 will be deleted from the original draft. I trust that Norman Mailer, John LeCarré, Isaac Asimov, Len Deighton, Richard Adams, Harold Robbins (to mention only a few of the struggling writers I have reluctantly refused a helping hand in the past) will appreciate my position and accept my apologies.

It has been a somewhat strange experience, writing

what I hope is my last book while a few meters away Mother was writing her first. (It was also pretty frustrating, when she was churning it out at five times my rate.)

I wish her the best of luck in her new career... as long, of course, as she doesn't try her hand at science-fiction.

Colombo, Sri Lanka
1978

Postscript: My mother wrote this book, which as the title indicates is more about horses, cows and sheep than human beings, at the age of eighty-six, two years before her death on 9 February 1980. It is the only work to bear the imprint of The Rocket Publishing Company, formed in 1953 to control my British and European rights. (Later, the name caused some confusion: the company frequently received mail and phone calls for Elton John's Rocket Records, and vice versa.)

My little joke about Norman Mailer and other "struggling writers" backfired when a not-very-bright journalist printed it as fact. As a result, John le Carré wrote a mildly indignant letter to the press, denying that he had ever appealed to me for assistance. I hope he duly received my explanation/apology.

The Web Between the Worlds

An Open Letter to the Bulletin of the Science Fiction Writers of America

Early in 1979 I published a novel, *The Fountains of Paradise*, in which an engineer named Morgan, builder of the longest bridge in the world, tackles a far more ambitious project—an "orbital tower" extending from a point on the equator to geostationary orbit. Its purpose: to replace the noisy, polluting and energy-wasteful rocket by a far more efficient electric elevator system. The construction material is a crystalline carbon fiber, and a key device in the plot is a machine named "Spider."

Introduction to *The Web Between the Worlds*, by Charles Sheffield (New York: Ace Books, 1979).

A few months later another novel appeared in which an engineer named Merlin, builder of the longest bridge in the world, tackles a far more ambitious project—an "orbital tower," etc., etc. The construction material is a crystalline silicon fiber, and a key device in the plot is a machine named "Spider"...

A clear case of plagiarism? No—merely an idea whose time has come. And I'm astonished that it hasn't come sooner.

The concept of the "space elevator" was first published in the West in 1966 by John Isaacs and his team at La Jolla. They were greatly surprised to discover that a Leningrad engineer, Yuri Artsutanov, had anticipated them in 1960; his name for the device was a "cosmic funicular." There have since been at least three other independent "inventions" of the idea.

I first mentioned it in a speech to the American Institute of Architects in May 1967 (see "Technology and the Future" in *Report on Planet Three*) and more recently (July 1975) in an address to the House of Representatives Space Committee (see *The View From Serendip*). However, although I had been thinking about *The Fountains of Paradise* for almost two decades, it was not until a very few years ago that I decided to use the orbital tower as its theme. One reason for my reluctance was, I suspect, an unconscious fear that, surely, some science-fiction writer would soon latch on to such a gorgeous idea. Then I decided that I simply had to use it—even if Larry Niven came out first...

Well, Charles Sheffield (currently President of the American Astronautical Association and V/P of the Earth Satellite Corporation) only missed by a few months with his Ace novel *The Web Between The Worlds*. (Incidentally, that would have been a good title for Brian Aldiss' marvelous fantasy *Hothouse* [a.k.a *The Long Afternoon of Earth*], which had *spiderwebs* linking Earth and Moon!) I am much indebted to Dr. Sheffield for sending me the ms. of his novel; and if you want another coincidence, I had just started reading his *first* novel, *Sight of Proteus* (Ace), when the second one arrived...

Anyone reading our two books will quickly see that the parallels were dictated by the fundamental mechanics of the subject—though in one major respect we evolved totally different solutions. Dr. Sheffield's method of anchoring his "Beanstalk" is hair-raising, and I don't believe it would work. I'm damn sure it wouldn't be permitted!

I'm writing this letter to put the record straight, and to divert any possible charges from Dr. Sheffield. But I'd also like to satisfy my own curiosity.

It still seems inconceivable to me that, in the eighteen years since it's been circulating, no one has used this idea in fiction—especially now that it is being taken more and more seriously in nonfiction, with a rapidly expanding literature. (I expect to give a survey paper on the subject at the annual International Astronautical Federation Congress, Munich, 20 September 1979). I no longer—alas— have time to read the S.F. magazines, or more than even a tenth of the good books published. So I'd appreciate any information on this point, before I get charged with plagiarism.

As for the rest of you—go right ahead. Charles Sheffield and I have just scratched the surface. The space elevator (and its various offspring, some even more fantastic) may be the great engineering achievement of the twenty-first century, making travel round the solar system no more expensive than any other form of transportation.

17 January 1979

Mysterious
World

Mysteries come in so many shapes and sizes that it is almost impossible to classify them. One useful way of doing so is to divide them into three categories, based on our current level of understanding. Borrowing shamelessly, let us call them Mysteries of the First, Second and Third Kind.

A Mystery of the First Kind is something that was once utterly baffling but is now completely understood. Vir-

Introduction to *Arthur C. Clarke's Mysterious World*, by Simon Welfare and John Fairley (published by Collins, London, and A & W Visual Library, NY, 1980).

tually all natural phenomena fall into this category; one of the most familiar, and beautiful, examples is the rainbow. To ancient man, this must have been an awe-inspiring, even terrifying sight. There was no way that he could explain it, except as the creation of some superior intelligence; witness the version in *Genesis*, when Jehovah tells Noah that he will set His sign in the heavens. . . .

The true explanation of the rainbow had to wait for Sir Isaac Newton's proof that "white" light is really a blend of all possible colors, which may be separated by a prism— or by drops of water floating in the sky. After the publication of Newton's *Optics* in 1704, there was no further mystery about the rainbow—but all its magic and beauty remained. Some foolish people think that science takes the wonder out of the universe; the exact opposite is the truth. *Genuine* understanding is not only more useful than superstition or myth; it is almost always much more interesting.

There are countless other Mysteries of the First Kind. Still more awe-inspiring than the rainbow is the aurora, and only since the dawn of the Space Age have we learned how that is created by electrified particles blasted out of the sun and trapped in the upper atmosphere by the Earth's magnetic field. Even now, there are still many details to be worked out; but there is no doubt about the general principles of the aurora.

Of course, as any philosopher will be glad to tell you, no "explanation" of *anything* is ever complete; beyond every mystery is a deeper one. The dispersion of light in the spectrum causes the rainbow—but what is light itself?—and so on, indefinitely. However, most of us are content to accept the common-sense or man-in-the-street attitude toward the universe, well summed up by the comedian Shelley Berman: "If you give a philosophy student a glass of water he says: *Is* this a glass of water? And if so, *why* is it a glass of water? And pretty soon he dies of thirst."

Mysteries of the Second Kind are what this book, and the television series on which it is based, are all about. They are mysteries which are *still* mysteries, though in some cases we may have a fairly good idea of the answers.

Often the trouble is that there are too many answers; we would be quite satisfied with any one of them, but others appear equally valid. The most spectacular modern example is, of course, the UFO phenomenon, where the range of explanations extends from psychic manifestations through atmospheric effects to visiting spaceships—and, to make matters even more complicated, the range of eager explainers runs from complete lunatics to hard-headed scientists. (There are some soft-headed scientists in this field as well.) All that I will say about the controversial subject of UFOlogy at this point is that, where there are so many answers, there is something wrong with the questions.

Another mystery, which does not arouse quite so many violent emotions, is the Great Sea Serpent. Most zoologists would be quite willing to admit that large unidentified marine creatures may exist—perhaps, as in the case of the coelacanth, even survivors from primeval times. And *if* they are still around, one day we should be able to prove it. (Though not necessarily; at this very moment, the last surviving Sea Serpent may be dying from an overdose of industrial pollutants....)

Barring such exceptional bad luck, most Mysteries of the Second Kind are eventually solved, and graduate to those of the First Kind. In witnessing this process, our generation is the most fortunate one that has ever lived. We have discovered answers to questions that have haunted all earlier ages—to questions, indeed, which once seemed beyond all possible solution. No more dramatic example could be mentioned than the Far Side of the Moon, once the very symbol of the unknowable. Now it has not only been completely mapped, but men have gazed upon its plains and craters with their own unaided eyes.

Yet there are some Mysteries that may remain forever of the Second Kind. This is particularly true where historical events are concerned, because once the evidence has been lost or destroyed, there is no way in which it can be recovered. One can conjecture endlessly about such famous enigmas as the true identities of Kaspar Hauser, or the Dark Lady of the Sonnets, or Homer. Unless someone invents a method of looking into the past—

extremely unlikely, yet not quite impossible—we may never know. Scientists are more fortunate than historians, for nature does not destroy evidence; all the questions they ask are ultimately answered—though in the process they invariably uncover new and more difficult ones.

Mysteries of the Third Kind are the rarest of all, and there is very little that can be said about them; some skeptics argue that they do not even exist. They are phenomena—or events—for which there appears to be *no* rational explanation; in the cases where there are theories to account for them, these are even more fantastic than the "facts."

Perhaps the quintessential M3K is something so horrible that—even if the material existed—one would prefer not to use it in a television program. It is the extraordinary phenomenon known as spontaneous human combustion.

There have been many recorded cases, supported by what seems to be indisputable medical evidence, of human bodies being consumed in a very short period of time by an extremely intense heat *which has often left the surroundings—even the victim's clothing!—virtually untouched*. The classic fictional case is in Dickens' *Bleak House*, but there are dozens of similar incidents in real life—and probably a far greater number that have never been reported.

The human body is not normally a fire hazard; indeed, it takes a considerable amount of fuel to arrange a cremation. There seems no way in which this particular mystery can ever be solved, without a great deal more evidence—and who would wish for *that*?

A less appalling, though sometimes very frightening, Mystery of the Third Kind is the poltergeist (from the German—literally, "noisy spirit"). Although a healthy skepticism is required when dealing with all paranormal phenomena, because extraordinary happenings require extraordinarily high standards of verification, there is impressive evidence that small objects can be thrown around, or even materialized, with no apparent physical cause. Usually there is a disturbed adolescent somewhere in the background, and although adolescents—disturbed or otherwise—are perfectly capable of raising hell by non-paranormal means, this persistent pattern over so many cultures, and such a long period of time, suggests that *something* strange is going on. If so, it is a complete mystery, and such labels as "psychokinesis" are only fig leaves to conceal our ignorance.

In this series, we have avoided M3Ks for several good and sufficient reasons. In the first case, there is no general agreement that they even exist, so discussions of their reality are inconclusive and unsatisfying. At best, the parties concerned agree to disagree; at worst, confrontations end up as slanging matches with charges of fraud or narrow-mindedness winging across the battle lines. This can be amusing for a while, but soon gets boring.

Secondly, such evidence as *does* exist is almost all in the form of eyewitness accounts—often fine for radio, but poor fare for television, unless one cheats and "reconstructs" reported events. Needless to say, none of *my* colleagues would ever be guilty of so heinous a crime....

Finally, even if the existence of a particular M3K is established, where does one go from there? Nothing could be more important than the *conclusive* demonstration of some anomalous event outside the frontiers of accepted science; it is by such discoveries that knowledge advances. However, until there is some plausible theory or working hypothesis to explain the phenomenon, there is little that one can say intelligently about it. Few things are more frustrating than isolated enigmas that seem to admit of *no* rational explanation. With the Mysteries of the Second Kind, we have at least something to get our teeth into.

If they are real, M3Ks quickly graduate to M2Ks, and eventually to M1Ks. A perfect example is the discovery of radioactivity at the end of the nineteenth century. The late Victorian scientists were amazed to find that certain uranium compounds continually emitted energy; the discovery was not only totally unexpected, but defied all that was then known about physics. However, the facts were swiftly established beyond controversy and led in a very short time to the first real understanding of atomic structure.

The fact that this process has *not* happened in the case of paranormal phenomena is one of the strongest arguments against their real existence. After more than a hundred years of effort, the advocates of the paranormal have still been unable to convince the majority of their scientific peers that "there is anything in it." Indeed, the tide now appears to be turning against them with recent revelations of fraud and incredibly sloppy techniques in what once seemed to be well-established results.

But the verdict is not yet handed down, nor will it be in our time. Those who think that science has accounted for everything are just as stupid—and that is not too strong a word—as those who accept the most fantastic stories on the flimsiest of evidence.

Which leads me to my final point. I said at the beginning that there were three kinds of Mystery; now let me add a fourth—Mysteries of the Zeroeth Kind....

The only mystery about *these* is that anyone ever thought they were mysterious. The classic example is the Bermuda Triangle, though this has not prevented countless writers, some of whom may even believe the rubbish they are regurgitating, repeating the same nonsense over and over again. The stories of vanishing aircraft and ships in this region, when the *original* sources are examined, usually turn out to be perfectly explicable and commonplace tragedies. Indeed, it is a considerable tribute to the Florida Coast Guard that there are so *few* disappearances in this busy area, among the legions of amateur sailors and weekend pilots who venture out across it, often with totally inadequate preparation.

A glance at any display of paperbacks will, alas, disclose a ripe collection of Mysteries of the Zeroeth Kind— the mental junk food of our generation. It is a pity that there is no way of labeling books that rot the mind— WARNING! READING THIS BOOK MAY BE DANGEROUS TO YOUR MENTAL HEALTH!—but the practical difficulties are obvious. What a pity it is not possible for some public-spirited benefactor to purchase copies of the latest flying saucer guide book, revelation from Atlantis, or pyramidal insanity, and then sue the author for incompetence. Even if he was awarded no more than the price of the book, it would be a lot of fun!

Sometimes it doesn't really matter, and there may even be occasions when the most rubbishy of books may open up a mind to the wonders of the universe (as bad science fiction can also do). But there are times when real harm can be done to serious and important studies, or to the elucidation of genuine mysteries, by the activities of frauds, cranks and hoaxers. Thus the idea that earth may have had visitors from space is a perfectly reasonable one; indeed, I would go so far as to say that it is surprising if it has *not* done so during the past billions of years of its existence. Unfortunately, books full of faked "evidence" and imbecile archaeology have scared serious researchers away from the field. So it is with the study of UFOs—which, despite all the nonsense that has been written about them, may yet turn out to be important and interesting.

It is my hope that this book, and the series on which it is based, will help all those interested in the truth to distinguish between real mysteries and fraudulent ones. True wisdom lies in preserving the delicate balance between skepticism and credulity. The universe is such a strange and wonderful place that reality will always outrun the wildest imagination; there will always be things unknowable.

Which is very lucky for us; because it means that, whatever other perils humanity may face in the future that lies ahead, boredom is not among them.

Colombo
January 1980

Writing
to Sell

The printed form which my secretary sends out in answer to 95 percent of my mail ends with these uncompromising words:

> So many publishers and authors have asked me to comment on books, or to write prefaces, that I am now forced to turn down *all* such requests, no matter how good the cause.

Introduction to second revised edition of *Writing to Sell*, by Scott Meredith (New York: Harper and Row, 1977). Some of the book synopses at the end were originally published in *The Worm Runner's Digest* Vol. XIV, No. 2, 1972.

Now Scott Meredith jolly well *knows* this, for his office also sends out skillions of these forms in the hope of heading the mailman off at the pass. So what the heck am I doing here?

I'll tell you exactly how it happened. It began with a phone call to Scott from my dear friend Isaac Asimov. "Scott," he said desperately, "I'm only 150 books ahead of Arthur—he's catching up. If you can slow him down just a bit, I'll give you the Lower Slobovian Second Serial Rights of *Asimov's Guide to Cricket*—without TV residuals, of course."

"Throw in that illustrated Braille *Kama Sutra* I know you're working on," Scott replied instantly, "and you have a deal."

"Done," said Isaac; whereupon Scott merely threatened to give my address to 589 people who want to know the real and secret message in *2001: A Space Odyssey*, and here I am...

It was, for heaven's sake, just over a quarter of a century ago that Scott and I first met in person as I stepped off the ocean liner (remember them?) onto the sacred concrete of Manhattan. At that time he looked about eighteen and wasn't *too* much older than that, and was thus only the second- or third-best literary agent in the United States; he was also still in a state of shock over the fact that he'd cabled to say that my book, *The Exploration of Space*, had just become a Book-of-the Month Club selection, and I'd replied by asking innocently, "What *is* the Book-of-the-Month Club?" And it's quite a shock to me, so many years later, to look at the copyright page and realize that he had already written, and Harper had already published, the first edition of the volume you, gentle would-be writer, are now holding in your hands....

Yet another shock, while we are about it. On going through what I laughingly refer to as my records, I've just discovered that it was thirty years ago next month that I sent Scott my first submission—the short story that later became the opening for *Childhood's End*. (See below.) I've long since forgiven him for insisting that it be rewritten; it probably needed it....

It sometimes seems to me that every writer I know is

represented by Scott, and acquired his basic skills as a staffer at Scott's agency.

I'm exaggerating, of course; I *know* that Norman Mailer and Ernest K. Gann and Jessica Mitford and Ellery Queen and Carl Sagan and Taylor Caldwell and hundreds of other Scott Meredith clients never worked for him. But he certainly seems to have had a hand in the beginnings and development of an apparently endless list of authors of present-day bestsellers. There's Harry Kemelman, for whose first novel Scott was only able to get an advance of $1000, but whose most recent contract—also, of course, negotiated by him—was for $475,000. There's Hank Searls, whose first sale via Scott was a short story to a now-defunct magazine for $50, and whose new novel, *Overboard*, is a best-seller, a selection of the Literary Guild, Reader's Digest Book Club and four other book clubs, with the paperback rights selling for hundreds of thousands of dollars, a bestseller in a dozen other countries as well, and a forthcoming motion picture. There's also the young Englishman named Clarke who came to Scott in 1947 with that short story which Scott sold, as I recall it, for $70, and whose most recent novel, *Imperial Earth*, was sold by Scott for—well, a bit more than that. And the list goes on and on.

Incidentally, Scott is no longer at 580 Fifth Avenue, his company address for twenty-six years, where I first met him; his agency has moved to larger quarters at 845 Third Avenue. However, the "scarred and lacerated spot on the wall" against which he beats his head from time to time, as mentioned in chapter 27, has been carefully framed and moved to the new premises. When he is not using it, he pretends it's a Jackson Pollock on loan from the Metropolitan Museum of Art.

In all seriousness, I do not believe that *any* writer, however experienced he may fondly consider himself to be, could fail to benefit from this book. The fact that it is also highly entertaining doesn't do any harm; several times, I found myself laughing out loud. It says a good deal for Scott's sense of humor that it has survived so many decades of contact with authors . . . not to mention editors.

It would be impertinent of me to add anything to Scott's hard-won advice—so, I'll be impertinent.

It's always seemed to me that the biggest single problem any author has to face is: When should I give up? Scott would say, "Never!" and, as he describes in "Inspiration, Perspiration, Desperation," he has a special padded cell, equipped only with typewriter and a good supply of paper, in which he occasionally locks up authors to prove this theory. But it really isn't as simple as that.

Agreed, authors have an amazing capacity for inventing excuses not to work. (Mine is a beautiful little monkey who cries piteously if not loved every hour, on the hour.) But there are times when no amount of staring at the typewriter and sweating blood will produce anything except frustration; you must learn to recognize those times.

Then you have two choices; you can switch to writing *something completely different* or, if that doesn't work, you must quit altogether. It was, I believe, Hemingway who said, "Writing is not a full-time occupation." That's true in more ways than one. You must live before you can write. And you must live *while* you are writing. But you mustn't kid yourself and make excuses to stop work by confusing laziness with that old standby "lack of inspiration." There is a lot of truth in the hard saying "A professional can write even when he doesn't feel like it. An amateur can't—even when he *does*."

The other big problem is to know when a job is finished. Sorry about all these quotations, but this is the most important yet: "No work of art is ever finished; it is only abandoned."

Old-time pros may snort indignantly at this; racing deadlines, they couldn't afford the time even for a second draft. Lester del Rey—another thoroughbred from the Scott Meredith stables, another staff editor at the agency who became and remains a Scott Meredith client—could sit at the typewriter and produce, *within two hours,* a pretty good six-thousand-word story. That's real professionalism, which I can only view with incredulous awe.

On another occasion, Lester sat down after breakfast and mailed off a twenty-thousand-word novelette the same night. He admits that it might have been better if he'd left it until next morning...but would it have been all that *much* better? You can go on tinkering and revising and polishing forever; sometimes it is as hard to *stop* work on a piece as it was to start in the first place. But unless you're a poet turning out one slim volume every twenty years, you must learn to recognize the point of diminishing returns and send your 99.99 percent completed masterpiece out into the cruel hard world. There's nothing wrong with amateurism (in the best sense of that misused word); but all serious artists are interested in money. And that means all *great* artists, too; take a look someday at Beethoven's correspondence with the London Philharmonic.

I'm in a generous mood this morning, possibly because of the $0.87 quarterly check I've just received for my five shares of COMSAT stock. So here, to give you inspiration, are a few ideas for books that I feel *somebody* ought to write. They cover a pretty wide range—biography, history, crime, science fiction, medicine—with a couple of guaranteed best-sellers thrown in:

JONATHAN LIVINGSTONE SEA-SLUG

The inspirational saga of one of nature's humblest organisms, an adventurous Abominable Sea Slug (*Mucus horribilis*). Jonathan, born—or rather, fissioned—in a sewer outlet off Flushing, feels a dim impulse for higher things and conceives the brave ambition of slithering upward to the glorious world above the waves. Unfortunately, despite the amazing camouflage which makes him almost indistinguishable from his surroundings, Jonathan is eaten by an even more revolting creature, the Squamous Scavenger Fish (*Scatophagus vomitous*), before completing his odyssey.

SCREAMING FLESH

The memoirs of a famous surgeon, pioneer of navel transplants, who is knighted by a grateful government when his revolutionary "brain by-pass" operation transforms the fortunes of a political party. The author recalls, with brutal frankness and in loving clinical detail, carefree days as a young medical student in the Terminal Accident Ward at St. Sepulchre's. Though there are lighter moments—such as the hilarious episode of the electrified bedpans—sensitive readers may not get past Chapter 2, which gives the book its striking title.

SUNSET ON THE BOULEVARD.

A moving account of the rescue work carried out by a rescue mission among the poor of Bel Air and Beverly Hills in the years following the Final Depression. There are harrowing stories of the destitute drinking the last drops of water in their swimming pools; maddened by hunger, trying to open Andy Warhol soup cans—and finally succumbing to fatal sunburn when the protective smog above Los Angeles vanishes.

DEFENDER OF THE DOOMED

The aptly entitled autobiography of the famous criminal lawyer whose courtroom exploits—hopefully—are never likely to be equaled. The author tells how he fought to save no less than ninety-eight clients from the gas chamber or electric chair—and lost them all. Now, for the first time, we learn exactly how he did it.

If you can't find something in *this* to trigger your imagination, perhaps you'd better stick to running your father's pre-stressed liverwurst business.

Just one minor point. Scott and I would *each* like 10 percent of the loot.

And 0 percent of the lawsuits.

Arthur C. Clarke

IV

From the Coast of Coral

Beneath the Indian Ocean

When you look at the map of India, you will see the island of Ceylon hanging from its southern tip like a teardrop or a pendant, pear-shaped jewel. It is the last outpost of the Northern Hemisphere; beyond it, across the equator and all the way to the icy walls of Antarctica, lies the greatest unexplored region of this world—the Indian Ocean. Though men have sailed it for at least three thousand years, the early mariners seldom ventured far from land. Even today, the

Originally published as "Ceylon: An Adventurer's Retreat" in *True Magazine*, April 1972, pp. 39, 42, 43.

only ships you are likely to find in the southern half of this great blank on the map are research vessels and the occasional whaler. The depths of the Indian Ocean may still hold their mysteries long after we have walked on the outermost of the planets.

Sea and space—to me these are two sides of the same coin. Looking back upon the last three decades, I now realize that it was my interest in astronautics that led me to the ocean. The process seems so inevitable that I grow more than a little impatient with those people who ask: "What *are* you doing underwater when you've written so many books about exploring space?"

Well, both involve exploration—but that's not the only reason. When the first skin-diving equipment started to appear in the late 1940s, I suddenly realized that here was a cheap and simple way of imitating one of the most magical aspects of spaceflight—"weightlessness." In those days, many physiologists were firmly convinced that the apparent absence of gravity would be fatal to the human organism: the blood would rush to the head, vertigo would be incapacitating, the heart would race out of control, etc., etc. We "space cadets," on the other hand, were equally certain that weightlessness would be a delightful experience—as, on the whole, it has turned out to be.

I can remember when I had learned to use the basic flipper-and-face-mask gear, how I used to dive to the bottom of the local swimming pool, close my eyes and spin around in the water until I had deliberately disoriented myself. Then I used to imagine that I was a space-man and ask myself the question, "Which way is up?" I never dreamed that, twenty years later, I would be taking *real* spacemen underwater.

In due course I graduated to scuba gear and to the open sea. (Well, to the English Channel, which in those days was not carpeted—top and bottom—with oil-tankers.) And in 1954 I sailed to Australia to write a book about the Great Barrier Reef—the largest coral formation in the world, and probably the only object of organic origin on this planet which is visible from the Moon.

In those days there *was* a Suez Canal, and the Pacific and Orient liner *Himalaya* stopped for an afternoon in Colombo, the capital and chief port of Ceylon. There was just time for a visit to the world-famous zoo, where I met the assistant director, Rodney Jonklaas—a trained zoologist and the only expert skin diver I know who *never* uses a snorkel (I think he can breathe through the back of his neck). He convinced me that if I survived the perils of the Great Barrier Reef, I should look at the seas of Ceylon. In 1956 I followed his advice, never imagining that I would get hooked and would make the island my home. For the last fifteen years I have left it only with great reluctance, and only for unavoidable reasons.

But Ceylon, although it is much better off than India, Pakistan and newly formed Bangladesh, is no earthly paradise; it has serious social and economic problems. Like New York, it is a fascinating place to visit, but anyone considering permanent residency should think twice. He must be prepared to face acute shortages of consumer goods—film, razor blades, suntan lotion, carbon paper, records—all the little necessities of life we take for granted in the West. Too, unless he has a fondness for ferocious curries, he may find the food rather monotonous. And, of course, it is very hot for much of the year, though the presence of the sea—never more than sixty miles away—has a moderating influence, and the hundred-plus extremes found in India are very rare. I have never been as uncomfortable in Ceylon as I have been in, say, Washington, DC.

Because the island is so close to the equator, the length of the day hardly varies throughout the year; it is always dark by 7 P.M., and there is not much to do after sunset. A few cinemas and modest nightclubs provide the available entertainment—and there is, as yet, no television. You're on your own as soon as the sun commits its spectacular nightly suicide.

I long ago accepted these disadvantages, such as they are; indeed, to a writer, many of them are positive boons. Over the years I have built up a large library, and, if all else fails, the Great Books could keep me busy until the 1980s. For other stimuli I have a small computer, a beloved German shepherd named Sputnik, a battery of cameras and a fully equipped darkroom, a Questar telescope and a thousand miles of coastline to explore. Thanks to good roads most of it is easily accessible, which is more than can be said of the Great Barrier Reef's immense coral universe.

During my first ten years in Ceylon, my colleague Mike Wilson and I collected material for several books and three underwater movies, starring Rodney Jonklaas and incredible numbers of fish. We visited the famous pearl beds between Ceylon and India (we didn't find any pearls, being too busy taking photographs) and explored the enormous harbor to Trincomalee, on the east coast of the island. For sixteen years, "Trinco" boasted one of the largest and most unusual wrecks in the world—a one-thousand-foot-long floating dock which was accidentally sunk during World War II while holding the thirty-thousand-ton battleship *Valiant*. The disaster was one of the British navy's most humiliating self-inflicted wounds, and the Lords of the Admiralty are still somewhat sensitive on the subject.

If you can imagine the Brooklyn Bridge sunk and full of fish—including groupers in the four-hundred-pound class—you may guess what it was like to dive along the submerged catwalks and soaring metal cliffs of this gigantic wreck. Alas, early in 1970 a determined entrepreneur managed to salvage two thirds of the dock and towed it away for scrap. About three hundred feet of the monster still remains, though at rather too great a depth for comfortable skin diving.

However, another of Trinco's unique attractions is more permanent. Around the base of a spectacular headland known as Swami Rock lie dozens of carved blocks, columns and porticos, cast centuries ago into the sea by earthquakes or landslides. This has long been a favorite diving site of mine, and in the summer of 1971 I took Commander Donald Walsh, USN, to visit it. Ten years earlier, Walsh had taken the bathyscaphe *Trieste* seven miles down into the Pacific on the deepest dive man has ever made—or ever will make, unless someone digs a deeper hole. (He lost his submariner's extra pay in the process, for the *Trieste* did not qualify as a submarine under navy regulations.) Our operations aroused a good deal of local interest, and when we got back to Colombo we found that an imaginative journalist had credited us with the discovery of Atlantis. Some other time, perhaps. . . .

Thousands of years of maritime commerce have left Ceylon surrounded by wrecks; it is virgin territory for the underwater archaeologist, and no one can guess what treasures lie off its shores. They will not be easy to find—in warm, tropical waters a wooden ship disintegrates within a few decades, and any remaining fragments of metal soon become disguised by a coating of coral.

Yet in 1961, by a combination of luck and skill, Mike Wilson discovered a 250-year-old wreck with all the storybook fittings—guns, cannon balls, a couple of dueling pistols, tens of thousands of beautiful silver coins—all straight from the mint of Surat (near Bombay) and bearing the Muslim date 1113 (A.D. 1702). We estimate that there is still a thousand pounds of silver in this wreck, which we have never been able to identify. I have thoughtfully given a map of the exact location in *The Treasure of the Great Reef*. We have also made arrangements with local authorities for the reception of unauthorized visitors.

A slightly more modern wreck lies in deeper water—near the safe limits of scuba diving—off the east coast of the island. H.M.S. *Hermes* was the first aircraft carrier ever built; she also has the ironic distinction of being the only British carrier to be sunk by aircraft, following an attack by the Japanese on 9 April 1942. For many years her location was uncertain, but Rodney Jonklaas was able to lead Peter Gimbel to her during his quest for the great white shark. The remarkable movie *Blue Water, White Death* contains several sequences shot at night in the gloomy recesses of the *Hermes*. She is a spectacular wreck but one I have no desire to visit; the currents are dangerous, and even a careful diver like Gimbel managed to get himself "bent" while working there.

While on the subject of sharks, it is a curious fact they have never killed even one diver or swimmer in the waters round Ceylon. Yet the island is almost at the center of the world-girdling "shark attack zone" which occupies the area between the Tropics of Cancer and Capricorn I have no plausible theory to explain this phenomenon, a fortunate one for the underwater tourist business.

A few years ago I started just such a business in an effort to get some mileage from all the expensive scuba gear gathering rust in my garage. Though "Underwater Safaris" hasn't paid the rent, it has given my Sinhalese companion Hector Ekanayake and me a lot of fun. Our most distinguished clients are undoubtedly the *Apollo 12* astronauts—Pete Conrad, Alan Bean and Dick Gordon—whom we took diving on an old wreck in Trincomalee Harbor. Recalling what had happened to the TV coverage on their mission, when I handed Alan Bean one of our underwater cameras I begged him: "Alan—*please* don't point it at the sun." He did not seem much amused.

Like all poor, developing countries, Ceylon is desperately trying to attract tourists, and dollar for dollar probably offers one of the best bargains in the world. Its wildlife and animal reservations are outstanding; with reasonable luck, the visitor can see elephants, crocodiles, leopards, bears and innumerable varieties of birds, all in a single afternoon. And besides its natural resources, the island can show the evidence of twenty-five centuries of continuous civilization and culture. Some of the great Buddhist shrines and ruined cities are contemporary with Rome.

I sometimes wonder if, in extolling Ceylon's charms, I am not helping to destroy them. The jumbo jets are already descending upon Colombo's Katunayake Airport, and the click of the Nikon is heard throughout the land. But there are still hundreds of miles of beach no tourist has ever seen, and virgin reefs where the fish gather round the diver with such fearless curiosity that he has to push them away before he can use his camera.

I am on my way to such a reef now, just before the first freezing winter fogs start drifting in from the Atlantic. It lies around a group of rocks half a mile out from a crescent arc of beach almost too perfect to be true—a classical composition of white sand, graceful palms and pure blue water.

There must be lost ships out there on the reef, because during the monsoon seasons those rocks are covered with a boiling mass of foam from which every few minutes walls of spray erupt twenty or thirty feet into the air. But from November through March there are days and weeks when the sea lies, all fury spent, smooth as oiled silk under the sun. Then the reef can no longer guard its secrets—whatever they may be.

For years that reef at Unawatuna has been a perpetual challenge to me—as the hidden side of the Moon was to astronomers before the age of space. I have never been able to reach it because I have always had to dash off to London or New York or some other place before I could take advantage of the calm season. But this *time*, I promise myself...

And if the monsoon frustrates me again there will be other opportunities. Impatience is a Western vice which cannot survive beneath the equatorial sun. The reef can wait, and so can I; there is no age limit to diving. I still intend to be snorkling down among the corals—even in the year 2001.

The
Last
Wilderness

A world which contained only human beings would not be worth living in; nor would it be habitable for very long. This is a lesson that our urban-centered, technologically oriented culture is painfully relearning, though our ancestors knew it well enough. A holy man once told the ruler of Ceylon: "O great King, the birds of the air and the beasts have as equal right to live and move about in any part of this land as thou. The land belongs

Originally published as "Sri Lanka's Wildlife Heritage" in *National Geographic Magazine*, August 1983.

to the people and all other beings; thou art only the guardian of it."

That was twenty-five centuries ago, when coexistence of man and beast presented few problems. But in the last twenty-five *years* the (human) population of Ceylon—now Sri Lanka—has doubled. Though the small island is not yet overcrowded, and much of its natural beauty is still intact, it now provides textbook examples of many modern dilemmas: development versus environment; farm versus forest; indigenous culture versus tourism....

It is impossible to return to the past, and no one would really wish to do so. For centuries, Ceylon's population was kept steady by the malaria-carrying mosquito: there are some forms of wildlife that should *not* be conserved. But there are countless beautiful, harmless and often valuable creatures whose very existence is now threatened by greed, indifference or ignorance. (And even by superstition: one local tortoise is prized for its flesh—those who eat it believe that their skin becomes equally well armored against injury!)

The elephant is, of course, the most spectacular as well as the most famous of Sri Lanka's animals; its enormous appetite for succulent greenstuffs puts it into direct competition with the farmer. It is impossible not to feel sympathy for a small cultivator who may be ruined overnight by a marauding herd—and can one blame him if he loads a blunderbuss with rusty nails to protect his crops? Fortunately the elephant is so useful—and so revered—that it is probably safe from total extinction.

But remembering what happened to the incalculable billions of passenger pigeons in the United States only a century ago, one cannot help fearing for the future of Sri Lanka's smaller and less publicized animals as the forests are cleared, the coral reefs smashed up to make lime, and the new industrial estates pollute land, air and water. Though some creatures seem to thrive in man-made environments, they are usually the less attractive representatives of the animal kingdom: crows, sparrows, rats, cockroaches... the beautiful birds and butterflies, the shy loris, the handsome leopard and its elegant prey the spotted deer all vanish before the advancing bulldozer. As do my own favorites of Sri Lanka's forest dwellers—its mischievous yet endearing monkey people. I still grieve for Silkie, a baby langur who spent most of her brief life nestled inside my shirt.

It has been wisely said that in wilderness is the preservation of the world. In Sri Lanka, we are engaged in the preservation of wilderness. For as King Devanampiyatissa was told five centuries before the birth of Christ, we are its guardians—*not* its owners.

The People of the Sea

I feel slightly apologetic in opening this Symposium, as I am certainly no expert on marine mammals, though I have sometimes considered myself one of them. My interest in the subject is strictly amateur and my experience very limited—and indeed rather uncomfortable. Once, while swimming off Hawaii, I was chased out of the water by a dolphin named Le-Le. There was no personal resentment on Le-Le's part, I hasten to add, but the researchers working with her

Keynote Address to the Symposium on Marine Mammals of the Indian Ocean, arranged by the National Aquatic Resources Agency, Sri Lanka, at Mount Lavinia Hotel, 22 February 1983.

had made several mistakes in the experimental program, so she'd just got fed up with stupid humans in general. I can assure you that it is a rather traumatic experience, seeing a large open mouth set with efficient-looking teeth approaching at high speed through the water, even if you are—fairly—sure that they didn't intend to bite you. At least, not very hard. . . .

Although I have dealt with whales and dolphins in two books—*The Deep Range* and *Dolphin Island*—they were written more than twenty years ago, and quite a lot has happened in that time. However, *The Deep Range*, published in 1957, is perhaps now even more topical than when it was written, since its main theme is whale conservation—and the attitude of the Maha Sangha toward the slaughter of animals, a subject which is still regularly featured in the papers here.

Dolphin Island was written a few years later, in 1962, and is set on Heron Island in the Great Barrier Reef, where I was one of the first SCUBA divers to visit in 1955. When I wrote it, I was quite impressed by the studies that had been made on the intelligence of dolphins—but now I have doubts on the subject. It seems to me that they cannot be *really* intelligent—they are much too friendly to man. . . .

More seriously, there is another argument against the intelligence of dolphins and many types of whales—the extraordinary and still mysterious way in which they permit themselves to become stranded on sloping beaches and trapped in fishing nets from which it would seem fairly easy to escape. Would really intelligent animals be fooled so often and so easily?

However, let us not feel too superior. What would intelligent visitors from space think of our nuclear arms race, in which so-called great power A feels insecure and in need of increased armaments because it can only destroy great power B a hundred times over, while B can destroy it one hundred and ten times over? I doubt if any of the marine mammals can match *that* degree of stupidity.

Yet whatever the truth about the exact level of intelligence among marine mammals, there are other attributes perhaps even more important. Many of us will admit that some of our nicest friends aren't all that bright, but then, we don't like them for their brains, but their characters and personalities. Strange though it may seem to use these terms of a mammal whose way of life is so different from ours, there's almost unanimous agreement that in the presence of dolphins—especially when swimming among them—people feel happy and relaxed—even joyful.

And this is not true only of the dolphins. It really is remarkable how charming and delightful most marine mammals are. The seals and walruses, the sea otters, the dugongs, the blue whales—most of the animals that have gone back to the sea, whether on a temporary or a full-time basis—seem to have characteristics that make them particularly endearing—friendlier than most land animals. Even the much-maligned killer whale has turned out to be astonishingly gentle.

In *Dolphin Island*, back in 1962, I felt I was risking ridicule by having my hero actually ride a killer whale. Now it's a regular act in oceanaria—and the trainer even put his—or often her—head inside the animal's mouth, between those huge teeth. I once saw a hair-raising television film in which a girl trainer was grabbed by a killer whale, who got hold of her by the leg and wouldn't let her go until her colleagues had prised open his jaws. He was just lonely and didn't want her to leave! I'm happy to say that the brave girl was back in the tank the next day.

There has certainly been a revolution in public attitudes toward marine mammals, as a direct result of underwater movies like Jacques Cousteau's famous films, the popularity of oceanaria and the explosion of interest in diving as a sport or hobby. I often wonder what Herman Melville would have thought of today's campaign to save the whale—especially the sperm whale, that ferocious monster he described so vividly in *Moby Dick*. I suspect he'd now wryly agree with that ironic French saying: "This animal is very vicious—when attacked, it defends itself."

How is it that we can so easily make friends with large and powerful carnivores in the sea—when we wouldn't dream of doing so on land? Anyone who behaved toward a lion, a tiger or a polar bear as divers have done countless times toward sperm whales, killer whales and dolphins wouldn't come back to tell the tale. I've never seen an answer to this question; perhaps someone at this symposium can enlighten me.

An even greater enigma is presented by the musical repertoire of the humpback whale, something unique in nature. In comparison, all bird songs are simple; they last only seconds, and are repeated mechanically year by year (though there are regional variations—perhaps the equivalent of human dialects). But whale songs last up to half an hour, and *change style in successive years*. To quote from Roger Payne's article in the January 1979 *National Geographic Magazine* (which incidentally features Sri Lanka in the same issue!), whales "compose as they go along, incorporating new elements into their old songs. We are aware of no other animal besides man in which this strange and complicated behavior occurs, and we have no idea of the reason behind it. If you listen to songs from two different years you will be astonished to hear how different they are. The songs we taped in 1964 and 1969 are as different as Beethoven from the Beatles."

Let's listen to them and judge for ourselves*.... The amount of information contained in one of these songs must be considerable; at a rough estimate, several kilobytes—the capacity of a small computer. How is it stored? What is its purpose? If they are intended merely for location, identification, warning, mating, these songs seem far more elaborate than necessity. After all, the birds manage rather well with a much simpler repertoire.... Are the humpback whales *really* musicians?

Astonishingly, they have turned out to be toolmakers—as far as we know, the only ones in the ocean. (Though the sea otters use stones to smash open sea urchins, that's tool-*using*, not toolmaking, a fundamentally different thing.)

How can an animal without hands—or their equivalent—make tools? (I've often wondered if the octopus or the squid may start to do this some day, if indeed it hasn't

---

*At this and other points in the talk, I played extracts from the recording bound into the January 1979 *National Geographic Magazine*.

already happened.) Well, the humpback whale uses its lungs, because the tool it creates is a very temporary one—made of air. It's a net of bubbles, designed to trap the shrimplike krill and small fish on which the whale feeds.

To quote again from the *National Geographic*: "Like a giant undersea spider spinning its web, the humpback begins perhaps fifty feet deep, forcing bursts of air through its blowhole while swimming in an upward spiral. Big bubbles, followed by a mist of tiny ones, rise to create a cylindrical screen that concentrates krill and small fish. Bubbles and food pop to the surface, followed by the gaping mouth of the whale as it emerges in the center of its net... two animals sometimes collaborate on a net perhaps a hundred feet across...."

I don't think anyone would have believed this, if Al Giddings hadn't photographed it. But seeing is believing—and so is listening. Here is a humpback whale spinning its net of bubbles.

Did the songs evolve from this technique, even though they are far more elaborate than any practical purpose would justify? (Exactly as we have gone from the simple vocalizations of human language, all the way to grand opera—though the latter certainly isn't absolutely necessary for our survival.) Whatever the explanation, their songs can link us emotionally to the humpback whales perhaps even more strongly than to the dolphins.

And it is a strange thought that the songs of the humpback whales are now, literally, on the way to the stars. The two Voyager spacecraft which flew by Jupiter and Saturn in 1979 carried with them gold-plated records on which were stored many of the characteristic sounds of earth, and messages in many languages. In his *Murmurs of Earth*, Dr. Carl Sagan tells how he contacted Roger Payne—some of whose recordings you have just heard. To quote Carl: "He was very excited by our desire to extend whale greetings on the record. When I told him that as a long overdue gesture of respect for these intelligent co-residents of Earth, we wished to include their salutations among those of the statesmen and diplomats, he was thrilled. He cried: "Wonderful! You can have everything I have. The most beautiful whale greeting was the one we heard off the coast of Bermuda in 1970. That's the one that should last forever." And so it was placed, with the other messages, aboard the two Voyagers.

In the benign and changeless environment of space, these records will still exist when all the other artifacts of man have been eroded by time and even the Earth itself has been consumed by the Sun when it goes nova at the end of its evolutionary sequence. So perhaps, millions of years hence, this song will be heard again, by creatures we cannot imagine, when they encounter our primitive space probe. And as Dr. Sagan remarks, how ironic it will be, if extraterrestrials a billion years hence grasp a message from fellow earthlings that has been incomprehensible to us.

Tourism: The Challenge of Change

In the widest sense of the word, including religious pilgrimages, tourism must be one of mankind's oldest recreations. The earliest tourist I can think of is Noah, though perhaps he was an involuntary one. It might even be argued that the tourist agent is a member of the *second*-oldest profession. . . .

But tourism, as we think of it now, is almost entirely

Keynote Address at Pacific Area Travel Association Workshop, Colombo, 19 January 1978. The quotation from COMSAT General's magazine *Marifacts* was first published in Vol 3, No.3, October 1977, p. 3 (reprinted in Vol. 7, No. 3, December 1981, pp. 6–7).

a by-product of modern technology, and is being continually changed by it. The steamship and the railway gave the first great impetus more than a hundred years ago; you will find that well recorded in the nonfiction writings of Mark Twain and Charles Dickens, amongst countless others. But perhaps the writer whom you should regard as your patron saint is Jules Verne. His *Round the World in Eighty Days*—published 105 years ago—had an immense impact. It made the folk back in the 1870s realize that they could see a great deal of the world, in reasonable comfort and safety, without sacrificing a large fraction of a lifetime to do so. I often wonder what Verne would have thought, could he have known that one day we would go round the world not only in eighty *hours*—but in eighty *minutes*... well, ninety....

Just thirty years after Verne's classic, in 1903, the first airplane staggered into the air for a few seconds. I very much doubt if anyone here, if he'd been watching the Wright brothers on that historic day, would have believed that their flimsy kite could have the slightest impact upon the tourist industry. Well...it would be interesting to have a poll, right now, of all the delegates in this hall who did *not* come here by airplane. I doubt if they'd fill one Microbus.

This certainly represents a revolutionary change, and it's occurred in three stages. First there was the propeller era—the DC3, and later the Constellations and DC6's. They started the age of aerial tourism, yet how primitive they already seem!

The introduction of the jets in the late 1950s, by doubling speed and more than doubling comfort, was the quantum jump that brought us to the period we're in at the present. And the third era—that of supersonic flight—is now having its painful birth.

The Concorde is the DC3 of the supersonic age—the necessary first step, and a vast improvement on anything that went before. I love the jumbos, but I don't mind telling you that if I've got to travel more than a couple of thousand kilometers, I'm going by Concorde—or I'm not going at all! So that gives me yet another good excuse not to leave Sri Lanka....

In another generation, when the bigger, faster, *quieter*

and more economical supersonics start doing to the Pacific what the jets did to the Atlantic, everyone will wonder what all the fuss was about. The people who opposed Concorde will look rather like those legislators who once insisted that a man carrying a red warning flag should walk in front of any motor car that ventured on the public highway.

Looking at the opposite end of the speed range—and perhaps a lot further into the future, maybe fifty or a hundred years because the factors here are economic rather than technical—I think it's quite likely that the passenger-carrying *airship* may make a comeback. Those who flew in them swear that the *Graf Zeppelin* and the *Hindenburg* provided unique standards of silent, luxurious transport. And with helium instead of hydrogen in the gas bags, there would, of course, be no possibility of fire. Even now, we could design perfectly marvelous cruise-airships showing five hundred passengers the world from a height of a couple of kilometers—the exact equivalent of the luxury ocean liner, but at five times the speed.

Communication and Tourism

Since my special interest is communication, in all its aspects, I'd like to say a few words about its impact upon future tourism.

Its *past* impact, of course, is enormous—I've mentioned Dickens and Twain and Verne, and there's a whole mountain of travel literature. This country, incidentally, has a share out of all proportion to its size; I've contributed to it myself, and indeed that's what brought me here in the first place. . . . And I recommend a fascinating book, recently published—*Images of Sri Lanka Through American Eyes*—accounts by travelers in the nineteenth and twentieth centuries, including Mark Twain, Andrew Carnegie, Thomas Merton and many others.

This century has seen the printed page rivaled by two new and highly effective media, cinema and television. The cinema must have contributed enormously to tourism, by showing people places they would like to visit—

and perhaps places they should carefully avoid. An earlier generation probably learned much about the world through James Fitzpatrick's lens…"And so we say farewell to gorgeous Bongo Bongo, as the sun sinks slowly in the east, doing it the hard way.…"

Sri Lanka has contributed to this genre with at least two classics, Basil Wright's *Song of Ceylon*—considered by some the finest documentary ever made—and David Lean's *Bridge on the River Kwai*. I am glad to see that filmmakers are now rediscovering the country;* that impressive lady Ursula Andress was here only a couple of weeks ago.

TV teams are also coming here with increasing frequency, and I'm going to show you an example of their work at the end of this talk. But now I want to ride my special hobby horse, *satellite* communication, because you may not realize how fundamental its effect on tourism has been—and will be in future.

Comsats have totally revolutionized the world telephone service. Three years ago, I sometimes had to book a call to London a couple of days in advance—and even *then* I wasn't sure that I'd be able to hear anything. Now I can get a perfect circuit in five minutes. I'm sure that being able to keep in touch with home and office will encourage tourists to visit places they would never have gone to otherwise. It will certainly help tourist guides and agents!

Which leads me to my next point, and I'd like to quote now from an article I recently wrote in COMSAT General's magazine *Marifacts*:

> A man's life cycle is determined by the technology of his age. Our century has been an explosion of technologies, and therefore, a proliferation of life styles. The automobile and the telephone provide the most striking examples, because they affect everybody. More recently, the rise of the "jet set" demonstrates how a single invention—the gas turbine—may make possible a model of existence which would have been fantasy a mere thirty years earlier.
>
> In 1976, with very little fanfare, another such revolution

---

*Including Steven Spielberg, who plans to make part of the sequel to *Raiders of the Lost Ark* here.

began; and this may ultimately involve a much larger—and more important—sample of humanity than the jet-setters.

It is not generally realized that, despite tremendous advances in electronics, the world's shipping is still in the Morse code era. Sometimes, when conditions in the ionosphere are bad, a ship may be out of touch with land for days on end. Such breakdowns in communication can cost hundreds of thousands of dollars—and occasionally, the entire ship. Even today, no ground radio station could guarantee to alert the *Titanic* in time.

But in early 1976, COMSAT General Corporation launched the two satellites of the Marisat System—one over the Atlantic, one over the Pacific—designed to provide high-quality communications to ships at any time, irrespective of ionospheric conditions. What its parent organization COMSAT has made possible on land—perfect intercontinental telephone calls, global TV—COMSAT General has started to do on the oceans. So far, only telephone and telex can be provided, but eventually everything available on land will be equally available at sea. Consider the implications of this....

A long sea voyage can be a most delightful experience, which many cannot share because of business responsibilities or family ties. The advent of first-class oceanic communications will change this—and may prevent the extinction of that splendid and endangered species, the great ocean liner.

Whole families could take to sea without interrupting the children's education; they could still be taught and graded every day by their friendly school computer, with a little on-board assistance. Retired people could become travelers for years at a time in floating hotels, knowing that they could still keep in touch with their friends and maintain all their intellectual interests; *The New York Times* and the *Wall Street Journal* (already satellite-distributed!) would be available in mid-Pacific as quickly as on Fifth Avenue. Only a few tears would be shed for the passing of that unique phenomenon, the Ship's Newspaper, with its tantalizingly brief glimpses of the outer world. (NEW ZEALAND SINKS IN EARTHQUAKE; BINGO 20.00 HOURS IN MAIN LOUNGE; PRESIDENT OF FRANCE ASSASSINATED; FANCY DRESS PHOTOS ON SALE B DECK. . . .)

Moreover, it might even be cheaper to live this way than on land—especially as voyagers who chose their registry and route with care could become citizens of the open sea, beyond the clutches of the IRS. Imagine the appeal to the businessman who has made it to the top but does not want to retire yet, of the "Luxury Executive Cruise." If he was in a high enough tax bracket, his permanent suite on the QE 2 would pay for itself. He would only have to spend a few hours each morning (or night, depending on the time zone he was in) dealing with the telex messages and making a few phone calls. He could run his business and see the world—while he was still young enough to enjoy it.

This sort of life would have suited the late Howard Hughes perfectly, had it been feasible a few years earlier. (He would have bought the whole ship, of course.) There is a particular irony in this—for the Marisats are built by the Hughes Aircraft Corporation.

There are of course, some people who will think that this is a perfectly dreadful idea, because the whole purpose of a sea voyage is to get-away-from-it-all. However, it will be a decade or so before every ship has these facilities, and many choices will remain for adventurous travelers. For a long time to come, Lower Slobovia's flagship, *Potemkin* (yes, THE *Potemkin*) will welcome up to ten decadent hard-currency passengers, as well as her usual cargo of guano and fermented yak butter.

And after that, of course, Thor Heyerdahl will still have a good line in rafts. . . .

Now let's look a little further ahead to something that I've called Telesafaris—a definite possibility for the next generation.

I envisage groups of perhaps twenty to a hundred people, using wide-screen color TV in their own homes, or perhaps in small local viewing theaters, hiring a guide who would take them on a tour of some exotic place. As he moved around, they would look over his shoulder, ask him questions, request close-ups of interesting objects—in fact share everything except the mosquitoes and the heat without leaving their armchairs! And, of course, if they liked the places they saw, they'd go there in person eventually. I think this kind of sample, or *preview* tourism may become a major industry—just another of the spin-offs from communications satellites.

Probably you're expecting me to say something about space tourism: Well, its exactly twenty-five years ago that I wrote a series of articles about this subject for *Holiday* magazine, and a couple of them have had interesting consequences.

One was called "Journey by Earthlight" and was about

the beginning of lunar tourism, which I put in 2076—
I'm sure that's *much* too pessimistic! I later worked this
material into a novel, *Earthlight*—and when they landed
on the Moon, the *Apollo 15* astronauts named a small
crater after this book and drove past in their lunar rover.
One of my proudest possessions is the relief map of this
area, with Earthlight marked, that Scott, Worden and
Irwin autographed and sent to me after their mission.

Another of the *Holiday* articles was about a vacation
in an orbiting space station. Ten years later, I was able
to get Stanley Kubrick to build the place I'd described—
the Orbiter Hilton—in our movie *2001*. Baron Hilton
was fond of showing slides of it...one day, it will exist.
After all, the space shuttle will start to take *passengers*—
not specially trained astronauts—up into orbit only two
years from now!* I recently told the new NASA administrator that the only thing that will get me back to the
States is the guarantee of a seat.

But let's return to Earth—and to Sri Lanka. Or at least
to the seas around it.

Another article I wrote for *Holiday* back in 1953 was
called "Underwater Safari." In that I described the "Reef
Hotel," where tourists could sit inside and watch the fish
or go out with diving gear. This sort of thing is obviously
possible right now, and I believe that some close approaches to it already exist.

Diving tours are already very big business, of course—
one unimagined before Cousteau and Gagnan invented
the Aqualung, about thirty-five years ago. Except, again,
by our old friend Jules Verne.

And I never dreamed, myself, that one day I would be
technical advisor for a company bearing the name of that
1954 *Holiday* magazine article—"Underwater Safaris"! I
hope that when you visit Coral Gardens, Hikkaduwa, you
go out in the glass-bottomed boat that we operate there.

But I don't know how much longer we'll be able to
run it. The reef, though still beautiful, is only a shadow
of its former glory. I suggest that when you drive south
along the Galle Road, you slow down at ninety kilometers
to observe one of the more unbelievable—but unadver-

*In 1983, it is *still* two years from now....

tised—attractions of this country. You will see small armies of men smashing up the reefs, piling up the coral by the roadside and burning it for lime—much of it to build tourist hotels! This is completely illegal and results in the government's having to spend millions for coast defenses to replace the ruined reefs. In some cases, you can see the coral miners actually working in the shelter of the protective groins!

Jacques Cousteau and Hans Hass have been pointing out for years the damage we are inflicting on the marine environment, and tourism may, I am afraid, add to it. And I am sorry, but the splendid sport of spear-fishing must be totally banned and any guns confiscated—at least in coastal areas or around small islands. (In the deep sea, it may be another matter.) So must shell, coral and tropical fish collecting, which have also been responsible for the ruin of many reefs.

So perhaps the *greatest* challenge to the tourist industry is this: How can it avoid destroying the attractions which are the very basis of its existence? You can all think of cases, I'm sure, where this has happened. I hope that the authorities here are aware of this danger, and will cooperate with you in avoiding it.

Finally, I'd like to close by showing you more of Sri Lanka in seven minutes than most of its inhabitants see in a lifetime. This film was put together for the Bell System when they asked me to host a TV special* celebrating the centennial of the telephone.

It includes the two main commercials I did—the second is probably the longest in the history of TV, almost three minutes! It was seen in about 40 million U.S. households last year, and I hope you'll admire the cunning way I duped the innocent Americans into paying for a commercial on Sri Lanka, when they *thought* that they were getting one on communications.

Ayu Bowan...

---

*This was the latest version of "The Man in the Iron Mask," starring Richard Chamberlain.

The Menace of Creationism

Today's mail brings a letter from a school-teacher in Anchorage, Alaska, with the request: "My students have been interested in the debate surrounding Evolution versus Creation. I would value your opinion...."

As it happens, my first scientific hobby was fossil-collecting, and I didn't gravitate toward astronomy until the ripe age of ten or so. But I always retained an interest in paleontology, which was considerably heightened when I met Louis and Richard Leakey during the production of *2001: A Space Odyssey*.

On that occasion, Dr. Leakey confided to me that he had written a play about an anthropologist who is sent back into the past by an African witch doctor, so that he can observe the origin of man. He would have been delighted to see how close his son came to achieving this in the magical opening of *The Making of Mankind*—where, in one breathtaking sequence, it seems that the TV camera has indeed gone back to the Dawn of Man, to gaze directly into the eyes of our ancestors.

But to return to the Alaskan teacher's question: the blunt answer is that Evolution versus Creationism is not a matter of *opinion*—mine or anyone else's. Evolution is a FACT, period.

What *is* a matter of opinion is Darwinism. That is a THEORY—and it's unfortunate that many people (sometimes deliberately, sometimes ignorantly) confuse the two.

The FACT of Evolution is now almost as well established as the shape of the Earth—which, incidentally, is still denied by some religious fanatics, because there are several passages in the Bible which imply that the Earth is flat. Of course, no one can *disprove* the hypothesis that the world was created six thousand years ago—or for that matter six thousand *seconds* ago!—so that it now appears as it is, complete with faked fossils and an infinite wealth of phoney yet utterly convincing evidence indicating an age of millions of years. But such a theory is also impossible to *prove*; and why should God perpetuate such a gigantic fraud—such an insult to the intelligence which is our noblest attribute?

As a tragicomic footnote to the history of science, the nineteenth-century naturalist Philip Gosse attempted to reconcile the fossil record with Genesis, by just such intellectual contortions—but even the pious Victorians laughed his book *Omphalos* to scorn. If there *is* such a crime as blasphemy, belief in this form of "Creationism" comes close to it. Einstein summed up the situation perfectly: "The Good Lord is subtle, but never malicious."

I find it almost incredible—and indeed tragic—that any intelligent person can possibly find the slightest threat to his religious beliefs in the concept of Evolution, or the immense vistas of time opened up by geology and astronomy. On the contrary—they are infinitely more awe-inspiring and wonderful than the primitive (though often fascinating and beautiful) myths of our ancestors. Indeed, some devout Christians (e.g., the Jesuit priest Dr. Teilhard de Chardin, to give the best-known example) have made them the very basis of their own faith.

So why do people who call themselves Christians object to Evolution? I suspect that the reason isn't very flattering: it damages their ego—their sense of self-importance. That same impulse made their counterparts, four hundred years ago, refuse to accept the now indisputable facts of astronomy.

That famous act of stubborn stupidity by the Catholic Church (though let's be fair—Galileo was a cantankerous genius who practically insisted on martyring himself, despite the attempts of his many clerical friends to stop him) did more than any other event in history to destroy the credibility of the Christian religion. It also brought Italian science to a full stop for centuries—a chilling reminder of what a victory for Creationism could do to American education.

And to American industry and security! It is not generally realized that there are also matters of enormous practical, commercial and even *strategic* importance involved in the Evolution-Creationism debate—it's not merely(!) a matter of religious belief. The discovery of new mineral resources and oil fields is now a branch of applied geology—a science which cannot be studied rationally without an understanding of the time scales and mechanisms involved. Although I've no doubt that there *are* some geologists who think that everything began around 4000 B.C., I'd invest in their companies just about as readily as I'd trust myself to an airline navigator who believes that the Earth is flat.

(Incidentally, I'm working on a theory that the attempt to persuade Americans that the world is six thousand or so years old is actually a diabolical Russian plot, because some KGB genius realizes that "Creationism" will ultimately destroy the U.S. oil and mining interests. The next move is to get Congress to pass a law making pi = 3, as is clearly stated in I *Kings* vii.23 and 2 *Chronicles* iv.2. Then Detroit will be forced to manufacture cars with elliptical wheels, etc. You can take it from there....)

One of the glories of the American way of life—the very reason the United States has attracted refugees from foreign tyrannies and still continues to do so—is that every citizen is allowed to express his own opinion. But there are limits; as a wise jurist remarked, freedom of speech doesn't include the right to shout, "Fire!" in a crowded theater.

I would defend the liberty of consenting, adult Creationists to practice whatever intellectual perversions they like in the privacy of their own homes; but it is also necessary to protect the young and innocent. Though it would be absurd—and inhumane—to suggest that a teacher who sincerely believes in Creationism should be excluded from the educational system, he should *not* be allowed to conduct classes in biology or the earth sciences—any more than a flat-Earther should be allowed to teach geography. (Though some flat-Earthers and Creationists might well serve as devil's advocates, challenging pupils to refute their arguments, and thus begin the painful process of thinking for themselves.)

The resulting debates would probably be no more heated than those going on right now between scientists who believe in Evolution but don't believe in Darwin— a situation which has been gleefully exploited by the Creationists. Darwin's theory (repeat, THEORY) states that the force or mechanism which drives the evolutionary process is natural selection; favorable modifications or adaptations survive, while the losers in the genetic lottery die out. No one doubts that this happens, but many biologists do not believe that it can explain all the truly fantastic phenomena (and creatures) that exist in the world of living things. For even a "simple" bacterium contains a greater degree of organization than New York City (no great compliment, perhaps). The evolution of life, particularly in its complex modern forms, seems to involve far too many improbable coincidences—even if the dice *are* biased by natural selection.

Yet in billions of years, even the most improbable coincidences *do* happen. For example: only an hour after I'd started writing this article, I had a visit from one of Darwin's most vigorous latter-day critics—the astronomer Dr. Chandra Wickremasinghe, who annoyed many of his fellow scientists by appearing at the recent Arkansas trial. But he probably upset the Creationists even more, for he has no doubt of the reality of Evolution and the huge time-scales involved.

In their 1981 book *Space Travellers: The Bringers of Life*, Dr. Wickremasinghe and his colleague Sir Fred Hoyle suggest that the universe is literally infested with bacteria—perhaps originating in cometary environments, which are exceedingly rich in water, carbon and all the essentials of life. Startling though this theory is, they have now gone on to propose a far more revolutionary idea, which in a way is an updating of William Paley's "argument from design," viz., "If you find anything as complicated as a watch—there must be a watchmaker."

Hoyle and Wickremasinghe argue that the marvelously adapted life forms on Earth (including us) were planned by a superintelligence which "seeded" our galaxy with spores, carefully designed to evolve into future higher organisms. The idea that God (or whatever you like to call our Creator) was a genetic engineer working with DNA a few billion years ago seems to me quite compatible with religious faith. Incidentally, the concept is not new; it was developed in Olaf W. Stapledon's magnificent history of the next 2 billion years, *Last and First Men*. (A book which profoundly influenced my own career and writing.)

Hoyle and Wickremasinghe's theories are, to say the least, stimulating; it will not be easy to prove or refute them. Even if they are wrong, they may be valuable in opening the eyes of biologists (and astronomers) to possibilities that have been overlooked—except by science-fiction writers. . . .

Finally, I would like to express my contempt for those who refuse to face the obvious fact that we are all part of the animal kingdom, and regard this as in some way demeaning. As Thomas Huxley said to poor Bishop Wilberforce when he demolished him at the famous 1860 Oxford debate: "I would far rather have a humble ape for an ancestor, than a man who used his talents to oppose the search for truth. . . ."

Technically speaking, of course, we *don't* have apes for ancestors; we both diverged from a common stock, hence the popular use of the word "cousin" for the relationship. As one who still mourns for two deeply loved little monkeys, I would be proud to claim an even closer kinship.

When one looks at the incredibly diverse pattern of terrestrial life from the *cosmic* viewpoint, the apes and monkeys no longer seem our cousins—but our brothers and sisters.

Who, then, are our cousins? Why, of course, the flowers and the trees....

Does anyone object to *that* relationship?

Soon after this article was written, I came across the following statement, issued just a few months earlier by a distinguished group of scientists:

> We are convinced that masses of evidence render the application of the concept of evolution to man and the other primates beyond serious dispute.

This should settle the matter, as far as those who call themselves Christians are concerned. For whatever their doctrinal differences, surely even the most fanatical Protestants will admit that the Vatican does speak with a certain authority on matters of faith....

Yes, the Pontifical Academy of Sciences summed it up very well. Evolution is now "beyond serious dispute."

About the Author

Arthur C. Clarke was born at Minehead, Somerset, England, in 1917 and is a graduate of Kings College, London, where he obtained First Class Honors in Physics and Mathematics. He is past Chairman of the British Interplanetary Society, a member of the Academy of Astronautics, the Royal Astronomical Society, and many other scientific organizations. During World War II, as an RAF officer, he was in charge of the first radar talk-down equipment during its experimental trials. His only *non*-science-fiction novel, *Glide Path*, is based on this work.

Author of fifty books, some twenty million-plus copies of which have been printed in over thirty languages, his numerous awards include the 1961 Kalinga Prize, the AAAS–Westinghouse science-writing prize, the Bradford Washburn Award, and the Hugo, Nebula, and John W. Campbell awards—all three of which were won by his novel *Rendezvous with Rama*.

In 1968 he shared an Oscar nomination with Stanley Kubrick for *2001: A Space Odyssey*, and his thirteen-part TV series "Arthur C. Clarke's Mysterious World" has now been screened in many countries. He joined Walter Cronkite during CBS's coverage of the Apollo missions.

His invention of the communications satellite in 1945 has brought him numerous honors, such as the 1982 Marconi International Fellowship, a gold medal of the Franklin Institute, the Vikram Sarabhai Professorship of the Physical Research Laboratory, Ahmedabad, and a Fellowship of King's College, London. The President of Sri Lanka nominated him Chancellor of the University of Moratuwa, near Colombo.